Japanese Monetary Policy

A National Bureau
of Economic Research
Project Report

Japanese Monetary Policy

Edited by   Kenneth J. Singleton

The University of Chicago Press

Chicago and London

KENNETH J. SINGLETON is C. O. G. Miller Distinguished Professor of
Finance at the Graduate School of Business, Stanford University, and a
research associate of the National Bureau of Economic Research.

The University of Chicago Press, Chicago 60637
The University of Chicago Press, Ltd., London
© 1993 by The National Bureau of Economic Research
All rights reserved. Published 1993
Printed in the United States of America
02 01 00 99 98 97 96 95 94 93   1 2 3 4 5

ISBN: 0–226–76066–9 (cloth)

Library of Congress Cataloging-in-Publication Data

Japanese monetary policy / edited by Kenneth J. Singleton.
    p.   cm.—(A National Bureau of Economic Research project report)
    "This volume is the result of a conference sponsored by the National
Bureau of Economic Research and held in Tokyo on 18–19 April
1991"—Pref.
    Includes bibliographical references and index.
    1. Monetary policy—Japan—Congresses.   I. Singleton, Kenneth J.
II. Series.
HG1275.J38   1993
332.4'952—dc20   92-38218
                                                                        CIP

Contents

Preface

This volume is the result of a conference sponsored by the National Bureau of Economic Research and held in Tokyo on 18–19 April 1991. The conference brought together scholars with an interest in Japanese monetary policy from the academic and financial corporate communities and the Bank of Japan. I would like to thank Martin Feldstein and Geoffrey Carliner for their helpful guidance at the organizational stages of this conference and the discussants for their constructive comments and suggestions on the manuscripts. In addition, I am grateful to Kirsten Foss Davis of NBER and Kunio Okina of the Bank of Japan for assisting in making local conference arrangements, Jane Konkel of NBER for guiding the manuscript through the various stages of editing and review, and Connel Fullenkamp of NBER for editorial assistance.

Funding for this conference has been provided by the Ford Foundation and the Mitsubishi Trust and Banking Corporation.

Introduction

Kenneth J. Singleton

How is monetary policy determined in Japan and what role did the policies of the Bank of Japan (BOJ) have in shaping the rapid economic expansion in Japan during the past twenty years? The authors of the papers collected in this book address these questions, with particular emphasis given to how monetary policy has evolved since the early 1980s in light of changing domestic and foreign markets for goods and assets.

The institutional context within which monetary policy has been conducted has evolved substantially over the past two decades. For instance, prior to the early 1970s there was a limited market for long-term national debt. The sizes of the capital markets have grown substantially, though the Japanese treasury-bill market still remains relatively undeveloped. Furthermore, there has been a marked disintermediation of Japanese financial markets: in 1970 approximately 97% of all corporate debt was held by banks and insurance companies, while by 1990 they held only 60% of this debt. In the Japanese money markets, markets for uncollateralized debt (e.g., commercial paper) did not develop until 1989. The maturity structure of all of these markets has also been expanded over time. Not surprisingly, the operating procedures adopted by the BOJ in the postwar period and the subsequent evolution of its operating procedures reflect this history, and differ from those of, say, the United States. Indeed, in some cases, the liberalization of markets in Japan was initiated by the BOJ in order to facilitate the implementation of monetary policy within the increasingly integrated global financial arena.

The central importance of bank credit in financing real investment in Japan and the influence that the BOJ has over the extension of bank credit suggest that monetary policy may have been an important determinant of the flow of

Kenneth J. Singleton is C. O. G. Miller Distinguished Professor of Finance at the Graduate School of Business, Stanford University, and a research associate of the National Bureau of Economic Research.

funds to corporations and, hence, real growth in Japan during recent decades. The following chapters explore this issue in detail, beginning with a comprehensive discussion of the daily operating procedures of the BOJ. This discussion is followed by an exploration of the effects of the instruments of monetary policy on interest rates and bank lending, as well as the effects of changing credit conditions on the investment decisions of firms. Finally, further evidence is presented on the relationship between monetary policy and aggregate fluctuation in Japan during the postwar period.

In the first two chapters, Kazuo Ueda and Kunio Okina discuss how special features of financial institutions and markets in Japan shape the formulation of policy. They stress several important characteristics of the BOJ's operating procedures: the BOJ has always attempted to control a short-term interest rate and not a monetary aggregate; the reserve accounting system in Japan is a hybrid of lagged and contemporaneous reserve accounting systems; and the discount window is the primary instrument for monetary control over short periods of time, not open-market operations. The latter feature arose in part because the short-term money markets were not sufficiently developed to absorb sufficiently large transactions by the BOJ for daily monetary policy activity. Furthermore, the settlement procedures and legal structure of gensaki (repurchase) agreements is very different than that, say, of the United States in ways that also hinder the use of money markets for open-market operations over short horizons.

While the BOJ's focus on interest rates has been widely discussed (e.g., Suzuki 1987), the BOJ's perceptions about the mechanisms by which it controls interbank call rates has been less extensively debated in the literature. Ueda and Okina provide complementary, though somewhat conflicting, interpretations of the control mechanism, and interesting insights into how the policy-setting process might be expected to evolve in the future. Okina stresses various institutional features of the reserve accounting system and the signaling of the BOJ's target levels of rates in characterizing the BOJ's control of call rates. Specifically, the BOJ signals a target rate for the end of a reserve maintenance period through public announcements and by the way it adjusts the actual relative to required reserves over the maintenance period. Okina argues that the BOJ can effectively achieve its target rate at the end of the period and hence that banks, in seeking to maximize their profits, will behave as if interest rates will converge to this target rate during the maintenance period. Ueda acknowledges the importance of market interventions during the maintenance period by the BOJ in controlling interest rates, but also raises the possibility that direct control of the call rate combined with moral suasion that discourages the flow of funds to other, higher-yielding markets may have been important, especially prior to 1988.

During the summer of 1988, market interest rates (e.g., the Euroyen rates) increased in the expectation of a future tightening of monetary policy. At the same time, the BOJ kept interbank rates at a relatively low level, so private transactions shifted to the higher-yielding markets. Subsequently, the gap between the call market and Euroyen markets did not narrow appreciably, because of constraints on the access of some institutions to both markets and differences in the maturity structures of the call and unrestricted markets. Consequently, the BOJ's control over market rates was weakened substantially. Accordingly, in November 1988 the BOJ announced major changes in the contract specifications for money markets, including the interbank market, in order to increase the degree of arbitrage between markets.

Ueda also addresses the transmission mechanism by which monetary policy affects real output in Japan. In particular, he provides some evidence on the relative importance of the credit view versus money view of the transmission of policy recently discussed, for instance, by Bernanke and Blinder (1990) and Romer and Romer (1990) for the U.S. economy. Japan is an interesting environment in which to explore this question, because a unique policy instrument is available to the BOJ; namely, it has at times directly controlled the amount of loans that financial institutions can write through "window guidance." Overall, the results suggest a more important role for changes in bank lending than for changes in the money stock in the transmission mechanism in Japan.

The role of BOJ guidance of commercial bank lending in the investment decisions of Japanese corporations is explored more extensively in the chapter by Takeo Hoshi, David Scharfstein, and Kenneth J. Singleton. Previous discussions of the effects of window guidance have often concluded that guidance typically does not change the availability of credit in the economy, but only the source. As such it should be neutral in its effects on real economic activity. Hoshi, Scharfstein, and Singleton argue that, when there are informational assymetries and capital market imperfections, alternative financing sources may not be perfect substitutes and, consequently, window guidance can have real effects. The empirical evidence using macrodata is consistent with this hypothesis. Moreover, the authors argue that guidance may have distributional effects depending on the relationship between firms and their many sources of credit. Consistent with their thesis, the analysis of firm-level data indicates that firms that are members of an industrial group (keiretsu) tend to invest more than independent firms during periods of tight window guidance.

Window guidance is a secondary instrument of monetary policy. The primary instruments are discount window lending and open-market operations. The effects of the primary instruments of monetary policy on real economic activity are typically viewed as arising from the BOJ's influence on the term structure of interest rates. Though in Japan the BOJ has a direct influence only on short-term interest rates, monetary policy may affect the entire yield curve and, thereby, the costs of capital and investment decisions of firms. Thus, as in many countries, there is considerable interest in Japan on the relationship between short- and long-term interest rates. John Y. Campbell and Yasushi Hamao investigate whether the expectations theory of the term structure of interest rates explains the comovements of the short and long ends of the yield curve. Given limitations on intermaturity "arbitrage" trading due to restrictions imposed historically by the Ministry of Finance, there are a priori reasons for doubting that the long rates are set as weighted averages of expected short rates in Japan. As Campbell and Hamao note, however, the bond markets have developed rapidly during the past decade, and therefore it is of interest to determine the proportion of variation in long-term rates that is explained by expected changes in short-term rates.

The expectations theory is rejected by the data on Japanese bond yields for both the short and long ends of the yield curve. However, Campbell and Hamao find a significant increase from the early half to the latter half of the 1980s in the correlation between the long-short yield spread and an unrestricted forecast from a vector autoregression of future short rate changes over the life of long-term bonds. Thus, while the long-short yield spread is consistently more variable than what is implied by rational forecasts of future changes in short-term rates, there has been an increase in the forecasting power of the term structure for long-term interest rate movements.

In the last two chapters, Hiroshi Yoshikawa and Kenneth D. West examine the relative importance of various aggregate shocks on real economic activity. Yoshikawa associates monetary policy disturbances with changes in the call rate, while West associates policy disturbances with the residual in an equation describing a monetary aggregate. Both studies find that monetary policy responded endogenously to economic developments in Japan, but that there was also a significant exogenous component as well to the BOJ's actions. Furthermore, they both find that foreign economic disturbances explain a substantial fraction of the variation in real output in Japan.

These studies reach opposite conclusions with regard to the importance of the contribution of monetary policy actions to real economic activity. Yoshikawa finds that monetary policy has had a substantial impact on real output, primarily through its effect on fixed investments and imports. In contrast, West finds that monetary policy has had a negligible effect on real output fluctuation. Reconciliation of these conflicting results may lie in their alternative interpretations of the BOJ's policy variables. As noted earlier, the BOJ has focused primarily on controlling short-term interest rates in Japan, which is consistent with Yoshikawa's use of the call rate as the policy variable. As West notes, if smoothing interest rates is an important objective of the BOJ, then some of the policy disturbances will be attributed to his aggregate demand shock, which is an important determinant of output fluctuation in Japan.

Taken together, the research presented in this book suggests that the institutional setting in which monetary policy has been set in Japan over the past twenty years has permitted an influence, perhaps a substantial one, by the BOJ on real economic activity in Japan. At the same time the authors catalogue important economic and political pressures both from within and outside Japan for changes in the legal and regulatory environments in which policy is set. As the liberalization of private financial markets has proceeded, there seems to have been a concurrent increase in the BOJ's reliance on market mechanisms, rather than moral suasion, for influencing bank lending activities and interest rates. This evolution has been especially notable over the past few years. In particular, there were substantial changes to money markets introduced in 1988, and many further changes are currently under discussion. One might expect a further weakening of the influence through moral suasion, and increasing reliance on market mechanisms, by the BOJ and Ministry of Finance, as corporations increasingly gain access to overseas markets and the accounting standards for Japanese companies change. Consistent with this view, the BOJ announced in June 1991 that it will no longer use window guidance in the conduct of monetary policy. If this change in policy is maintained, it would constitute another example of a shift from direct administrative guidance of bank behavior to reliance on market mechanisms for controlling loans.

The forms of future liberalization (e.g., the development of a domestic secondary market for corporate bonds) may well have important implications for the degree and channels by which monetary policy affects real economic activity in Japan and, therefore, warrant close observation. In this regard, Japan provides a very interesting and potentially revealing economic environment in which to study the way various "frictions" in credit and other financial markets influence the effects of monetary policy.

There are some very important issues related to monetary policy that are not addressed in these studies. One of the most intriguing of these is the role of monetary policy in the relatively rapid inflation of real asset values (land and common stock) in Japan, and the subsequent rapid decline in their values. Others include the implications of increased coordination among monetary authorities of different countries for the formulation and implementation of policy, and the relationship between the political process and monetary-policy setting in Japan. It is hoped the papers in this book will provide a useful background for addressing these and other important issues related to Japanese monetary policy.

This book is the culmination of a research project on Japanese monetary policy initiated by the National Bureau of Economic Research in 1990. As part of this project, the papers were presented to a small research forum comprising academics from Japan and the United States and several authorities from Japanese financial institutions in Tokyo during April 1991. The authors benefited from the comments of formal discussants as well as discussion with other participants.

References

Bernanke, Ben, and Alan Blinder. 1990. The federal funds rate and the channel of monetary transmission. NBER Working Paper No. 3487. Cambridge, MA: National Bureau of Economic Research, October.

Romer, Cristina D., and David H. Romer. 1990. New evidence on the monetary transmission mechanism. *Brookings Papers on Economic Activity,* no. 1:149–213.

Suzuki, Yoshio. 1987. *The Japanese Financial System.* Oxford: Clarendon Press.

1   A Comparative Perspective on Japanese Monetary Policy: Short-Run Monetary Control and the Transmission Mechanism

Kazuo Ueda

Three major building blocks of the analysis of a country's monetary policy are the reaction function of the central bank, or the ultimate targets of policy; short-run monetary control; and the transmission mechanism. Japanese monetary policy has been unique in all three aspects. This paper analyzes the special features of the second and third of these building blocks of Japanese monetary policy, but not the first. That is, it discusses the daily monetary control of interest rates and the mechanism by which interest rate changes affect the real economy, but does not address the question of what causes a change in policy instruments.

In my analysis of short-run monetary control and the transmission mechanism, I try to relate the discussion, to a maximum extent, to current research on the same topics in the United States. A perspective relevant for both aspects is that Japanese monetary policy has been moving very rapidly over the past few years from old-fashioned direct control through moral suasion of interest rates and quantities of transactions to one with heavier reliance on the price mechanism in money and capital markets. In this sense, the present study is in line with previous studies on Japanese money and financial markets, such as Suzuki (1980), Feldman (1986), and Cargill and Royama (1988), but it adds to the literature by providing a more rigorous statistical analysis of the Japanese interest rate and money-supply data and by discussing more carefully institutional aspects of the Bank of Japan's short-run monetary control process.

The Federal Reserve (henceforth the Fed) has alternated between controlling the federal funds rate and bank reserves. The funds rate volatility was

Kazuo Ueda is associate professor of economics at the University of Tokyo.

The author would like to thank A. Horiuchi and K. Okina for useful comments on an earlier version of the paper. Financial support from the Ministry of Education under grant 02451079 is gratefully acknowledged.

much higher during 1979–82—the period of bank reserve control. In either case, the Fed uses open-market operations to hit its target. Operations are "defensive" ones in which the Fed accommodates short-run temporary fluctuations in the demand for high-powered money, and "dynamic" ones directed toward changing the level of the target.[1]

Has the Bank of Japan (BOJ) controlled bank reserves? How stable is the call rate relative to the funds rate? How important are "defensive" and "dynamic" operations? What are the instruments available to the BOJ for controlling the call rate or bank reserves? These are the major questions I address in my comparative analysis of Japanese monetary control.

I argue that the BOJ, in its daily operations, has long targeted the call rate and other interbank rates. It has never targeted bank reserves in the sense of setting target growth ranges for reserves and reaching them within a short period of time such as a few months. I show this first by presenting evidence of the stability of interbank rates in Japan relative to the United States and then by pointing out the importance of "defensive" operations by the BOJ in stabilizing interbank rates.

An important consequence of interbank rate targeting in Japan is that the stock of high-powered money has been an endogenous variable. That is, the BOJ has been accommodating fluctuations in the demand for high-powered money at target levels of interbank rates.

Another feature of Japanese monetary policy is that for both "defensive" and "dynamic" operations the BOJ uses changes in lending at the discount window very extensively. That is, discount window lending is an important daily instrument for the BOJ. This differs from the role of borrowing from the Fed, which moves more or less passively in response to the requests of commercial banks. The difference results from the absence of large-scale open markets in Japan.

An important question discussed in the literature is whether the call rate has been at the correct level to clear the market for high-powered money. I do not offer a definitive answer. But I supply casual evidence pointing to the importance of more direct control, possibly through moral suasion, of interbank rates by the BOJ, at least for certain subperiods of the postwar period. I discuss in a related context the new operating procedure introduced in 1988, which has allowed less restricted movement of interest rates and funds.

In section 1.2 of the paper, I look at the transmission mechanism of Japanese monetary policy. The analysis is again related to current research on the topic in the United States. The controversy between the credit and money views of the transmission mechanism is receiving renewed interest in the recent literature, although conclusive evidence has yet to be offered. The topic is even more interesting in Japan because of the availability of a unique policy instrument, window guidance, by which bank loans are directly controlled by

---

1. See, for example, Roosa (1956) for "defensive" and "dynamic" operations.

the BOJ. Hence, loans may be important not only as a channel of policy transmission but also as an instrument of policy.

I apply techniques used in the recent U.S. literature to analyze Japanese data. I find two important conclusions. First, the results of time series analysis of Japanese data involving monetary aggregates are extremely sensitive to the choice of prefiltering technique. Hence, robust results are rather hard to obtain. Second, despite the sensitivity to the methods used, I find support for the importance of loans in the transmission mechanism of Japanese monetary policy.

I also find that both the call rate and bank loans cause other monetary indicators in the Granger sense. Hence, we might characterize the behavior of the BOJ as using both the call rate and window guidance to move bank loans and other interest rates, which in turn change other monetary aggregates and real variables of the economy.

The BOJ announced in June 1991 that it would discontinue its use of window guidance. Perhaps this was part of the new strategy of the BOJ to rely more heavily on the price mechanism in money and capital markets for carrying out monetary policy. Whether such moves will be permanent and whether they will be successful has yet to be determined.

Section 1.1 starts with a brief summary of the Fed's operating procedure. I then compare it with the BOJ's operations. Detailed analysis of the behavior of interest rates and bank reserves is presented. I turn to the analysis of the transmission mechanism of Japanese monetary policy in section 1.2. I carry out time series analysis of monetary indicators, paying particular attention to the comparison of the predictive power of money and lending. Section 1.3 summarizes the major conclusions of the paper.

1.1 The Short-Run Monetary Control Technique of the BOJ

In this section I try to relate the daily operating procedures of the BOJ and associated issues as much as possible to the procedures of U.S. monetary control. I briefly summarize what appears to be the consensus view of the Fed's operating procedure and then explain the operating procedure of the BOJ, highlighting the similarities and dissimilarities between the operating procedures of the two central banks.

It is important to keep in mind the time unit of analysis. Some of the discussion below refers to daily operations of the central banks, some abstracts from daily movements and looks at averages over reserve accounting periods, and some is not affected by the time unit.

1.1.1 The Operating Procedures of the Federal Reserve

It will be useful for later purposes to discuss the operating procedures of the Fed. The following discussion owes much to Federal Reserve Bank of New

York (1981, 1988), Kanzaki (1988), and Partlan, Hamdani, and Camilli (1986).

A convenient starting point is the balance sheet of the Fed, shown in table 1.1. From the equality of total assets and liabilities, we have

(1) $S = R + VC + CU + DG - (BL + FL + NA),$

where S is security holdings, R is member-bank deposits, VC is vault cash, CU is currency held by the public, DG is treasury deposits, BL is discount window lending, FL is float, and NA is other net assets. This can be rewritten as

(2) $S = (TR - BL) + RF = NBR + RF,$

where TR is total reserves defined as $R + VC$; RF is reserve factors, which is the sum of all the other items on the righthand side of (1); and NBR is nonborrowed reserves. By taking the first difference of (2), we obtain an identity involving open-market operations, OMO:

(3) $OMO = d(TR - BL) + d(RF) = d(NBR) + d(RF),$

where $d(x)$ indicates the first difference of x.

The Fed derives its objective for NBR or $d(NBR)$ by estimating the demand for required and excess reserves consistent with medium-term targets for monetary aggregates, and then subtracting the estimate of the level of discount window borrowing. This sets the "dynamic" objectives of the Federal Open Market Committee—the first part of the righthand side of (3), with $d(NBR)$ equal to its targets. The second term, $d(RF)$, in addition to being volatile and uncertain, is believed by many central bankers to be beyond their control in the very short run, for example, at the daily level. Therefore, it would be best to estimate as precisely as possible the fluctuations in RF and offset them using open-market operations in order to avoid unnecessary volatility in short-term interest rates.[2] This is the so-called defensive part of open-market operations.

Most observers of the Fed's operating procedures suggest that borrowing at the discount window is not rationed even if the discount rate is below the federal funds rate. Member banks pay surveillance costs, which are increasing in the amount of discount window borrowing. Hence, rational behavior on the part of member banks suggests that BL is determined at a finite level and is increasing in the difference between the federal funds rate and the discount rate.

Assuming that total reserves are a decreasing function of the federal funds rate, equation (3) gives the equilibrium condition of the federal funds market.

2. The reason for central bankers' aversion to interest-rate volatility is a question yet to be answered in the literature. But it has played a major role in the daily operations of many central banks. In the U.S.-Japan context, there is more aversion on the part of the BOJ, as the following analyses reveal.

Table 1.1   **The Fed's Balance Sheet**

Assets	Liabilities
BL (discount window lending)	R (member-bank deposits)
S (security holdings)	VC (vault cash)
FL (float)	CU (currency held by the public)
NA (other net assets)	DG (treasury deposits)

To the extent that "defensive" operations fail to fully offset changes in reserve factors, the Fed will observe unexpected changes in discount window borrowing.[3] The Fed tightens its stance by decreasing the "dynamic" part of open-market operations. This creates a rise in the federal funds rate and increased borrowing at the discount window.

It is widely recognized that the Fed targeted nonborrowed reserves during the 1979–82 period and the federal funds rate in other periods.[4] However, the difference lies more in emphasis than in substance. Obviously, the Fed cannot set targets for reserves on a day-to-day or even month-to-month basis and hit them exactly. If this policy were tried, it would create enormous movements in interest rates and confusion in short-term money markets. Targeting reserves merely means more frequent adjustments of the "dynamic" part of open-market operations in response to the deviations of actual reserves from their targets and, consequently, more fluctuations in the federal funds rate than in the case of targeting the federal funds rate.

1.1.2   The BOJ's Operating Procedures

Let us turn to the description of the BOJ's operating procedures, using the argument in the previous section as a benchmark.

Some institutional features of the Japanese money markets and bank regulations should be noted at the outset. Japanese banks are required to hold reserves as deposits at the BOJ; therefore, vault cash is not included in the calculation of legal reserves. The treasury bill (TB) market is not comparable in size to that of the United States. In addition, the current accounting system implies that an operation in the TB market on a certain day is settled three days later. Because of these problems, TB operations are not very useful for daily adjustments of bank reserves.[5]

---

3. Spindt and Tarhan (1987) show that discount window borrowing responds in this sense to fluctuations in other items. They show for the 1979–82 period that changes in money, which create changes in *TR*, cause discount window borrowing in the Granger sense.

4. See Meulendyke (1988) for a more careful, historical review of the Fed's operating procedure.

5. See Okina's paper in this volume for a more careful description of the Japanese short-term money markets. The report of the Committee on Short-Term Money Markets (1990) discusses other institutional problems, including the effects of taxation on money markets.

Let us reproduce equation (1) for the BOJ, ignoring the float and net assets:

(4) $BL + S = R + VC + CU + DG.$

A favored rearrangement of this equation by the BOJ is

(5) $d(R) = d(BL) + OMO - d(VC + CU + DG).$

Some of the differences between the BOJ's and the Fed's operating procedures are already apparent. The Japanese counterpart to $d(RF)$—technical reserve factors—is the third term on the righthand side of (5), and unlike (3) it includes vault cash. This is because vault cash cannot be used to meet legal reserve requirements. It also implies that the BOJ regards vault cash as exogenous in the short run. Just as the Fed regards $d(RF)$ in equation (3) as exogenous, the BOJ treats the $d(VC + CU + DG)$ term as exogenous in its daily operations.

Another difference between equations (3) and (5) is that BL is not subtracted from R to arrive at nonborrowed reserves. In fact, the concept of nonborrowed reserves has never been used in Japan.[6] This reflects the use of discount window borrowing as a control variable by the BOJ. The discount rate has always been lower than the call rate. Therefore, discount window lending has been rationed in Japan. And the level of lending has been changed at the initiative of the BOJ, not of private banks.[7] In fact, this has been the major policy instrument of the BOJ, as shown below.

The BOJ calls the $d(VC + CU + DG)$ term of equation (5) the shortage (or surplus if negative) of funds in the money market. The "defensive" operations of the BOJ are directed toward offsetting the effects of changes in this term. The BOJ devotes considerable effort to estimating the shortage of funds. Funds are supplied either through the BOJ's discount window, $BL,$ or by openmarket operations, $OMO.$ For "defensive" operations, both instruments are usually used.

The difference between the total supply of funds from the BOJ and the amount of "defensive" operations is accounted for, of course, by the "dynamic" operations of the BOJ, and this difference determines the change in bank reserves. Assuming that the demand for reserves by banks responds to the call market rate, we see that equation (5) determines the equilibrium call rate.

1.1.3   Interbank Rate Targeting in Japan

What has been the target of the BOJ's operations? As far as I know, the BOJ has never targeted bank reserves or high-powered money.[8] In a sense, short-

6. Interestingly, more than all reserves are borrowed; that is, nonborrowed reserves are negative in Japan. In 1990 reserves were about 4.9 trillion yen, while BOJ lending stood at 6.3 trillion yen.
7. Royama (1971) was one of the first to point this out. Although the situation in which the interbank rate is higher than the discount rate is the same in the United States, private banks may borrow at their initiative from the Fed in the United States, while this is not the case in Japan.
8. Many, including Dotsey (1986), Cargill and Royama (1988), and Bryant (1990), have made a similar observation. In particular, Dotsey's work compares the variability of interest rates be-

term (month-to-month) control of bank reserves is almost impossible in Japan because of the lagged reserve accounting system and the near absence of excess reserves.[9] Since the mid-1970s, the BOJ has paid attention to the behavior of broader monetary aggregates as intermediate targets of monetary policy. However, it seems that it has never used information on monetary aggregates to calculate target levels for bank reserves or interbank rates in a mechanical way.

The short-term operating target of the BOJ has long been interbank interest rates. During normal times, when tightening or loosening of monetary policy is unnecessary, the BOJ stabilizes interbank rates. A change in the stance of monetary policy creates new target levels for interbank rates. New targets are almost immediately achieved by "dynamic" operations as explained in section 1.1.4. The precise manner in which the BOJ calculates the target levels of interbank rates has never been disclosed. I doubt that it uses any quick formula to do this. As stated above, it has never targeted bank reserves. But it does pay close attention to the level of the reserve supply relative to required reserves on a daily basis in order to achieve interest rate targets. This will be explained below.

I now show more formally that the BOJ has targeted interbank rates. First I show that, as a statistical matter, the call rate has been much more stable than the federal funds rate. Second I argue that the stability of the call rate is a result of the "defensive" operations of the BOJ rather than a result of the stability or high interest rate elasticity of the demand for high-powered money.

The relative stability of Japanese interbank rates is shown in table 1.2, where the standard deviations of daily interest rates for the periods since the late 1970s are presented for the United States and Japan. Clearly, interest rate volatility is higher in the United States. The differences in the standard deviations between the two countries are significant for all three interest rates on the basis of the usual F-test on two variances.

The difference in the degree of volatility is largest for the interbank rates. The volatility of the federal funds rate for the entire period is affected by the increased volatility in the 1979–82 period, when the Fed paid more attention to the control of reserves. However, the volatility of the call rate is lower than that of the federal funds rate even in periods that exclude 1979–82. The numbers in parentheses are standard deviations calculated from the sample, excluding Wednesday observations. They are presented because the volatility of the federal funds rate is much affected by its behavior on the last day of the reserve accounting period—Wednesday. However, the volatility of the federal funds rate is still much higher than that of the call rate. Though significant,

---

tween Japan and the United States, as I do in table 1.2, and concludes that in both countries interbank rates are targeted. Because he uses quarterly data, however, he does not find as large a difference in interbank rate variability as I do.

9. For the period 1967–87, excess reserves were, on average, 1.225% of required reserves in the United States and 0.142% in Japan. It is possible, though, that this near absence of excess reserves is the result of passive accommodation of reserve demand by the BOJ.

Table 1.2   **The Volatility of Daily Interest Rates**

Period	Interbank Rate[a]	3-Month Rate	Long-Term Rate
	United States		
1977:1:1–1991:2:11	.523 (.466)	.221	.143
1977:1:1–1979:10:7	.211 (.159)	.180	.0581
1979:10:8–1982:10:22	.841 (.738)	.402	.239
1982:10:24–1991:2:11	.437 (.400)	.111	.112
	Japan		
1978:1:1–1991:2:14	.139	.0725	.121
1978:1:1–1979:4:30	.125	.047	
1979:5:1–1988:10:31	.147	.0801	.136
1988:11:1–1991:2:14	.102	.0254	.0877

Notes: Entries are the variance of deviations of each rate from its centered moving average with ten observations on each side. The interest rates are: the federal funds rate, TB rate, and the seven-year-bonds rate for the United States and the call rate, the CD rate, and the 10-year-bond rate for Japan.

[a]Entries in parentheses are calculated by excluding Wednesday observations.

Table 1.3   **The Volatility of Currency in Circulation**

	Japan 1963–90	United States 1967–90
Seasonally adjusted data	$3.0 * 10^{-4}$	$7.5 * 10^{-6}$
Unadjusted data	$5.6 * 10^{-3}$	$8.0 * 10^{-5}$

Note: Entries show the variance of the monthly rate of change in currency in circulation.

the difference in the volatility of long-term rates between the two countries is not very large.

Consequently, the stability of Japanese interbank rates evidenced in table 1.2 must come from one of three possibilities: the shortage or surplus of funds in Japan is more stable than U.S. reserve factors; the interest rate elasticity of the demand for high-powered money is higher in Japan; or the BOJ carries out more accurate "defensive" operations.

Table 1.3 shows the variability of currency in circulation, the largest component of high-powered money in both countries. Unambiguously, the demand for currency by the nonbank public fluctuates more in Japan than in the United States. Okina's paper in this volume presents evidence, though less formally, of the larger volatility of other components of high-powered money in Japan as well.

Estimates of the interest elasticities of the components of high-powered money—currency held by the public and bank reserves—are presented in table 1.4. The specification of the demand functions is the conventional one of partial adjustment, in which the righthand side of the demand function

Table 1.4   **Interest Rate Elasticities of the Components of High-Powered Money**

	Japan 1963–90	United States 1967–90	Activity Variable
CU (currency in circulation)	− .0014	− .00097	IP
	− .0022	− .000516	C
TR (total reserves including vault cash)	.0032	− .0013	IP
	− .62 ∗ 10^{-4}	− .62 ∗ 10^{-3}	RR

Notes: The equations estimated are, for example, the log of *CU* regressed on a constant, the call (or funds) rate, the log of an activity variable, and the lagged dependent variable. Both *CU* and *TR* are deflated by the CPI. Entries are short-term (semi-) elasticities. IP = index of production; C = sales of department stores deflated by the CPI; RR = required reserves deflated by the CPI.

includes the lagged dependent variable. The table shows only short-run elasticities, that is, the response of *CU* or *TR* within a month of a change in the interest rate. The magnitude of the elasticity of *CU* is about the same across the two countries, but that of reserves is smaller in Japan.

We have seen no evidence of greater stability or higher interest elasticity in the demand for high-powered money in Japan. Consequently, accurate "defensive" operations by the BOJ must have been the key to achieving stable interbank interest rates in Japan. A back-of-the-envelope calculation will help us to understand the magnitude of interest-rate fluctuations in the absence of "defensive" operations. Monthly variations in the *RF* term can easily come close to a few trillion yen. Suppose that the Bank of Japan did not accommodate these and that the elasticity of *CU* + *TR* was at most .002 based on table 1.4. High-powered money stands at about 40 trillion yen. One would need to change the call rate by close to 100 percentage points to bring about a few trillion yen change in the demand for high-powered money.

Fortunately, the daily data on the shortage or surplus of funds and its previous day's expectation, both published by the BOJ, enable us to check the accuracy of "defensive" operations. If they are successful, they would purge interest rates of any systematic response to the shortage or surplus of funds. Therefore, I regressed daily changes in the unconditional/collateral call rate on the shortage or surplus of funds for the same day, using its forecast of the previous day as an instrument. The results are

$$d(i_c) = .00713 + .00690 * d (VC + CU + DG), \text{D.W.} = 1.99,$$
$$(.071) \quad\quad (.080)$$

where i_c is the overnight call rate, the sample is 1990:8:9–1991:1:10, and t-statistics are in parentheses. The equation rejects the existence of any systematic effect of the shortage or surplus of funds on the call rate. The operations of the BOJ must have been accommodating these fluctuations in the demand for high-powered money.[10]

10. Bernanke and Blinder (1990) offer similar evidence for the United States, using weekly data for the period of funds rate control.

To summarize, the BOJ has deliberately aimed at stabilizing the call rate around its target level. To achieve this, the BOJ has used "defensive" operations extensively. An important consequence of this policy, of course, has been that the stock of high-powered money has been an endogenous variable responding to changes in the demand for high-powered money.

1.1.4   Changing the Target Level of the Call Rate

Adjustment of the Reserve Progress Ratio

"Dynamic" operations are the mechanism by which the BOJ changes the target level of the call rate. Toward the end of the 1980s, many new types of operations became available to the BOJ, such as operations in TB, financial bills, (FB) and commercial paper (CP) markets. However, these markets are too small for the BOJ to carry out large-scale operations. Consequently, the BOJ has depended on changes in lending at the discount window and operations in the bill market when it carries out "dynamic" operations.[11]

Table 1.5 presents some regression results highlighting the use of *BL* as the most important instrument of "dynamic" operations. Equation (2) in the table explains the (daily average of the) call rate in any month, using the discount rate and the share of *BL* in high-powered money, both measured at the end of the previous month. The regressors are lagged by one month in order to avoid biases stemming from the correlation between the regressors and the error term. The estimation result shows that, as more funds are supplied through the discount window, the call rate will be lower. Equation (3) shows a similar result in first difference form. These results are at least consistent with the hypothesis that a lowering of interest rates is initiated by an increase in discount window lending.

On the other hand, the correlation between the federal funds rate and discount window borrowing is positive in the United States, as shown in equation (1) of the table. Such a pattern of correlation will result if open-market operations are used as the vehicle of monetary policy and borrowing responds passively to the resulting movements in the funds rate.

During periods of monetary tightening or loosening, the BOJ changes the time path of reserve supplies within one reserve accounting period.[12] Both the BOJ and the market pay attention to the reserve progress ratio, the cumulative sum of actual daily reserves since the beginning of the current reserve accounting period relative to the required reserves of the period. During normal times, this ratio is assumed to start at zero and to increase by about 1/30 every day to reach 1 at the end of the period. A "dynamic" initiative by the BOJ to tighten (loosen) its stance is reflected in a slowing (quickening) of the pace of

---

11. Operations in the bill market are not "open"; that is, the BOJ picks a bank with which it trades bills. In this sense, operations in the bill market are closed to discount window lending.

12. See, for example, Kanzaki (1988) or Suzuki, Kuroda, and Shirakawa (1988) for a more detailed description of this process.

Table 1.5   **Discount Window Lending and Interbank Interest Rates**

SMPL	Left-hand-side Variable	Right-hand-side Variables	
(1)[a] 1967:1–1987:12	$\log(BL/p)$	$.257 * i_f - .171 * i_d$ (2.19) (−1.00)	$k = .867$ (28.4)
(2)[b] 1966:11–1989:10	i_c	$.792 * i_d(-1) - 1.50 * (BL/H)(-1)$ (11.2) (−2.56)	$k = .949$ (55.1)
(3)[b] 1966:11–1989:10	$d(i_c)$	$.667 * d(i_d)(-1) - .216 * d(\log(BL(-1))$ (9.13) (−3.56)	$k = .0884$ (1.46)

Notes: Constant terms are also included in the equations. Numbers in parentheses are t-statistics. BL = borrowings at the central bank; H = stock of high powered money; i_c = call rate; i_d = discount rate; i_f = federal funds rate; k = estimated coefficient of the first-order serial correlation of the error term; p = index of CPI.
[a]Equation (1) is estimated by Fair's method using the log of real nonborrowed reserves as an instrument.
[b]Equations (2) and (3) use the maximum likelihood method to correct for serial correlation.

the increase in this ratio relative to the normal pattern of increase. This is accomplished by, for example, a decrease (increase) in BOJ lending.

When the BOJ slows the pace of increase in the reserve progress ratio, it sends a signal of monetary tightening to the market, forcing private banks to borrow more funds in the call market and thus achieving the policy objective of raising the call rate.

I make one final remark on the endogeneity of high-powered money. I pointed out in section 1.1.3 that high-powered money is endogenous during normal times because of interest rate targeting. The above interpretation of "dynamic" operations suggests that a process of tightening is begun by a decrease in the stock of high-powered money. By the end of the reserve accounting period, however, the BOJ will be obliged to supply (because of lagged reserve accounting) a predetermined amount of reserves, albeit at a higher interest rate.[13] The total stock of high-powered money will decrease to the

13. Many have discussed what would happen if the interest elasticity of high-powered money were zero. In that case, one could argue that the BOJ may not be able to change the call rate because it cannot change the stock of high-powered money. Private banks may just as well wait until the BOJ supplies enough reserves, making changes in the reserve progress ratio an ineffective tool of monetary control. Suzuki (1980) and Okina (1987 and in this volume) have pointed out the high cost of discount window borrowing close to the end of a reserve accounting period as an important vehicle for the control of the call rate. For example, the BOJ may charge two days of interest (at the discount rate) for a twenty-four-hour loan from the discount window on the last day of the accounting period. In such a case, the daily interest rate is double the usual discount rate and easily exceeds the call rate. Market participants point out another form of penalty for private banks that do not take enough funds in interbank markets. (See Ueda and Uekusa 1988.) The penalty is the calling off of discount window lending. Since BOJ lending is done at a subsidized rate (that is, a rate lower than the call rate), such banks would lose part of the subsidies they receive from the BOJ. The BOJ does not have to impose these penalties all the time. It suffices to create the expectation of such a possibility by using the penalty once in a while. These are inter-

extent that a higher interest rate will decrease some other components of the demand for high-powered money—for example, the demand for currency by the nonbank public. But the amount of the response is usually very small. Hence, most of the movements in the stock of high-powered money are driven by demand-side factors, even in periods when a strong "dynamic" initiative is exercised by the BOJ.

An Alternative View of Interest Rate Control

An alternative explanation of interest rate control by the BOJ is that the BOJ determines the call rate at whatever rate it desires and sometimes forces market participants to take undesired positions. This view has been fairly strong among market participants (for example, Asami 1963) and academics (for example, Horiuchi and Kato 1989). Of course, direct pegging of the call rate by the BOJ would not be much different from the control mechanism explained in the previous section, if the BOJ accommodated all changes in the demand for high-powered money at the quoted call market rate. However, there are reasons to believe that the call market was not in equilibrium at least until 1988.

Direct pegging of the call rate by the BOJ has been achieved by the following mechanism, although the BOJ is not a player in the call market. The BOJ has exerted strong influence on the behavior of the call loan dealers (Tanshi Gaisha) who act as brokers and dealers in the call market. Under the *tatene* system, that is, until 1979, every day after the close of the market the BOJ and a representative call loan dealer met and discussed the next day's call rate; in effect, the BOJ told the dealer the call rate. The rate would be announced the morning of the next day. Under the *kehaichi* system, between 1979 and 1988, the role of the BOJ in the determination of the call rate was officially weakened but actually remained the same.

The next question is whether the call rate that had been quoted was clearing the market. Anecdotal evidence abounds that it did not. Large city banks have been chronic borrowers of funds in the call market. Interviews with these bankers reveal that their daily demand for reserves is interest inelastic. They claim that they only take funds supplied by call loan dealers. This would occur if the call rate were set by the BOJ at artificially low levels so that the market was in a state of excess demand. On the other hand, suppliers of funds in the interbank markets have an incentive to move funds into more flexible markets such as Euromarkets. They speak of informal guidance by the BOJ asking them not to move large quantities of funds away from the interbank markets.

Direct transactions among banks in the call market have been strictly pro-

---

esting arguments, but they rely on special features of the current reserve accounting system, such as the absence of a carry-over procedure, or on lagged reserve accounting and/or the discount rate being lower than the call rate. Moreover, the issue itself disappears if the interest rate elasticity of high-powered money is nonzero, as shown in table 1.4.

hibited. Such a regulation would be necessary if the call rate quoted by the BOJ was not at the equilibrium level.

Table 1.6 shows the chronology of regulations on interbank rates. During the years before 1988, the only period in which the BOJ did not quote the call rate either directly or indirectly was between August 1955 and June 1957. I have calculated the variance of monthly changes in the call rate for each period. Clearly, the variance is much higher for this period than for the others. This fact and the anecdotal evidence discussed above raise doubts about the explanation that the stability of Japanese interbank rates is the result of accurate defensive operations by the BOJ. The call rate may well have been stable because it was set by the BOJ and because movements of funds between markets were limited by nonmarket forces such as moral suasion. Horiuchi and Kato (1989) also present evidence consistent with a similar interpretation of the stability of interbank rates.

The Liberalization of Short-Term Money Markets

In a sense, the BOJ admitted to such heavy use of moral suasion when it introduced a new operating procedure in November 1988. (See BOJ 1990 for the details of the new procedure.) In the summer of 1988, short-term rates in open markets, such as the CD rate and Euroyen rates, increased as a result of an expectation of a future tightening of monetary policy. But the BOJ wanted to keep interbank rates at relatively low levels. The difference between inter-

Table 1.6   **Chronology of Regulations on Interbank Rates**

Period[a]	Regulations[a]	Variance[b]
1948:1–1955:7	The BOJ sets guidance rates for the call rate at levels not higher than the maximum indicated in the Temporary Law for Interest Rate Adjustment.	
1955:8–1957:6	Guidance rates are abolished.	4.18
1957:7–1967:8	Private banks (under the strict guidance of the BOJ) set the *jishuku* rate.	0.31
1967:9–1979:4	Call loan dealers, in consultation with the BOJ, set tatene for the call rate daily and announce it to market participants.	0.17
1979:5–1988:10	Interbank rates are set daily by the BOJ, and dealers announce it as kehaichi.	0.20
1988:11–	The new monetary control regime is introduced. But the kehaichi system for the call transactions with collateral remains until 1990:10.	0.04

[a]From Horiuchi and Kato (1989), my translation.
[b]The variance of monthly changes in the unconditional call rate with collateral.

bank and open-market rates widened, as illustrated in figure 1.1, and transactions shifted to open markets. However, the large gap between the two types of rates and the existence of transactions in both markets implies that implicit regulations existed that prohibited at least part of the arbitrage between the markets.

In November 1988 the BOJ announced that it would liberalize transactions in the interbank markets and arbitrage between open and interbank markets. The alleged purpose of such a policy change was to increase the degree of arbitrage between interest rates and to encourage more free determination of interbank rates.

Since then, the difference between interbank and open-market rates has never been as large as it was in the summer of 1988. In that sense, the new procedure has increased arbitrage between markets.[14] However, the variability of the call rate has not increased, as is shown in table 1.6. Calculations using daily data also show that the volatility of the call rate has decreased since 1988. This is partly attributable to the decline in the volatility of long-term rates, which is shown in table 1.2. That is, it has been a relatively calm period.[15] But more research needs to be carried out on this point.

To summarize the discussion so far, the call rate has been the target of BOJ policy for most of the postwar period. It has been much more stable than the federal funds rate. The major reason for the stability has been the extensive and accurate use of "defensive" operations by the BOJ. However, the heavily used practice of the BOJ's directly quoting the call rate, together with moral suasions discouraging arbitrage between markets, might also have played a role.

1.2   The Transmission Mechanism

Let us now turn to the analysis of the transmission mechanism of Japanese monetary policy, again comparing it with the U.S. transmission mechanism.

Recent research in the field has centered on the question of the credit-versus-money view of the transmission mechanism of monetary policy. Thus, on the one hand Bernanke and Blinder (1990) present evidence for the importance of bank loans, while King (1986) and Romer and Romer (1990) argue for the importance of bank liabilities. In addition, Bernanke and Blinder report the interesting finding that the federal funds rate is a good indicator of monetary policy. That is, the funds rate is markedly superior to various mon-

14. Even as of early 1991, however, market participants admit that there is guidance given by the BOJ and the Ministry of Finance regarding the proportion of funds participants in the noncollateral call market relative to the collateral market.

15. The practice of the BOJ's setting the call rate indirectly—the kehaichi-sei—remained for the collateral rate until November 1990. But the difference in the volatility of this rate before and after November 1990 is very small.

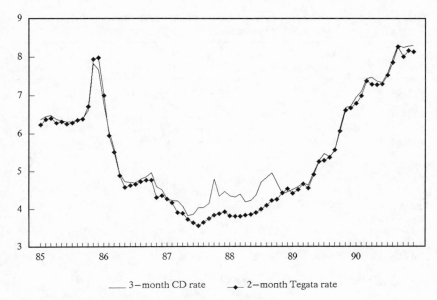

_____ 3−month CD rate   _⬦_ 2−month Tegata rate

Fig. 1.1   Tegata (bills discount) rate and CD rate

etary aggregates and other interest rates as a forecaster of major macroeconomic variables.

The analysis of the Japanese monetary transmission mechanism is especially interesting in the context of such recent developments. A unique policy instrument available to the BOJ is so-called window guidance, whereby the BOJ controls the amount of bank loans directly. This may increase the importance of bank loans in Japan relative to countries in which such an instrument is not used.

The stability of the call rate relative to the federal funds rate, analyzed in section 1.1.4, may imply that the call rate is a very good indicator of Japanese monetary policy and at the same time a good predictor of macrovariables. The predictive power of the call rate in Japan may be higher than that of the federal funds rate in the United States.

Unfortunately, the statistical relationships between the call rate and other monetary variables or macrovariables are very unstable. Time series analyses involving monetary aggregates and other macroeconomic variables are extremely sensitive to the choice of end-of-period versus average-of-period data as well as to the way the series are detrended and seasonally adjusted. It almost seems as if one can come up with any conclusion by choosing different ways of prefiltering the data.

Tables 1.7 and 1.8 show the results of money-versus-loan causality tests and a comparison of the predictive powers of various monetary variables. In

Table 1.7   **Predictive Power of Monetary Indicators in Bivariate Regressions with Index of Production**

Data	Seasonal Adjustment	Dependent Variable	H	M_1	M_2	L	i_c	SMPL[a]
Average	y	level	y	y	y	y	y	1
			y	—	y	—	—	2
Average	y	FD	—	—	—	—	y	1
			y	—	—	—	—	2
Average	dummy[b]	level	y	y	—	y	—	1
			—	—	—	—	—	2
Average	—	annual change	y	y	—	—	—	1
			—	—	—	—	—	2
End of period	y	level	—	—	y	—	y	1
			—	y	y	—	y	2
End of period	y	FD	—	—	—	—	y	1
			—	y	y	—	y	2
End of period	dummy	level	—	—	—	—	—	1
			—	—	—	—	—	2
End of period	—	annual change	—	—	—	—	—	1
			—	y	y	y	—	2

Notes: The dependent variable is the log of the index of production plus the log of the CPI. The money-supply data are also differenced in the same way. Twelve lags were used for all dependent and independent variables. *Annual change* indicates the log annual change; *FD* means the log difference; *level* is the regression including a linear time trend; y indicates significance at the 5% level. H = high-powered money; L = bank loans; i_c = call rate.

[a]1 = estimation for 1969:1–1979:4; 2 = estimation for 1979:5–1989:10.

[b]Monthly dummies are included as independent variables.

table 1.7 the predictive power, in the Granger sense, of monetary indicators is shown in bivariate regressions involving the pace of economic activity (the log of the index of production plus that of the CPI) and one of the indicators. The data are monthly, and twelve lags of each variable were included in the regression.

As warned above, the results are amazingly sensitive to small changes in the data or the specification. Thus, it would be better to use seasonally adjusted data in order to find strong effects of monetary indicators, and better to use nonadjusted, end-of-month data in level form with a time trend in order to support perhaps the real business cycle theory. The use of monthly averages of daily data implies strong effects for indicators in the 1970s; end-of-period data imply strong effects in the 1980s. Money supply measures (M_1 and M_2) appear to exert strong effects on the economy, in terms of the number of times they are significant in the table, as does the call rate.

In table 1.8 I carry out an exercise similar to the one performed by Bernanke and Blinder (1990). When more than one indicator was significant in table 1.7, I included all the indicators in the regression to compare the predic-

Table 1.8   **Marginal Significance Levels of Monetary Indicators for Forecasting the Index of Production**

Data	Seasonal Adjustment	Dependent Variable	H	M_1	M_2	L	i_c	Period[a]
Average	y	level	.012	.093	.212	.120 **	.165	1
			.008	.103	.009	.012 **	.030	2
Average		annual change	.147 *	.045	.242	.646 *	.564	1
End of period	y	level	.010	.010 *	.011 *	.795	.002	1
			.467	.115	.009	.030	.021	2
End of period		annual change	.501	.097	.011 *	.277 *	.116	2

Notes: Regressions in this table include twelve lags of all the monetary indicators. Results are shown only for those cases in which more than one indicator was significant in table 1.7 and at least one indicator was significant when all indicators were included. * means the indicator had the highest explanatory power in terms of variance decomposition either in the order appearing in the table or in the reverse order; ** means the indicator had the highest explanatory power in both decompositions. *Annual change* indicates the log annual change; *FD* means the log difference; *level* is the regression including a linear time trend; *y* indicates significance at the 5% level. H = high-powered money; L = bank loans; i_c = call rate.

[a]1 = estimation for 1969:1–1979:4; 2 = estimation for 1979:5–1989:10.

tive power of each more accurately. In contrast to the finding of Bernanke and Blinder that the federal funds rate is unambiguously the best indicator. I find mixed results. None seems to be markedly superior to the others.

The results of the variance decomposition shown in the table, however, are less ambiguous. Even with reordering of equations, bank loans possess the highest explanatory power in 80% of the cases. This result is, at least, suggestive of the importance of bank loans in the Japanese monetary transmission mechanism. In other words, bank loans affect the real economy through their effects on other indicators such as monetary aggregates, and this accounts for their predictive power in the Granger sense.

Such an interpretation is broadly consistent with the perception of the staff of the BOJ and of market participants about the transmission mechanism. Their perception is conveniently summarized in a flowchart (fig. 1.2) used occasionally by the BOJ. In the middle of the chart we see that the call rate is the most important direct target (or instrument) of policy, and it is controlled mainly by BOJ lending, open-market operations, and the discount rate. This was discussed in section 1.1. Changes in the call rate cause changes in other interest rates, including the loan rate. These changes, together with the effect of window guidance, will affect bank loans and real variables. This has long been the established view of Japanese monetary policy, and it highlights the importance of bank loans. The chart also includes the direct effects of the

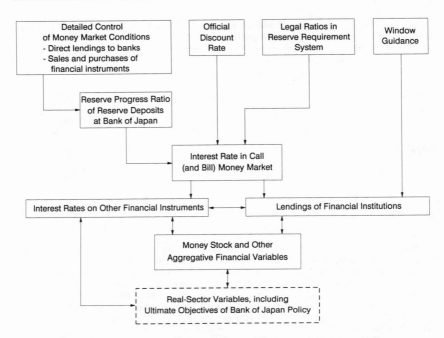

Fig. 1.2 Schematic diagram of the conduct of Japanese monetary policy

money supply and other interest rates on the real sector, but these have not been regarded as the centerpiece of the transmission mechanism.

Slightly more robust time series evidence than that presented in table 1.7 is shown in table 1.9. Here we check for Granger causality among monetary indicators only, and we find exactly the pattern of causation expected from the above discussion. That is, loans and the call rate are not caused by the other variables except for minor cases, while these two indicators help predict other variables.[16]

One additional piece of evidence on the importance of loans is offered, using the technique employed by Romer and Romer (1990). In their study of the money-lending-output correlation they focus on periods when the Fed deliberately shifted to tighter monetary policy. This focus allows them to avoid confusion between the effects of monetary indicators on output and the effects working in the reverse direction.

The dates of deliberate shift to tighter monetary policy are easy to identify in Japan. Most people assume that a change in the discount rate provides such information. (Such dates are March 1957, December 1959, July 1961, March

16. Hutchison (1986) finds causality running from the call rate to M2 in a three-variable system of M_2, the call rate, and nominal retail sales. But he does not check for the importance of bank loans.

Table 1.9   **Granger Causality among Monetary Indicators**

	M_1	M_2	H	L	i_c
M_1	—	n,n	n,y	y,y	n,y
M_2	n,y	—	n,y	y,n	n,y
H	y,y	y,n	—	n,n	y,y
L	n,n	n,n	n,n	—	n,n
IC	y,n	n,n	n,n	n,n	—
M_1	—	n,y	n,y	n,y	n,y
M_2	n,n	—	n,y	n,y	n,y
H	n,n	n,n	—	n,n	y,n
L	n,n	n,n	n,y	—	n,n
IC	n,n	n,n	n,n	n,n	—

Notes: Entries indicate significance in the Granger sense in the regression of a row variable on the column variables. The upper half uses the average of daily data, while the lower half uses end-of-month data. The sample is 1969:1–1979:4 for the first half of the paired entry and 1979:5–1989:10 for the second half. All regressions included twelve lags of each variable and a time trend. Monetary aggregates were seasonally adjusted. H = high-powered money; L = bank loans; i_c = call rate. y = significance at the 5% level; n = insignificance.

1964, September 1967, September 1969, April 1973, April 1979 and May 1989.) In certain cases window guidance preceded an increase in the discount rate. But I do not make adjustments here, in order to preserve the clarity of the criterion.

Essentially, Romer and Romer first calculate the forecast errors of money and bank lending from a regression of each on its own lags immediately after the shifts to tighter monetary policy. The forecast errors (actual minus predicted) are, of course, negative because of the sudden shifts to tightening. However, the errors contain two parts: the independent decrease in money or lending and the response of money or lending to output. The latter may be large in magnitude because tighter policy decreases output over time. In the second part of their analysis they recalculate the forecast errors from a regression of money or lending on its own lags and output. The larger the forecast errors from the second exercise and the smaller the difference between the two exercises, the more important that a monetary indicator is in the transmission mechanism of monetary policy. Based on such an analysis, they conclude that money is more important than lending.

Figures 1.3 and 1.4 present the results of the same analysis using the Japanese data. For money I used M2, and bank loans are the total loans of the banking accounts of all banks—that is, bank loans do not include loans that are backed by money and other trusts of trust banks. The data are monthly, end-of-month, and not seasonally adjusted. The regressions run are money (lending) on a constant, monthly dummies, twelve lags of money (lending), and in some cases the index of production. Variables are in log difference form. I show the forecast errors from regressions that do not include output in

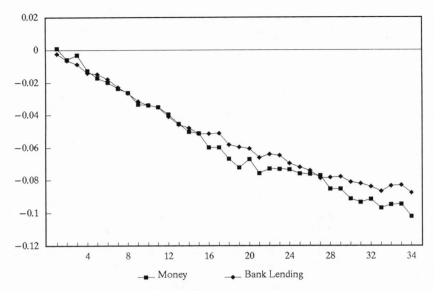

Fig. 1.3   Average forecast errors for money and lending after tightening

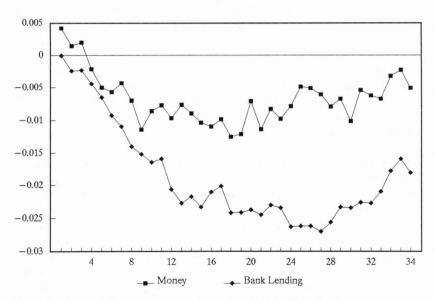

Fig. 1.4   Average forecast errors, given actual path of production

figure 1.3. The errors move in almost the same way for money as for lending, although during the first few months the errors in lending move ahead. (This is already somewhat different from the Romer and Romer finding in which the errors for lending are much larger than, but initially lag behind, those for money.)

The forecast errors from the regressions involving output, presented in figure 1.4, are significantly different between money and lending. Both are much smaller in absolute value than in figure 1.3, but more so for money. Moreover, the peak in the forecast error occurs after eighteen months for money, but after twenty-three months for lending. The errors from the lending regression to monetary tightening respond more quickly than do those from the money regression, which is more evident in figure 1.4 than in figure 1.3. This is also in sharp contrast to Romer and Romer. They find that the error from the lending regression does not become significantly negative until after fifteen months of tightening.

The results in figures 1.3 and 1.4 are supportive of a more important role for bank lending than for money in the transmission mechanism. Also, they are consistent with the interpretation that bank lending itself is an instrument of monetary policy. The results are not sensitive to whether the data are seasonally adjusted or to the choice of monetary aggregate, M1 or M2.

One needs to appreciate fully the important implication of the exogeneity of bank loans together with their high explanatory power for real variables. Bank loans are important not only because monetary policy affects real variables through loans. They also have been under the more direct influence of the BOJ—hence the exogeneity. The BOJ uses both instruments—the call rate and window guidance—to affect real variables.

1.3   Conclusions

In its daily operations, the BOJ's policy target has been the call rate. It has never targeted bank reserves. The call rate has been much more stable than the federal funds rate even for periods during which the Fed targeted the funds rate. Because of this, the stock of high-powered money is an endogenous variable.

The BOJ stabilizes the call rate by using "defensive" operations extensively, which accommodate movements in the shortage or surplus of funds. Although the BOJ also fully accommodates changes in the demand for bank reserves at the monthly level, it carries out "dynamic" operations at the daily level to change the target level of the call rate. Changes in BOJ lending at the discount window are an important instrument for this purpose.

The possibility of more direct control of the call rate by the BOJ has also been pointed out. In some periods the BOJ quoted the call rate either directly or indirectly, at the same time preventing arbitrage between markets through moral suasion. The importance of such non-market-oriented control of the call rate and the change in its importance over time need to be more carefully studied.

Bank loans play an important role in the transmission of monetary policy in Japan. I find stronger support for the credit view in Japan than in the United States. The interpretation of this finding, however, involves more than merely pointing out that monetary policy affects the real sector through its effects on bank loans.

The call rate is not the best indicator of monetary policy in the sense of being the best predictor of real-sector activity in the economy. Monetary aggregates and loans also predict real variables fairly well. However, the call rate and bank lending cause other monetary indicators in the Granger sense. This is plausible, because the BOJ uses window guidance to control bank lending directly during times of monetary tightening.

Abstracting from daily operations, we may say that the call rate and bank lending are the instruments of monetary policy in Japan.[17] Changes in these will create changes in other interest rates and monetary aggregates, in turn moving real variables.

References

Asami, Shinzo. 1963. *Koru-shijo no Kaisetsu: Nihon no Koru Shijou* (in Japanese). Nikkeibunko 42, Nihonkeizaishinbun-sha.

Bank of Japan. 1990. Developments in Financial and Other Sectors of the Japanese Economy in 1989 (in Japanese). *Monthly Report of the Research and Statistics Bureau* (May): 1–60.

Bernanke, Ben, and Alan Blinder. 1990. The Federal Funds Rate and the Channel of Monetary Transmission. NBER Working Paper No. 3487. Cambridge, MA: National Bureau of Economic Research, October.

Bryant, Ralph C. 1990. Model Representations of Japanese Monetary Policy. June. Mimeo.

Cargill, Thomas F., and Shoichi Royama. 1988. *The Transition of Finance in Japan and the United States.* Stanford, CA: Hoover Institution Press, Stanford University.

Committee on Short-Term Money Markets. 1990. *Wagakuni Tanki Kinyuushijouno Gennjou to Kadai* (The current state of Japanese short-term money markets and their problems). Tokyo: Ministry of Finance and the Bank of Japan. June.

Dotsey, Michael. 1986. Japanese Monetary Policy: A Comparative Analysis. *Bank of Japan Monetary and Economic Studies* 4 no. 2 (October): 105–28.

Federal Reserve Bank of New York. 1981. Monetary Policy and Open Market Operations in 1980. *Quarterly Review* 6 (Summer): 56–75.

———. 1988. A Review of Federal Reserve Policy Targets and Operating Guides in Recent Decades. *Quarterly Review* 13 (Autumn): 6–17.

Feldman, Robert A. 1986. *Japanese Financial Markets.* Cambridge, MA: MIT Press.

17. At the end of June 1991, the BOJ announced that it will no longer use window guidance. The implication of this decision for the conduct of the BOJ's monetary policy is a topic for future study.

Horiuchi, Akiyoshi, and Masaaki Kato. 1989. Monetary Policy and the Interbank Money Markets in Japan (in Japanese). *Journal of Economics* (University of Tokyo) 55, no. 3 (October): 58–72.

Hutchison, Michael M. 1986. Japan's "Money Focused" Monetary Policy. *Federal Reserve Bank of San Francisco Economic Review*, no. 3:33–46.

Kanzaki, Takashi. 1988. Tanki Shijo Kinri no Kettei mekanizumu ni tsuite—Nichibei Kinyu Chosetsu Hoshiki no Hikaku Bunseki. *Kinyu Kenkyu* 7, no. 2 (August): 1–60.

King, Stephen R. 1986. Monetary Transmission: Through Bank Loans or Bank Liabilities? *Journal of Money, Credit, and Banking* 18, no. 3 (August): 290–303.

Meulendyke, Ann-Marie. 1988. A Review of Federal Reserve Policy Targets and Operating Guides in Recent Decades. *Quarterly Review* 13, no. 3.

Okina, Kunio. 1987. Short-Term Interest Rates and Monetary Control in Japan: A Reconsideration of the BOJ Theory. Discussion Paper No. 157. Institute of Economic Research, Hitotsubashi University, March.

Partlan, John C., Kausa Hamdani, and Kathleen M. Camilli. 1986. Reserves Forecasting for Open Market Operations. *Quarterly Review* 11, no. 1 (Spring): 19–33.

Romer, Cristina D., and David H. Romer. 1990. New Evidence on the Monetary Transmission Mechanism. *Brookings Papers on Economic Activity* no. 1:149–213.

Roosa, Robert V. 1956. *Federal Reserve Operations in the Money and Government Securities Markets*. Federal Reserve Bank of New York.

Royama, Shoichi. 1971. Wagakunino Kinyu Mekanizumu. In *Nihon no Kinyuu*, ed. T. Shimano and K. Hamada. Tokyo: Iwanami Shoten.

Spindt, Paul A., and Vefa Tarhan. 1987. The Federal Reserve's New Operating Procedures: A Post Mortem. *Journal of Monetary Economics* 19, no. 1 (January): 107–24.

Suzuki, Yoshio. 1980. *Money and Banking in Contemporary Japan*. New Haven: Yale University Press.

Suzuki, Yoshio, Akio Kuroda, and Hiromichi Shirakawa. 1988. Monetary Control Mechanism in Japan. *Monetary and Economic Studies* 6, no. 2 (November): 43–65.

Ueda, Kazuo, and Kazuhide Uekusa. 1988. Kinyuu-Chousetsu no Mekanizumu. In *Gendai Keizaigaku Kennkyuu*, ed. Y. Onitsuka and K. Iwai. Tokyo: University of Tokyo Press.

2   Market Operations in Japan: Theory and Practice

Kunio Okina

This paper outlines Japan's short-term money markets, the conduct of the daily operations of the Bank of Japan, and the theoretical framework behind such operations.

The modi operandi of monetary policy in recent decades have experienced several regime changes. First, from 1960 to the early 1970s, lending by financial institutions rather than the money stock was considered the most important variable linking operating variables and the ultimate objectives of monetary policy. The second period began in the early 1970s when the immediate impact of the first oil crisis had dissipated, and ended in the mid-1980s. The bank shifted its emphasis from financial institutions' lending to the money stock, especially M_2. It was in July 1978 that the Bank of Japan started publishing forecasts of broad money supply developments. Finally, since the mid-1980s, M_2 + CDs (certificates of deposit) has not declined gradually as it did during the second period, but has continued to grow around 10% per year until very recently. At the same time, the prices of goods and services have remained stable.[1]

Kunio Okina is a senior economist at the Institute for Monetary and Economic Studies of the Bank of Japan.

This paper was prepared for the NBER Conference on Japanese Monetary Policy 18–19 April 1991, in Tokyo. The author is indebted to Wataru Takahashi for his great help with respect to sections 2.1 and 2.2. The author is also grateful to Akiyoshi Horiuchi, Takatoshi Ito, Mitsuru Iwamura, Motonari Kurasawa, Hiroshi Yoshikawa, and Kazuo Ueda for their helpful comments. The opinions expressed are solely those of the author and do not necessarily express the views of the Bank of Japan.

1. One possible explanation of this phenomenon is the recent financial deregulation and innovation in Japan. Another plausible explanation lies in the sharp appreciation of the yen since October 1985 and the stock market crash of October 1987, which killed inflationary expectations. Under the sharp appreciation of the yen and rapid growth of the money supply, a combination of stable prices of goods and services (which partly reflected lower prices of tradable goods) and the rapid inflation of land prices (a nontradable factor of production) was observed. See Ito (1991).

The Bank of Japan has never committed itself to a certain rate of growth of monetary aggregates as an intermediate target and often reiterates that it watches a variety of economic indicators such as interest rates, price indices, indicators reflecting corporate liquidity conditions and the general business outlook, and the yen exchange rate. However, the Bank of Japan's monetary policy *always* begins with controlling interest rates in short-term money markets. Thus, in this paper, I will concentrate on the mechanism for controlling the operating targets, that is, short-term interest rates. Neither the relationship between the intermediate (or final) and the operating targets nor how the desired operating targets are chosen by the bank will be discussed.

In order to control short-term interest rates, central banks are supposed to change the level of the monetary base through open-market operations. However, it is difficult to apply this textbook explanation to actual market operations, especially in Japan. The reason for this is as follows. High-powered money consists of banks' reserve deposits in central bank accounts and bank notes. On the one hand, because the lagged reserve system was adopted in Japan, the demand for reserves in a given month is predetermined. On the other hand, the demand for bank notes, including vault cash, is quite insensitive to market interest rates in the short run. Therefore, the aggregate demand curve for high-powered money in any month is virtually vertical. In order to clear the market for high-powered money, the Bank of Japan has no option but to accommodate the demand for required reserves and bank notes.

Put differently, under the current institutional framework, the Bank of Japan is obliged to supply a sufficient amount of high-powered money, at least as a monthly average, so that all banks can meet their reserve requirements; hence, it will not be able to effect textbook-type operations.

Of course, over periods longer than a month, the demand for many components of high-powered money will become more interest elastic. However, this does not imply the possibility of short-term textbook-type operations. Interest rate determination in this kind of market needs an explanation more elaborate than the simple textbook story. The one given in this paper emphasizes the role of signals for equilibrium rates transmitted by the Bank of Japan.

Although the issue of the mechanism of interest rate control may appear to be technical, it has important macroeconomic implications. For example, according to the interest rate control mechanisms discussed in this paper, the level of short-term interest rates does not necessarily depend on the quantity of high-powered money or on monetary aggregates. Thus, the validity of empirical studies that use innovations in the money stock as a proxy for changes in the monetary policy stance in Japan must be called into question.

Section 2.1 is a brief review of recent developments in the short-term

---

In such circumstances, the Bank of Japan has gradually corrected its monetary policy stance, which had remained very expansionary for several years. In May 1989 the discount rate was raised by three-quarters of a percentage point, the first increase since early 1980.

money market and an explanation of the market's characteristics. Section 2.2 examines the supply and demand of high-powered money in the money market, which is the basic consideration behind the Bank of Japan's daily operations. This is followed by a detailed discussion of operating procedures and tools and their limitations. In section 2.3 the relationship between the daily operations of the Bank of Japan and the formation of overnight interest rates is explained, with special attention given to how the bank controls overnight rates through accommodative operations. Section 2.4 deals with the relationship between overnight rates and longer-term interest rates, and assesses the impact of the money market reforms of November 1988. The paper concludes with a brief summary and some caveats.

2.1   Recent Developments in the Short-Term Money Markets

2.1.1   Money Markets in Japan: the Status Quo

Short-term money markets in this paper are defined as those in which assets have a maturity of less than one year and are traded by market participants (rather than through bilateral negotiations), with the call, bill, bond repurchase (gensaki), certificate of deposit (CD), commercial paper (CP), and treasury bills and financial bills (TBs, FBs) markets being considered representative.[2]

As shown in table 2.1, short-term money markets in Japan have grown rapidly in recent years, especially since 1985 (annual rate of growth in 1975–85, 11.8%; after 1985, 29.5%), and posted a total outstanding figure of 80 trillion yen at the end of 1989. This rapid expansion is the combined result of economic growth, the creation of new money markets stimulated by deregulation and globalization, and money market reforms promoted by market participants and the Bank of Japan.

Several new short-term money markets have come into operation since 1985: (1) the uncollateralized call market (July 1985); (2) the TB market (February 1986); and (3) the CP market (November 1987).

The main recent reform measures affecting the money markets have been (1) reduction of the minimum denomination of CDs (a gradual lowering from 500 million yen to 50 million yen); (2) extension of CD maturities (a gradual widening from three to six months originally to a two-week- to two-year interval today); (3) reduction in the minimum transaction amount for TBs and FBs (from 100 million yen to 50 million yen in August 1987, and from 50 million yen to 10 million yen in April 1990); and (4) diversification of TB maturities (from six months only to three months and six months, September 1989).

---

2. Yen-denominated deposits in Japan's offshore market and yen-conversion market could also be included. In addition, though there is no official data with respect to market size, CD and CP gensaki markets may satisfy the definition in this paper.

Table 2.1 Money Market Assets Outstanding (end of fiscal year, in 100 million yen)

	1975	1985	1986	1987	1988	1989	Share (%)
Interbank market	71,575	159,097	223,364	268,549	338,369	384,031	46.2
Call	50,271	87,408	131,581	186,414	211,563	287,214	34.5
Collateralized	(50,271)	(78,982)	(112,755)	(158,080)	(140,324)	(161,544)	(19.4)
Uncollateralized	(—)	(8,426)	(18,827)	(28,335)	(71,239)	(125,670)	(15.1)
Bills	21,304	71,689	91,783	82,135	126,806	96,817	11.6
Open market	73,995	159,722	217,088	273,089	355,647	447,871	53.8
Certificates of deposit	16,708	96,335	112,630	135,235	182,881	211,362	25.4
Commercial paper	—	—	—	26,373	90,530	132,163	15.9
Treasury bills	—	10,236	20,226	20,007	24,014	55,028	6.6
Financial bills	—	10,000	25,000	29,000	10,000	10,000	1.2
Securities gensaki[a]	57,287	43,151	59,232	62,474	48,222	39,318	4.7
Total	145,570	318,819	440,452	541,638	694,016	831,902	100.0

Source: Short-Term Money Market Study Group (1990).

[a]Excluding TB and FB gensaki.

Meanwhile, practices in the short-term money markets have been reviewed extensively, especially since November 1988, by the Bank of Japan and market dealers (see table 2.2).

2.1.2   Characteristics of Short-Term Money Markets in Japan

For historical and institutional reasons, money markets in industrialized countries have their own characteristics. Japan's money markets are marked by the following features.

First, the size of the markets as measured by the ratio of outstanding amounts of the traded instruments to GNP is relatively small, though recent developments have brought the ratio to GNP closer to that of the other large industrialized countries (see table 2.3).[3]

Second, the size of short-term government paper relative to the total outstanding amount of the market is smaller than in the United States (at the end of September 1989, 7% in Japan versus 26% in the United States) and closer to that of the United Kingdom and West Germany. In addition, this ratio shows wide month-to-month fluctuations in Japan. Though the amounts of short-term government debt and CP outstanding have recently been increasing, bank liabilities such as call money, bills, and CDs still dominate Japan's market.[4]

2.2   The Short-term Money Markets and Daily Market Operations

2.2.1   The Surplus or Shortage of High-Powered Money and Market Operations

The short-term money market is where short-term lending and borrowing among various economic agents (business firms, central and local governments, financial institutions, etc.) take place. Like the central banks of other developed countries, the Bank of Japan implements monetary policy through market operations aimed at adjusting the aggregate surplus or shortage of high-powered money ("funds"[5]) in short-term money markets. I will discuss its operating practices from two perspectives: (1) the relationship between the surplus or shortage of high-powered money and market operations; and (2) daily operating procedures.

The surplus or shortage of an individual bank arises from various financial transactions such as the settlement of bills and checks, domestic exchange,

---

3. From the end of 1985 to the end of 1988, this ratio went from 9.1 to 17.4% in Japan, 32.0 to 32.7% in the United States, 32.6 to 25.5% in the United Kingdom, and 17.9 to 18.0% in West Germany. As mentioned earlier, there are no official statistics for either CD or CP gensaki outstanding. If such figures were added to the outstanding amounts, the gap in market size between Japan and other countries would narrow.

4. The ratio of bank liabilities to the total amount outstanding in the market decreased from 80.4% at the end of 1984 to 70.8% at the end of 1989.

5. In Japan the hypothetical change in aggregate reserves held by financial institutions if the Bank of Japan were not to conduct any operations is called "the surplus or shortage of funds."

Table 2.2   **Money Market Reforms since November 1988**

Item	Before Reform	After Reform
1988		
Nov		
Bill maturities	1–6 months	1 week–6 months
Collateralized call money maturities	Unconditional–3 weeks	Unconditional–6 days
Uncollateralized call money maturities	Overnight–3 weeks	Overnight–6 months
Maturities of bills eligible for BOJ operations	1–3 months	1 week–3 months (mainly 1–3 weeks)
1989		
Jan		
Unit for call money and bills	1/16%	1/32%
Apr		
Bill maturities	1 week–6 months	1 week–1 year
Uncollateralized call money maturities	Overnight–6 months	Overnight–1 year
May		
CP operations	—	Introduced
Aug		
Disclosure of demand/ supply of funds and market operations	—	Figures for the previous day and revised estimates for the day: 10 A.M. Results for the day and estimates for the following day: 4 P.M.
Advanced acceptance of bills used as collateral for bill operations	Not accepted	Commencement of "roll-over" of bill operations
Dec		
Borrowers of collateralized credit extended by BOJ	City banks, long-term credit banks, major regional banks, etc.	Shinkin banks, foreign banks, and some others added
Disclosure of demand/ supply of funds and market operations	Results for the day and estimates for the following day: 4 P.M.	Results for the day and estimates for the following day: 3 P.M. Offered operations of the day (recorded services): 10 A.M.
1990		
Jan		
TB operations	—	Introduced
Feb		
Limitations on use of uncollateralized call loans by investment funds	Up to 30% of total amount of call loans incorporated in funds	Up to 50% of the aggregate amount of call loans and bills incorporated in funds
Apr		
Securities eligible as collateral for BOJ advances	Publicly offered municipal bonds	Some non-publicly offered municipal bonds added
Jun		
Auction schedules of TB operations, rotative bond purchases, and bond repos	From offers to notice of bids 3 hrs., 30 mins.	From offers to notice of bids 2 hrs., 50 mins.

Table 2.2   (continued)

Item	Before Reform	After Reform
Aug Disclosure schemes for fund demand/supply and market operations	Disclosure of figures based on increase/ decrease in bank notes	Disclosure of figures based on surpluses/ shortages in the market Commencement of disclosure of difference between current reserve amount and required reserves not satisfied
Nov Collateralized call rates	Quotation system	Commencement of offer/ bid system

Source: Nakao and Horii (1991).

deposit withdrawals, government expenditures, and so forth. However, if the surpluses or shortages among banks are added up, the aggregate net surplus or shortage of high-powered money simply corresponds to that of the government sector and the demand for cash (bank notes) by the private sector.

Since the interest elasticity of the demand for high-powered money for daily settlements is negligibly small, central bank open-market operations are essential to establish daily market equilibrium and to avoid volatile interest rate movements.

This can be confirmed by checking the budget constraints of market participants. Suppose the financial sector consists of m banks, where the simplified budget constraint of the ith bank ($i = 1, \ldots, m$) is assumed to be

$$(1) \qquad\qquad R_i = D_i - L_i - C_i + B_i,$$

where R_i = ith bank's deposits with the Bank of Japan; D_i = ith bank's deposits outstanding; L_i = ith bank's loans outstanding; C_i = ith bank's other financial assets, (if negative, other financial liabilities); and B_i = Bank of Japan lending outstanding to the ith bank. By aggregating over all banks, the following budget constraint for the financial sector is attained:

$$(1') \qquad (1)'\ \sum_i R_i = \sum_i D_i - \sum_i L_i - \sum_i C_i + \sum_i B_i.$$

Next, the simplified budget constraint for the jth agent ($j = 1, \ldots, k$) in the nonfinancial private sector is assumed to be

$$(2) \qquad\qquad L_j + W_j = D_j + C_j + N_j + V_j,$$

where L_j = jth agent's borrowing outstanding; W_j = jth agent's net wealth; D_j = jth agent's deposits outstanding; C_j = jth agent's financial assets (if negative, financial liabilities); N_j = cash (bank notes) held by the jth agent; and V_j = jth agent's real capital.

Table 2.3   **Money Markets of Some Large Industrialized Countries (end September 1989)**

Country		Share (%)	Country		Share (%)
Japan (trillion ¥)			United States (billion $)		
Call	25	32.3	Federal funds and RPs	178	11.5
Bills	11	14.6	CDs[a]	396	25.5
CDs	20	25.7	CPs	507	32.7
CP	11	14.3	Bank acceptances	64	4.1
TBs	3	4.3	TBs	407	26.2
FBs	2	2.6			
Securities gensaki	5[b]	6.3			
Total	77	100.0	Total	1,551	100.0
Ratio of total to nominal GNP		19.6	Ratio of total to nominal GNP		29.4
West Germany (billion DM)			United Kingdom (million £)		
Call	311	79.2	Call	10,913	6.7
Bills	71	18.1	Interbank deposits	87,406	53.5
TBs	10	2.6	Bills	5,472	3.3
Total	392	100.0	£ demonimated CDs	43,556	26.7
			£ denominated CP	3,126	1.9
Ratio of total to nominal GNP		7.3	TBs	12,891	7.9
			Total	163,364	100.0
			Ratio of total to nominal GNP		32.0

Source: Short-Term Money Market Study Group (1990).
[a]Large-denomination time deposits (over $100,000).
[b]Excluding TB and FB gensaki.

By aggregation, we have

$$(3) \qquad \sum_j L_j + \sum_j W_j = \sum_j D_j + \sum_j C_j + \sum_j N_j + \sum_j V_j.$$

If we ignore, for the sake of simplicity, the government sector, then the balance sheet of the private sector can be described as follows.

After aggregating over the entire private sector, without open-market purchases of securities by the central bank the net supply of financial assets in the private sector is zero; that is,

$$(4) \qquad \sum_i C_i + \sum_j C_j = 0.$$

Similarly,

$$(5) \qquad \sum_i L_i = \sum_j L_j,$$

and

$$(6) \qquad \sum_i D_i = \sum_j D_j.$$

And since net wealth in the economy corresponds to real capital, we have

(7)
$$\sum_j W_j = \sum_j V_j.$$

Putting all these constraints together, we have

(8)
$$\sum_i B_i = \sum_j N_j + \sum_i R_i.$$

This equation simply shows that, in spite of the existence of various markets, the macroeconomic conditions determining the quantity of high-powered money held by the private sector (deposits with the central bank and bank notes) boil down to the budget constraint of the central bank. That is, in order to satisfy the demand for high-powered money, the Bank of Japan's lending $(\sum_i B_i)$ should equal the demand for banknotes $(\sum_j N_j)$ plus aggregate reserves $(\sum_i R_i)$ if no market operations are conducted.

In reality, the government sector affects the budget constraint of the Bank of Japan, and the Bank of Japan not only lends but also purchases financial assets. However, these do not affect the fundamental nature of market equilibrium. In fact, daily open-market operations by the Bank of Japan are based on a straightforward extension of equation (8), which includes the government sector and is expressed with flow variables:

(8′)
$$\Delta R = \Delta B + \Delta G - \Delta N,$$

where ΔR = increase in reserves held by financial institutions; ΔB = increase in Bank of Japan credit; ΔG = increase in net expenditures by the government sector; and ΔN = increased bank note issuance.

Equation (8′) is an identity. However, since the interest elasticity of ΔG and ΔN is quite small on a daily basis, these variables can be regarded as exogenous. ΔB is a policy variable determined by the Bank of Japan daily, according to its desired level of ΔR.[6]

Hence, market operations commence from the estimation of the shortage of funds $(\Delta N - \Delta G)$. In Japan, since the surplus or shortage fluctuates quite widely (figure 2.1 shows the weekly fluctuation in the surplus or shortage of funds in Japan and the United States during 1988), the prediction of a surplus or shortage plays an important role in conducting appropriate market operations. A brief explanation of the Bank of Japan's prediction schedule will be given, with the reservation that it is often changed following a change in market practice. The explanation that follows is, in principle, based on the situation as of January 1991.

The monthly surplus or shortage of funds for the following month, taking into account seasonality, business conditions, and information acquired from

---

6. As mentioned later, on the final day of the reserve period the Bank of Japan must extend enough credit to satisfy the aggregate reserve requirement.

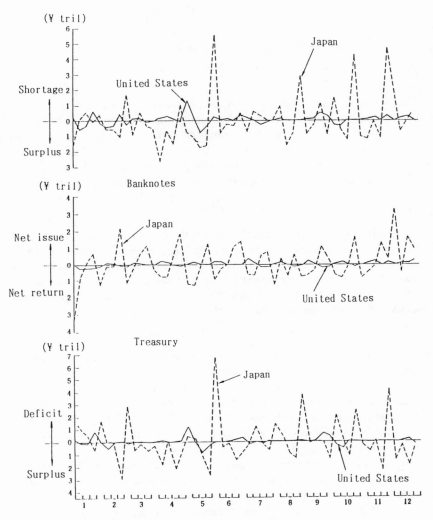

Fig. 2.1   Fund markets in the United States and Japan (1988, weekly)
Source: Short-Term Money Market Study Group (1990).

market participants and others, is predicted and announced at the end of the current month. These figures may be revised shortly afterward on the basis of new information.

Estimates of daily shortages and surpluses, which are based on the information available at the Bank of Japan's head office, are announced each day around 3 P.M. On the morning of the day concerned, revised estimates are released with details of the bank's planned operations. In the afternoon the figures for government net expenditures and the net demand for bank notes are revised, and preliminary figures are published around 3 P.M.

2.2.2   Schedule of Daily Market Operations

The next question is when and how the Bank of Japan enters the market. Table 2.4 shows the Bank of Japan's typical market-operation schedule in January 1991. There are two focal points during a business day that are especially important for the Bank of Japan's market operations: (1) the bill clearing settlement at 1 P.M., and (2) the final settlement at 3 P.M.

Before noon, call money transactions, mainly overnight, are usually quite active, as are various bill transactions. In the early morning, the Bank of Japan offers CP and bill operations (for the final settlement of the day) and lending; later, it offers bond, bill, and TB operations for the next business day and after. At 1 P.M., bill clearing settlement, domestic exchange settlement, and call and bill settlements are carried out. Financial institutions having insufficient reserves for such settlements must raise money by the specified times. In Japan there exist intraday call transactions—financial institutions that do not have enough reserves for settlement at 1 P.M., but that expect to receive funds by 3 P.M. (final settlement), for example, utilize second-half intraday call transactions. After 1 P.M., the total surplus or shortage in the market for the final settlement gradually becomes known. The Bank of Japan carries out its final market adjustment to offset part of the surplus or shortage of funds. The primary tool for this final operation is Bank of Japan lending to financial institutions.[7] At 3 P.M., yen-based settlements in categories such as foreign exchange and net government expenditures are effected.

2.2.3   Bank of Japan Market-Operation Instruments and Their Limitations

Presently, the Bank of Japan possesses several tools for market operations: bill purchases, CP purchases, TB purchases, FB sales, bond gensaki, and long-term government bond purchases (see tables 2.5 and 2.6).

These instruments are used for different adjustment purposes. The roles of these respective instruments in the 1980s were roughly as follows:

• Bill operations and lending by the Bank of Japan are mainly used to correct the daily surplus or shortage.[8] On some occasions, CP operations are employed for the same purpose.

7. In Japan, Bank of Japan lending is considered a primary market operation tool. Such lending is not carried out passively, according to the demand of private banks; rather, it is almost completely determined by the Bank of Japan.

8. Dotsey (1986) and Ueda (chap. 1 in this volume) emphasize that the Bank of Japan uses discount window lending as a tool of "dynamic" operations. Though the weight of discount window lending is substantial, usually the Bank of Japan does not consider it a tool for dynamic operations. Rather, since Bank of Japan lending involves minimal administrative work, it is considered the most convenient tool for final adjustment.

Table 2.4   **Schedule of Market Operations for January 1991**

Time	Market Transactions	BOJ Operations	BOJ Announcements
09:00	Uncollateralized call Collateralized call Bill Euroyen 90	Offer of bill operation for final settlement of the day	
09:30	80	Offer of BOJ lending	
10:00	100 (approx.)	Securities purchases and gensaki (settled the fourth business day) TB purchases (settled the third business day	Revised fund surplus/ shortage for the day and actual figure for the prior day Operation plan for the day and actual operations the prior day Prior-day difference between required reserve and accumulated reserve
11:00		Bill operation (settled the next business day)	
12:00			
13:00	(Bill clearing and domestic exchange settlement)		
14:00	10 20		
		Offer of BOJ lending for final settlements	
15:00	(Final settlement)		Publication of preliminary surplus/ shortage for the day and prediction for the next business day Preliminary announcement of operations for the day

Table 2.4   (continued)

Time	Market Transactions	BOJ Operations	BOJ Announcements
16:00	|		
17:00		Offer of FB operations for the next business day	Preliminary announcement of the difference between required reserve and accumulated reserve

Source: Research and Statistics Department, Bank of Japan.

Notes: While CD and CP transactions are effected almost simultaneously with Euroyen transactions, transactions tend to be concentrated in the late afternoon for next-day settlement. Bar graph figures indicate the weight of transactions normally carried out within the given time span ("guesstimation" based on the views of market participants; %).

Table 2.5   **Instruments of Monetary Control**

Instrument	Bank of Japan lending[a]	Bill operations (1) Purchase of commercial bills (3) Sale of commercial bills
Commencement	November 1962	June 1972
Intervention rate	Official discount rate	Bill rates determined in the interbank bill market
Objectives	Adjusting short-term fund shortages/surplus	Credit accommodation for short-term fund shortages
Characteristics	BOJ advances to banks are made and called back solely upon the BOJ's initiative; amounts also determined by the BOJ. This makes BOJ lending a very flexible and attractive instrument for controlling the reserve supply in the money market. (From the viewpoint of borrowing banks, they always have to anticipate that BOJ advances might be called back at any time.)	The BOJ purchases bills held by financial institutions through money market dealers[b] (bill terms: 1 week–3 months) Different from BOJ lending, in that sellers (financial institutions) do not have to worry about repurchases. (The BOJ rarely resells bills to others.)
Instrument	Bill operations (1) Purchase of commercial bills	FB operations Sales

(continued)

Table 2.5   (continued)

	(2) Sale of commercial bills	
Commencement	August 1971	May 1981
Intervention rate	Bill rates or call rates determined in the interbank bill market	Bill rates
Objectives	Absorption of short-term fund surpluses	Absorption of short-term fund surpluses
Characteristics	The BOJ issues bills, payee being the BOJ itself, and sells them to money market dealers. (1) To the call market (term: several days; rates: call rates [in this case dealers do not resell]). (2) To the bill market (term: 1–3 months; rates: bill rates [in this case dealers resell bills to financial institutions]).	The BOJ sells financing bills (short-term government bills) to money market dealers with repurchase agreements. Dealers resell to financial institutions or securities firms; which in turn distribute them to various banking and nonbanking institutions. This instrument enables the BOJ to intervene in the open market directly. Since the BOJ is able to manage only sales operations, however, FB operations are not sufficient as a monetary control measure.
Instrument	Outright purchase of bonds	Purchase of bonds with repurchase agreement
Commencement	November 1962	December 1987
Intervention rate	Rate determined by auction	Rate determined by auction
Objectives	Supply of currency necessary for economic growth	Credit accommodation for short-term fund shortages
Characteristics	The BOJ buys government bonds from financial institutions and securities companies. The current operating method (in which a purchase offer of a relatively small size is made to a limited number of institutions chosen by the BOJ on a rotation basis) was introduced in June	The BOJ buys securities (in practice, long-term government bonds) from financial institutions and securities companies with repurchase agreements.

Table 2.5   (continued)

	1984 in order to mitigate the impact on the bond market	
Instrument	CP operations Purchases	TB operations Purchases
Commencement	May 1989	January 1990
Intervention rate	CP repo rates, or call rates	Rate determined by auction
Objectives	Control of overnight interest rates	Credit accommodation for short-term fund shortages
Characteristics	The BOJ purchases CP (with due date within 3 months from operation date via money market dealers) with repurchase agreements.	The BOJ purchases securities (in practice, TBs or short-term government bills) from financial institutions or securities firms with resale agreements.

Source: Nakao and Horii (1991).

[a]In addition to the types of loans listed here, a limited amount of lending is available upon request (the lending takes the form of discounting eligible commercial bills and import settlement bills).
[b]The BOJ usually purchases bills issued by financial institutions and those backed by other commercial bills as collateral.

- Seasonal factors (such as monthly or quarterly surpluses or shortages) are mainly corrected by FB and securities gensaki operations.
- Long-term government bond purchases are employed to accommodate the demand for money originating from economic growth.

It should be emphasized again that the role of each operational tool is not fixed. Rather, it changes in accordance with changes in the financial environment and changes in market practice.[9]

The Bank of Japan has various tools for intervening in the money markets. There is criticism that the bank should concentrate instead on operations in a core market. In Japan, however, there is neither a core market nor a core operating tool such as the repurchase market in the United States.

The primary prerequisites for an operating tool to become a core tool are

1. The respective market should have sufficient depth.

2. Operational instruments should be homogeneous.

3. The administrative work involved in the operation should be minimal and same-day settlement ensured.

9. In fact, as shown in table 2.2, CP and TB operations were introduced in the late 1980s.

Table 2.6   BOJ Credit and Bank Reserves (100 million yen)

	1987	1988	1989	1989				1990
				September	October	November	December	January
Surplus or shortage of funds	−6,710	−12,889	−57,284	−25,762	−17,232	49,716	−92,233	26,285
Bank notes	−23,019	−31,315	−51,017	−398	698	−6,083	−71,919	61,032
Treasury funds	2,965	6,087	3,992	−23,193	−16,450	55,590	−19,797	−33,987
Bank of Japan credit								
Lending	442	19,071	−15,288	3,088	6,054	−20,750	28,507	−14,218
Commercial bills purchased	993	3,007	41,000	22,000	1,000	3,000	10,000	−3,000
CP purchased	—	—	—	−3,000	—	3,000	−3,000	3,000
Sales of TBs	—	—	—	—	—	—	—	4,035
Sales of FBs	−2	−996	9,947	72	14,882	−44,807	49,767	−9,972
Short-term sales of securities	1,783	416	3,051	−1,556	—	3,065	2,185	−3,281
Sales of securities	7,380	4,215	17,154	—	1,255	3,633	1,022	2,212
Total	10,596	25,713	55,864	20,604	23,191	−52,859	88,481	−21,224
Reserves	3,886	12,824	−1,420	−5,158	5,959	−3,143	−3,752	5,061

1990

	February	March	April	May	June	July	August	September
Surplus or shortage of funds	16,460	7,611	45,278	43,034	−48,705	−21,566	12,095	−5,895
Bank notes	−4,432	−17,696	−11,112	34,681	−25,029	9,441	7,460	−2,609
Treasury funds	20,342	28,739	55,627	8,317	−24,669	−33,594	2,308	−4,913
Bank of Japan credit								
Lending	5,920	−7,742	−7,946	−9,613	6,339	1,309	−19,891	20,762
Commercial bills purchased	−6,000	−14,000	−21,000	6,000	21,000	−6,000	−17,000	−5,000
CP purchased	−3,000	—	—	—	3,000	2,000	−5,000	—
Sales of TBs	−1,064	−1,873	5,536	−697	−1,257	4,015	−924	2,264
Sales of FBs	−14,805	14,813	−21,732	−40,919	22,007	23,795	11,958	9,900
Short-term sales of securities	1,935	−2,361	−1,543	1,493	159	—	−15	—
Sales of securities	1,886	1,340	1,663	1,737	1,723	2,045	1,967	2,046
Total	−15,128	−9,823	−45,022	−41,999	52,971	27,164	−28,905	29,972
Reserves	1,332	−2,212	256	1,035	4,266	5,598	−16,810	24,077

Source: Bank of Japan (1990).

Note: A minus sign indicates the following in each row: row 1 = shortage of funds; row 2 = increase of notes in circulation; row 3 = net receipts of the Treasury; row 4 = net repayment to the Bank of Japan; rows 5–7 and 9 = net resales by the Bank of Japan; rows 8 and 10 = net sales by the Bank of Japan; row 11 = decrease of credit; and row 12 = decline in reserves.

4. The assets to be acquired should have creditworthiness and liquidity appropriate for being assets of the central bank.[10]

In light of these four conditions, short-term government bills are potentially the most suitable tools for money market operations. At present, however, there are some difficulties in using government bills as core instruments. In Japan, two types of short-term government bills are issued: TBs and FBs. The amount of TBs outstanding was about 4 trillion yen as of the end of December 1989, accounting for only 5.0% of the money market. For the TB market to become a core area of operations, expansion of its volume is essential. However, in light of the structural change in the money flow, for example, the decline in the total issuance of government bonds, it seems to be difficult to increase TB issuances rapidly.[11]

In order for the short-term government bill market to become the primary area of operation, it is necessary to maintain sufficient market size at all times. Since the issuance volume of TBs cannot grow very rapidly, a second option would be to expand the FB market. FBs are bills issued by the government to meet its temporary shortage of funds. FBs outstanding at the end of December 1989 totaled 28 trillion yen, more than five times the outstanding stock of TBs. At present, however, FBs are issued through fixed-rate public subscription, where the Bank of Japan underwrites the remaining FBs. In practice, the Bank of Japan must underwrite the bulk of the FBs issued: this means that the Bank of Japan cannot purchase FBs before selling them to the private sector.

Thus, due to the absence of a primary tool of operation, the Bank of Japan is at present heavily dependent on lending.[12] Introducing a public auction system for the issuance of FBs would change this situation.

2.3   The Relationship between Market Operations and the Control of the Overnight Interest Rate: A Theoretical Interpretation

2.3.1   The Reserve Requirement System and Market Operations

Ueda's paper in this volume criticizes the explanations (including the one in this paper) of interest rate determination that are given by the staff of the Bank of Japan for all sharing the problem of relying too much on the special

10. These four conditions were mentioned by the Short-Term Money Market Study Group (1990).

11. There are two other problems: (1) TBs are settled on the third business day; and (2) profit gained from the redemption of TBs, as well as other discounted securities, is subject to an 18% withholding tax at the time of issuance. This is rarely observed in other countries and may be a reason that TBs have not become important yen-denominated assets for nonresidents.

12. Constraints with respect to other tools of operations are (1) CP and bills are issued by various private companies. Therefore, their creditworthiness is not homogeneous, and additional administrative work is necessary, making them not appropriate as primary tools of operation; and (2) long-term government gensaki are subject to a securities transaction tax and are settled on the fourth business day.

features of the current reserve accounting system. Indeed, the explanation given below relies heavily on the institutional framework of the present reserve system, though I do not think it is an analytical problem. In fact, if institutional features are not taken into account, misleading conclusions will result.

Thus, in order to understand the techniques of the Bank of Japan's monetary policy, some knowledge of the reserve requirement system in Japan is indispensable. The system requires financial institutions to keep deposits with the central bank in certain proportions to their deposits and other liabilities. This system was introduced in 1957, under the Law concerning the Reserve Deposit Requirement System, and in 1959 reserve ratios were established for each category of financial institution.[13] When the system was introduced in Japan, it was considered to be an instrument that directly affected the liquidity position of private banks by changing their reserve requirement ratios. Today, however, the Bank of Japan rarely employs this tool to affect monetary conditions in the economy, April 1981 being the last occasion. Still, the reserve requirement system supplies a basic framework for market operations by the Bank of Japan.

2.3.2   Interest Rate Control under a Lagged Reserve System

The Profit-maximizing Behavior of Private Banks under a Lagged Reserve System

Ordinarily, the reserve requirement system requires commercial institutions to maintain deposits in certain proportions to their deposits and other liabilities in non-interest-bearing accounts at the central bank. In Japan, private banks' required reserves are calculated as the product of the reserve ratio and average deposits outstanding in a calendar month, with the reserve "maintenance period" beginning on the sixteenth day of that month and ending on the fifteenth day of the following month. Therefore, the Japanese reserve requirement system is a mixture of a "lagged reserve system" and a "contemporaneous reserve system." But to understand its role in controlling short-term interest rates, it could essentially be viewed as a lagged reserve system. This system is more suitable for controlling short-term interest rates than for controlling reserves.[14]

To see this, let us consider the mechanism of interest rate determination under a lagged reserve system. For the sake of simplicity, we assume that the maturity of all financial assets is overnight (i.e., the only interest rate in the economy is the overnight rate) and ignore the existence of the government sector as well as the demand for bank notes from the nonfinancial private

13. For details on the introduction of the reserve requirement system in Japan, see the Bank of Japan (1985).

14. This does not imply that a lagged reserve system is essential to interest rate control. This is self-evident when we recall that there was no reserve requirement in Japan before 1959.

sector. In reality, both the government's financial balance and bank note demand are interest rate inelastic in the short run. In order to maintain the smooth functioning of the money markets, the Bank of Japan partially accommodates them on a daily basis and completely accommodates them over the "maintenance period." Therefore, neglecting them poses no problem in discussing the nature of the lagged reserve system.

Let us consider the profit-maximizing behavior of private banks before the last day of the reserve maintenance period. The optimum strategy for the banks would be to borrow from the market and accumulate reserves when the interest rate is low, and to become a lender when the interest rate is high. Thus, on each business day, banks compare the interest rate for the day and the expected interest rate for the remainder of the maintenance period. Through this kind of intertemporal arbitrage, the daily interest rate converges to the expected interest rate for the rest of the reserve maintenance period.

If the daily reserve demand (except on the final day) in a reserve maintenance period is perfectly substitutable, such arbitrage works completely. In other words, the interest rate elasticity of daily reserve demand is infinite at the level of cumulative required reserves. Therefore, the actual quantity of daily reserves supplied by the central bank is not important as such for controlling the daily equilibrium interest rate. Rather, the market's expectation of future interest rates is the dominant factor in the determination of the current interest rate. In this setup, once the central bank's ability to control market interest rates is established, the expectations of market participants are formulated around the inferred target range of the central bank. Thus, signals about the target range of interest rates emanating from the central bank are what actually determine market rates.

The "Anchor" Rate and the Reserve Market on the Final Day of the Maintenance Period

The theoretical essence behind the credibility of the central bank is that it is the lender (and borrower) of last resort, which is easily understood by looking at the reserve market on the final day of a reserve maintenance period.

On the final day, the demand for reserves will become highly interest inelastic because financial institutions are obliged to satisfy the reserve requirement. In Japan, if a bank fails to meet the reserve requirement, the shortfall is subject to a penalty interest rate 3.75 percentage points per annum above the discount rate. Moreover, since a failure to satisfy the reserve requirement is quite exceptional and is viewed as disgraceful, banks consider the nonpecuniary cost to be more serious. Thus, on the final day, these financial institutions try to raise funds to satisfy the reserve requirement at any cost. Therefore, if there is an aggregate shortage in the market, interest rates will skyrocket without reaching market equilibrium unless the central bank intervenes in the market as the lender of last resort.

On the other hand, if there is an aggregate surplus on the final day, banks will try to lend excess reserves, and the interest rates will drop to zero unless the central bank absorbs funds as the borrower of last resort.

Hence, with a net surplus or shortage on the final day of the maintenance period, the net supply or demand curve for aggregate private banks' reserves becomes vertical, and therefore the market interest rate will be determined by the rate at which the central bank supplies or absorbs reserves from the market.

As mentioned above, however, the central bank has an obligation to supply reserves to private banks so that they can meet reserve requirements. Therefore, if it cannot choose interest rates (e.g., if lending at a fixed discount rate were the only way to supply credit), the interest rate control mechanism mentioned above would not work. But usually central banks have many options through which to control interest rates on their credit, the most standard one being open-market operations with prices determined by the central bank. The Bank of Japan usually utilizes lending for the final adjustment; the expected effective rate of this instrument is also controllable, if necessary.

For example, lending by the Bank of Japan is calculated according to the "both ends–counted method" (a historically typical lending practice in Japan) in which a loan of a week is counted as an eight-day loan, that is, the actual length of the loan plus one day. If private banks try to exploit a profit opportunity by using the discount window on the final day, the Bank of Japan can thus penalize them by asking them to return the funds immediately after the final day of the maintenance period. This would raise the effective cost of borrowing from the Bank of Japan to a level significantly above that indicated by the official discount rate. Even if this penalty is only rarely utilized, its mere existence is sufficient to provide the Bank of Japan credibility in the eyes of market participants.[15]

Under the implicit assumption that market participants recognize the strong influence of the central bank on interest rates on the final day, the interest rates on other days converge to the expected (central bank's final day target). In this setup, private banks try to maximize profits daily, continually bearing in mind the expected rate on the final day (the "anchor"), and such behavior is the key to formulating the daily rate. This game is repeated every month. The art of central banking here is to transmit information about the anchor to market participants in an effective way.

15. Ueda's paper (chap. 1 in this volume) emphasizes the role of heavy reliance on discount lending for interest rate control under the current framework. He argues that expectations of the cancellation of discount window lending are important. Since the official discount rate is usually lower than market interest rates and since banks rely heavily on discount window lending, this could work as an effective punitive deterrent. Theoretically speaking, the structure of this explanation is quite similar to the "both ends–counted" story given in this paper. However, anecdotal evidence suggests that, when the final day of the maintenance period comes just before a weekend, it becomes more difficult for the Bank of Japan to control interest rates because the penalty from using the "both ends–counted" rule becomes unfeasible. Therefore, heavy reliance on discount window lending in itself is not a necessary condition for controlling interest rates.

Of course, since the maintenance period in Japan is one month, and since the daily market rate depends on expected targets, the overnight rate is not perfectly controllable. For example, given a situation in which the yen is rapidly depreciating, market participants may be confident that the Bank of Japan will raise the official discount rate and try to raise short-term interest rates within the current maintenance period. This expectation would actually raise interest rates, even if the Bank of Japan tried to transmit the signal that it wanted to keep rates at current levels, for example, by supplying reserves. In the present world with abundant information, the problem is whether the signals transmitted by the central bank can acquire credibility among market participants.[16]

2.3.3 Interest Rate Control under Alternative Reserve Systems

Length of the Maintenance Period and the Role of Defensive Operations

The importance of accurate "defensive operations" (operations aimed to offset changes in aggregate reserves) differs just as reserve systems differ. One example of a system in which defensive operations are essential is the case of Italy before 14 October 1990. Reserve requirements were maintained each day of the maintenance period until 14 October 1990; every day was a kind of "final day" of the maintenance period. As a result, interest rates were quite sensitive to the market operations of the Bank of Italy.

When the Bank of Italy supplied excess reserves, for example, overnight rates dropped to near 0%. Because of these problems, on 15 October 1990 the Bank of Italy shifted its reserve requirement system to a monthly average requirement. When there is no reserve requirement system, or when a required reserve ratio is quite low and is not a binding constraint on banks, as it was in Japan before 1959, the situation is similar to that in Italy because the demand for the high-powered money required for daily settlements cannot be interest elastic. Thus, it is not surprising that the nonregulated call rate in Japan before 1959 was volatile.[17]

If precise defensive operations are not essential in controlling interest rates under the current lagged reserve framework, the question arises why the Bank of Japan makes every effort to estimate the shortage or surplus of funds every day, as explained earlier.

My tentative interpretation of this phenomenon is that the so-called reserve progress ratio is used in Japan as a means of signaling the anchor rate to market participants.[18] The reserve progress ratio is the ratio of reserve deposits accumulated from the first day of a maintenance period to the total cumulative reserve deposits required for that period. Suzuki, Kuroda, and Shirakawa

---

16. The problem of consistency among the signals transmitted by the central bank will be discussed again in section 2.5.1.

17. See Ueda's paper (chap. 1 in this volume).

18. For further discussion of this interpretation, see Okina (1987).

(1988) argue that the ratio increases by 3.3% a day in a standard path along which required reserve deposits are equally maintained every day during a given maintenance period. A faster pace would emit a signal of easier, and a slower pace tighter, money market control. In order to avoid transmitting confusing signals, accurate estimation of the shortage or surplus of funds each day would be important.

Interest Rate Control under a Contemporaneous Reserve System

So far, I have assumed a pure lagged reserve system. In reality, however, the Japanese reserve requirement system is a mixture of a lagged reserve system and a contemporaneous reserve system. Do I have to modify my arguments about interest rate control if this fact is taken into account? To answer this question, consider the function of the contemporaneous reserve system.[19]

Under a lagged reserve system, the required reserve for a given maintenance period is a predetermined variable. On the other hand, under a contemporaneous reserve system, it has been argued that, since private banks can change their deposits by changing lending levels, they can control the level of required reserves. Therefore, the central bank need not transmit signals regarding the target interest rate to market participants. This is why a contemporaneous reserve system is advocated when total reserve targeting is attempted.

Even in the United States, however, where a contemporaneous reserve system has been adopted, reserve demand on the final day of the maintenance period is highly interest rate inelastic, and the federal funds rate often shows volatile movement on that day.

Of course, the reserve requirement system in the United States is not purely contemporaneous.[20] But even if we adopt a purely contemporaneous reserve system, it would not be easy for the central bank to avoid affecting interest rates directly, for as the maintenance period comes closer to its end, it becomes more difficult for private banks to adjust required reserves. Actually, at the very last moment such adjustment should be practically impossible, and the demand for reserves is bound to become highly interest rate inelastic. Therefore, unless the central bank is willing to accept severe interest rate vol-

19. One practical problem of a contemporaneous reserve system is the difficulty in calculating required reserves. Partly due to this, a contemporaneous system was avoided in Japan. In 1957, the Report of the Committee for Financial System Research argued that it was appropriate to have some lag between the maintenance period and the period of calculation for cash and deposits, for the convenience of data collection. As a result, the fifteen-day lag of the current system was decided upon.

20. Since February 1984, U.S. depository institutions have been required, on average, to maintain given reserves for over fourteen days. Since the average reserve requirement against transaction deposits is computed by using the average over the fourteen days ending two days before the end of the maintenance period, and since the relative weight of transaction deposits in the reserve requirement calculation is high (reserve requirements against other liabilities are lagged by nearly four weeks, compared with those against transaction deposits), the system is usually considered to be essentially contemporaneous.

atility, it has no option but to accommodate the demand for reserves, and in that process it will have to reveal its anchor.[21]

One might argue that private banks could quickly adjust their deposits, by repurchasing CDs, for example. In Japan, however, the share of CDs in all deposits of private banks is only a few percent, and the required reserve ratio for CDs is only 1.75%. Therefore, in order to offset a reserve shortage, the required amount of CD repurchases would be approximately fifty-seven times the initial reserve shortage. Moreover, there is no incentive for a bank with a shortage of reserves to repurchase the CDs: such action would reduce the level of required reserves for the concerned bank and for the banking system as a whole; for the individual bank, however, the outflow of reserves caused by the repurchase will be much larger than the reduction in required reserves. Thus, CD repurchases may not be a practical solution.

In sum, even under a contemporaneous reserve requirement system, the central bank may still have to act as a lender (and borrower) of last resort. If so, market participants are very likely to attach great importance to the level of interest rates that they consider the central bank to be targeting, and the techniques of central banking used to guide market rates will be very similar to those used under a lagged reserve system. In Japan, although the reserve system is a mixture of "two weeks lagged" and "two weeks contemporaneous," the art of central banking is intrinsically closer to a pure lagged reserve system.

Effects of Carry-over Options

Since reserve carry-over is not permitted in Japan and the Bank of Japan would accommodate any potential shortages during a given maintenance period, private banks have no incentive to hold excess reserves. Thus, sometimes it is argued that the absence of carry-over is an important feature of the reserve system in Japan.[22] However, the carry-over in the reserve system is not necessarily essential. The existence of carry-over options in the Japanese reserve requirement system, such as those in the United States, would have a negligible impact. In the United States, banks are allowed to carry forward any deficiency in reserves up to two percentage points of the reserve requirement, but this deficiency must be made up by holding additional reserves in the next maintenance period. Under the current system in the United States, this option is used only for technical adjustments made by the bank, and the impact of the federal funds rate on the carry-over amount is quite limited.

---

21. The Fed seems to be relatively less interested in defensive operations. In fact, it effects market operations only once a day, around 11:30 A.M. Therefore, if it misestimated the surplus or shortage of funds, it would affect the market rate. However, in the United States, volatile movements in the federal funds rate are mostly observed on the final day of each maintenance period. The implication of this fact is that the importance of defensive operations differs between a usual day and the final day.

22. See Ueda's paper (chap. 1 in this volume).

Indeed, in spite of the existence of this carry-over allowance, the federal funds rate in the United States shows considerable volatility on the final day of the maintenance period.

In addition, if the two-percentage-point limit on the carry-over option were to be lifted, it would simply mean that the length of the maintenance period would be doubled, becoming two months rather than one. All of this indicates that carry-over is not necessarily as important as has sometimes been argued.

2.3.4   The Equilibrium Overnight Rate in a General Equilibrium Model

In this paper I concentrate on the determination of the overnight rate within a given one-month maintenance period. If I tried to discuss the transmission mechanism of monetary policy from operating targets to intermediate and final targets, I would need to construct a dynamic general equilibrium model and accumulate empirical knowledge of the parameters involved. However, the discussion in this paper is not necessarily imperfect just because my analysis is based on a partial equilibrium setup. In what follows, I will briefly expand on this point.[23]

Consider a dynamic general equilibrium model that includes markets such as the high-powered money market, the deposit market, the bank lending market, and the securities market. It might be desirable to include the real sector as well, but I omit that sector for the sake of simplicity. The time unit t represents one reserve requirement maintenance period (one month for Japan). In this model, interest rates such as lending and deposit rates should be determined simultaneously. Equilibrium in the high-powered money market, ignoring the government sector, is given by

$$(8'') \qquad \sum_i R_{it} + \sum_j N_{jt} = B_t,$$

where R_{it} = reserves of the ith bank at the tth maintenance period; N_{jt} = demand for bank notes of the jth nonfinancial agent at t; and B_t = credit supplied by the central bank at t. Under a lagged reserve system,

$$(9) \qquad \sum_i R_{it} = \sum_i \gamma D_{it-1} \ (= R_t^*),$$

where D_{it-1} = deposits outstanding of the ith at $(t-1)$; γ = reserve requirement ratio; and R_t^* = aggregate required reserve at t.

Equation (9) implies that the reserve demand at t is predetermined. The demand for bank notes is both insensitive to interest rates and volatile, as shown in figure 2.1. Thus, if we denote the aggregate demand for bank notes at t as N_t^*,

$$(10) \qquad N_t^* = \sum_j N_{jt},$$

---

23. Iwamura (1992) deals with a similar problem by using a standard general equilibrium model. Ueda (1984) has pursued a related argument.

then N_t^* is almost exogenous. As a result, the central bank must accommodate reserve requirements and the demand for bank notes at time t. Namely,

$$(11) \qquad\qquad B_t = R_t^* + N_t,$$

which means that the credit supplied by the central bank is determined by the predetermined reserve requirement and the exogenous demand for bank notes. Note that these variables are not affected by any variables determined by other sectors in the model. Since the demand for reserves is predetermined and the supply of reserves is accommodative, the equilibrium interest rate in the money market is seemingly indeterminate. However, the central bank can choose the level of interest rates, as explained earlier. In sum, since R_t^* and N_t are predetermined or exogenous and are not simultaneously determined in the whole general equilibrium model, the Bank of Japan can guide interest rates even if it completely accommodates the demand for high-powered money.[24]

2.4 Determination of Longer-Term Market Rates and Money Market Reform in Japan

2.4.1 Longer-Term Interest Rates and Overnight Rates

So far, I have assumed that money market transactions are only effected overnight. In reality, however, there are also other maturities of money market transactions. For example, the maturities of transactions in commercial bills run from one week to one year.[25]

The standard theory of the term structure suggests that longer-term interest rates are equal to the expected average of overnight rates in the period concerned plus a risk premium, which is determined by the market and which reflects such factors as the preferred maturity of market participants, the degree of risk aversion, and the expected volatility of overnight rates.[26]

If the money market is efficient, it should not be possible for the Bank of Japan to effect successfully a "twist operation" within a given maintenance period. Suppose the Bank of Japan carries out at the same time an overnight CP operation and a one-week bill operation seven days before the final day of the maintenance period. Through the latter operation, it may try to transmit a signal regarding the average future level of overnight rates during the maintenance period. Market participants will compare this rate with the overnight rate, however, and if the signals conveyed by the overnight CP operation are

---

24. Thus, in constructing a general equilibrium model, we need a reaction function that explains how the Bank of Japan determines its target level for short-term interest rates. Regarding the reaction function of the Bank of Japan, see Bryant (1991).

25. In this section, we are mainly concerned with interest rates in short-term money markets. However, interest rates on assets with maturities of longer than one year are not excluded from the argument, because some empirical analysis suggests that information regarding longer-maturity interest rates is more abundant than that for shorter-term rates.

26. One example of a recent empirical study of the term structure in Japan is Campbell and Hamao's paper (chap. 4 in this volume).

inconsistent with those of the bill operation, market participants would be puzzled. If market participants believed that the intention of the Bank of Japan was to realize a different overnight rate on the final day of the maintenance period, arbitrage would simply offset the effect of the CP operation.

Let us consider the case in which there occurs a "twist operation" that goes beyond a particular maintenance period. Since the demand for reserves in each of the two periods concerned are not directly linked, it should in principle be possible to have longer-maturity operations reveal the expected future anchor without affecting the expected anchor in the current maintenance period. This kind of operation by the central bank may sometimes become meaningful. But even in this case, market participants would be puzzled, unless the signal included in each type of operation is established as a market practice.

If the possibility of a "twist operation" is limited, the central bank must select one maturity from the whole term structure as its operating target. The criteria in selecting an operating target are (1) ease of control by the central bank; (2) the market information sacrificed by using that particular instrument as a target; and (3) its relationship with intermediate and final targets. If the emphasis is placed on the first two criteria, it is natural to select the overnight rate as an operating target. In this case, the overnight rate would directly reflect the policy stance of the central bank. Longer-term interest rates, in turn, would reflect the expected overnight rate formulated by market participants based on their expectations of business conditions and monetary policy in the future, and would thus provide the central bank with important information about market sentiments.

The framework of interest rate determination would be formulated by the following feedback rule: overnight rates affect longer-term rates via the expectations of market participants and, observing these rates, the Bank of Japan readjusts overnight rate targets.

Suppose the Bank of Japan keeps the overnight rate at an inappropriately low level. Theoretically, it could maintain this situation in any maintenance period. However, doing so would create inflationary expectations and the anticipation of a future increase in overnight rates (i.e., changes in the future policy stance), and interest rates for longer maturities would rise.[27] This rise would reflect pressure for a policy change stemming from market participants. Thus, although longer-term rates naturally have a stronger influence on the real economy than do overnight rates, it may not be a good strategy for the central bank to choose a longer-term rate as the operating target unless it contains no useful information and only noise.[28]

27. Nakao and Horii (1991) argue that market rates in Japan are noisy and not a credible indicator of future inflation. On the other hand, Kato (1991) uses a method similar to that of Mishkin (1989) and reports that spreads between short- and long-term interest rates in Japan can perhaps suggest the course of future inflation.

28. Although longer-term interest rates may contain valuable information that could be used in formulating monetary policy, a problem in attaching too much importance to them is the possible

Of course, from the central bank's viewpoint, the market may not always react appropriately. Market participants sometimes overreact to variables such as the exchange rate, stock prices, interest rates abroad, and speeches by government officials at home and abroad, and they sometimes misperceive the true intentions of the central bank.

In order to avoid such misunderstanding, the Bank of Japan manifests its policy intentions not only in various market operations but also in many other ways. Examples are the governor's speeches and his press conferences every other week, and official comments on statistics compiled by the bank (wholesale prices, the money supply, the Short-Term Economic Survey of Enterprises, or TANKAN). The publication of the *Quarterly Review* (since 1987 in both English and Japanese) is also used as a means of explaining the current monetary policy stance.[29]

When the central bank transmits various signals, it is important that market participants identify the one that is the most fundamental. In Japan, the official discount rate is considered to be the most basic signal. Therefore, flexible and timely changes in the official discount rate are highly desirable.

2.4.2   An Interpretation of Money Market Reforms in 1988

Until November 1988, the maturity of the bill operations frequently used by the Bank of Japan was two to three months. Under this situation, interest rate differentials between bill rates and the Euroyen or CD rates widened in the summer of 1988, when the expansion of the economy was evident and market participants expected a future increase in short-term interest rates. Thus, the bulk of money market transactions shifted to outside the bill market.

Against this background, practices in the interbank market were jointly reviewed in November 1988 by the Bank of Japan as well as market participants. One of the major items that came under review was the extension of the transaction period for bills (from a range of one to six months to a range of one week to six months; see table 2.2). With this proposal, the Bank of Japan made clear its intention to shorten the maturity of market operations, while leaving the formation of long-term rates to market arbitrage, so as to reflect the expectations of market participants. As a result of the adoption of these reforms, the interest rate differentials between bill rates and Euroyen or CD rates disappeared and transaction volume in the bill market was restored, as shown in figure 2.2. One interpretation of this reform is that it was an attempt to use long-term interest rates as an indicator of the state of the economy.

---

indeterminacy of the operating target and the resultant instability. Similarly, Dornbusch (1986) argues that there exists the possibility of instability due to exchange-rate-oriented endogenous monetary policy.

29. Since 1989, data on money market transactions including reserves and on the volume of operations by each instrument are published daily and monthly (see table 2.5). Also see Nakao and Horii (1991).

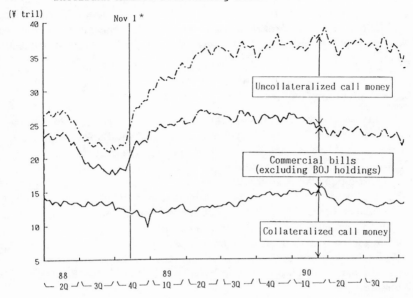

Interbank Market Outstanding Stock

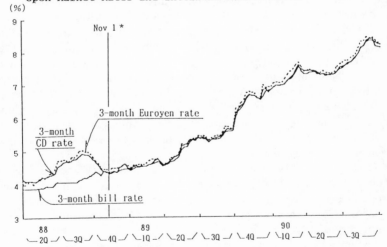

Open Market Rates and Interbank Market Rates

Fig. 2.2   Results of the money market reform
* = Effective date of reform.
Source: Short-Term Money Market Study Group (1990).

Reform of the short-term money market has progressed since November 1988. For example, overnight CP operations and one-month TB operations were introduced. Since financial liberalization and globalization is still under way, market reform must proceed in order to maintain the efficacy of monetary policy.

2.5   Concluding Remarks

In this paper I have discussed (1) the structure of the short-term money market in Japan, (2) the daily market operations of the Bank of Japan in this market, and (3) a possible theoretical interpretation of the role of such operations in formulating market interest rates.

The main points of the third issue are

1. In principle, the Bank of Japan can control overnight rates by transmitting signals regarding the "anchor" rate (the overnight rate on the final day of the reserve maintenance period) to market participants.

2. Since the span of the reserve maintenance period in Japan is one month, however, market rates are formulated around the anchor rate expected by market participants, which does not necessarily reflect the exact intention of the Bank of Japan.

3. Since the most crucial element in determining the overnight rate is the expectation of the anchor, the supply of daily reserves itself is not necessarily important, except on the final day of the maintenance period.

4. If the overnight rate is selected as the operating target, long-term interest rates can be used by the central bank as valuable economic indicators.

Of course, these conclusions are not without some reservations. First, regarding the controllability of interest rates, I have argued that, in principle, the Bank of Japan can control the overnight rate. But if the bank tries to maintain an inappropriate rate (e.g., an inflationary rate), the market may not believe the signal, or the central bank may lose credibility in the market. In other words, the central bank cannot control interest rates as if the rate of interest were a perfectly exogenous variable.

Usually, central banks do not directly indicate the level of the target rate. This fact may partly be due to a concern over political pressure. In addition, some theorists have suggested that the central bank cannot transmit signals that are too precise, because otherwise it would have an incentive to pursue a "time-inconsistent" policy.[30]

I believe that there is another reason why central banks are hesitant to quote the target rate directly. They tend to consider the process of pursuing monetary policy to be a dialogue between themselves and the market, and thus believe that interest rates should have an element of being endogenous. If this philosophy is extended too far, the system may become indeterminate; on the other

30. See Stein (1989), for example.

hand, if controllability of interest rates is overemphasized, the actuality of market operations is lost.

Second, the influence of international capital flows has been ignored in this paper. One justification for this is that the topic of this paper is mainly the determination of overnight rates. Since exchange rate risk is large compared with the daily speculative return in the money market, it might not be unrealistic to regard Japan's money market as being effectively isolated from international capital flows.

However, this would not apply to a fixed exchange rate regime. Since interest rates are firmly linked by arbitrage, interest rate controllability by the central bank is restricted. By the same token, a perceived strong commitment to a target exchange rate restricts interest rate controllability.

Also, the development of the Euromarket can be exploited to avoid domestic regulation, including reserve requirements. The latter problem is also important from the viewpoint of monitoring by the monetary authorities and financial system stability.

References

Bank of Japan. 1985. *Nihon Ginko Hyakunenshi* (Centennial history of the Bank of Japan). Vol. 5. Tokyo: Bank of Japan.

———. 1990. Financial Markets September 1990. Tokyo: Bank of Japan, October.

Bryant, R. C. 1991. Model Representations of Japanese Monetary Policy. *Bank of Japan Monetary and Economic Studies* 9, no. 2:11–61.

Dornbusch, R. 1986. *Dollars, Debt, and Deficit*. Cambridge, MA: MIT Press.

Dotsey, M. 1986. Japanese Monetary Policy: A Comparative Analysis. *Bank of Japan Monetary and Economic Studies* 4, no. 2.

Ito, T. 1991. Monetary Policy in the Age of Financial Innovations: The Case of Japan 1985–1990. Paper presented at the NBER conference on Japanese Monetary Policy, April.

Iwamura, M. 1992. The Determination of Monetary Aggregates and Interest Rates. *Bank of Japan Monetary and Economic Studies* 10, no. 1:65–93.

Kato, K. 1991. The Information Content of Financial and Economic Variables: Empirical Tests of Information Variables in Japan. *Bank of Japan Monetary and Economic Studies* 9, no. 1:61–86.

Mishkin, F. 1989. A Multi-country Study of the Information in the Term Structure about Future Inflation. NBER Working Paper No. 3125. Cambridge, MA: National Bureau of Economic Research, September.

Nakao, M., and A. Horii. 1991. The Process of Decision-making and Implementation of Monetary Policy in Japan. Special Paper No. 198. Bank of Japan, March.

Okina, K. 1987. Tankikinyushizyo Kinri to Kinyu Chosetsu (Short-term interest rates and monetary control in Japan). Discussion Paper No. 157. Institute of Economic Research, Hitotsubashi University, March.

Short-Term Money Market Study Group. 1990. *Wagakuni Tanki Kinyu Shijono Genjo to Kadai* (Japan's short-term money market and its issues). Tokyo: Kinyu Zaisei Jijo Kenkyukai.

Stein, J. 1989. Cheap Talk and the Fed: A Theory of Imprecise Policy Announcements. *American Economic Review* 79 (March): 32–42.

Suzuki, Y., A. Kuroda, and H. Shirakawa. 1988. Monetary Control Mechanism in Japan. *Bank of Japan Monetary and Economic Studies* 6, no. 2:1–27.

Ueda, K. 1984. Kashidashi Shijo to Kinyu Seisaku. (Lending market and monetary policy) *Osaka Daigaku Keizaigaku* 34, nos. 2, 3:160–79.

3 Japanese Corporate Investment and Bank of Japan Guidance of Commercial Bank Lending

Takeo Hoshi, David Scharfstein, and Kenneth J. Singleton

Throughout the postwar period of rapid economic growth in Japan, the Bank of Japan (BOJ) has guided lending by financial institutions. This "window guidance," as it is called, sometimes takes the form of restrictions on lending by major financial institutions, particularly during periods of tight monetary policy (Suzuki 1987). In this paper, we explore the impact of these direct credit restrictions on the borrowing and investment activity of Japanese corporations. We take two approaches. At the macroeconomic level, we first explore the extent to which Japanese firms substitute alternative sources of funds for bank borrowing when it is restricted by window guidance. Then we examine whether this guidance has real effects on investment in capital and inventories. At the microeconomic level, we analyze a panel of Japanese firms to determine whether there are any distributional effects of window guidance. In particular, we are interested in whether some firms have preferential access to capital and are more prone to invest during episodes of tight monetary policy.

Window guidance is used by the BOJ to supplement its main monetary policy instruments—loans through the discount window and open-market operations. In principle, if firms have alternative financing sources that are unrestricted by window guidance, it is difficult to see how such guidance can have much effect on investment decisions. But if firms do not have alterna-

Takeo Hoshi is assistant professor at the Graduate School of International Relations and Pacific Studies, University of California, San Diego. David Scharfstein is associate professor of finance at the Sloan School of Management, Massachusetts Institute of Technology, and a research associate of the National Bureau of Economic Research. Kenneth J. Singleton is C.O.G. Miller Distinguished Professor of Finance at the Graduate School of Business, Stanford University, and a research associate of the National Bureau of Economic Research.

The authors are grateful for comments from Professor Akiyoshi Horiuchi of the University of Tokyo and other participants at the NBER Conference on Japanese Monetary Policy held in Tokyo in April 1991. Helpful research assistance was provided by Yoshito Sakakibara.

tives, or those alternatives are substantially more costly, then window guidance could have a large impact on corporate borrowing and investment. In fact, prior to the mid-1980s, Japanese companies were quite restricted in their ability to raise funds outside the banking sector. Most corporations—even large ones listed on the Tokyo Stock Exchange—were effectively prohibited from issuing bonds domestically and abroad. Their only feasible alternative financing sources during this period were the financial institutions that were not restricted by window guidance, such as insurance companies. This changed in the mid-1980s, when the Ministry of Finance relaxed a series of restrictions on bond financing. The result has been a marked disintermediation of Japanese financial markets: in 1970, 97% of all corporate debt was held by banks and insurance companies; by 1990, they held only 60% of the outstanding corporate debt. So window guidance may have had an important effect on corporate borrowing and investment, particularly before the mid-1980s.[1]

The macroeconomic effects of monetary policy are examined in the context of a vector autoregression (VAR) in which real economic activity is measured by the growth rate of the real stock of capital and the growth rate of the real value of inventories. Since we do not have a long time series on BOJ guidance of bank loans, our measure of the impact of window guidance must necessarily be indirect. We argue that the proportion of loans to corporations from financial institutions that are restricted by guidance to total loans by financial institutions is an informative indicator of the stance of window guidance.[2] This ratio declines substantially during the two episodes in our sample when window guidance was constraining, and is relatively high or rising during periods of monetary ease. The mix of external financing may, of course, also be influenced by open-market operations and lending through the discount window. Indeed, our information-based motivation for examining the loan mix suggests that imposing window guidance enhances the effectiveness of monetary policy and reinforces the use of the loan mix as a measure of the stance of monetary policy more generally. As a more traditional measure of the stance of monetary policy, we also include the change in the interbank call rate, which is strongly influenced by the BOJ, in the VAR.[3] The evidence supports the conclusion that monetary policy generally and window guidance in particular had an important effect on aggregate inventory accumulation and the growth rate of the aggregate capital stock during our sample period.

1. See Hoshi, Kashyap, and Scharfstein (1990a) for an analysis of the increased use of bond financing.

2. Kashyap, Stein, and Wilcox (1991) use a similar mix variable based on bank loans to corporations and transactions in the commercial paper market as a measure of the stance of U.S. monetary policy. We will compare our findings for Japan to their results for the United States in section 3.3.

3. The call market is the market for interbank loans in Japan. City banks were consistently net borrowers in the call market until the 1980s (Suzuki 1987). The regional banks, who had fewer large corporations as their customers, consistently invested their surplus funds in the call market. The interest rate on call loans was one of the few interest rates that was not regulated by the Ministry of Finance during this period.

This macroevidence may mask potentially important distributional effects of window guidance on corporate investment activity. Some firms may have an easier time finding alternative financing sources or may be given preferential access to bank credit. In particular, firms with close bank relationships or those affiliated with banks and insurance companies through the keiretsu system may be favored in receiving financing. This could be because banks prefer to allocate capital to firms they already know well or to those in which they own equity. Moreover, insurance companies—the largest of which are in a keiretsu—may also prefer to lend to other keiretsu firms with whom they have dealt before and in whom they own equity. The empirical question that we address is whether the investment activities of firms that are members of a keiretsu are hampered less by restrictive window guidance policies than are those of independent firms.

The evidence we present is consistent with this view. We examine the investment response of keiretsu and nonkeiretsu firms to restrictive window guidance in 1979 and 1980. We find that, all else equal, keiretsu firms tend to invest more than nonkeiretsu firms during the 1979–80 period, but this is not the case when window guidance is lax. In addition, nonkeiretsu firms appear to be liquidity-constrained in their investment; they tend to cut capital expenditures when they have relatively low cash flow. This is not the case for group firms. Interestingly, during 1979 and 1980 nonkeiretsu firms appear to be even more liquidity-constrained than do keiretsu firms. This evidence is also consistent with the view that group firms get preferential access to capital.

The remainder of this paper is organized as follows. In section 3.2 we describe the concept of window guidance in more detail and review the implementation of this guidance by the BOJ during the past thirty years. In section 3.3 we explore the macroeconomic relations among monetary policy, capital investment, and inventory accumulation. In section 3.4 we analyze the investment behavior of a panel of Japanese manufacturing firms. Concluding remarks are presented in section 3.5.

3.2   The Historical Use of Window Guidance

Window guidance by the BOJ has taken several forms during the past thirty years. Operationally, the BOJ receives information from its client financial institutions about the actual loan and borrowing positions of these financial institutions. Based on this information, the BOJ provides guidance to these institutions regarding their lending positions. The guidance may take the form of regulation of increases in loans or of limitations on overall loan positions.

In the conduct of monetary policy by the BOJ, window guidance has been used as a supplementary instrument for monetary control. The primary instruments have been lending through the discount window and open-market operations in securities markets. For the control of very short-term fluctuations in reserves, lending by the BOJ through the discount window, mainly to city banks, has been the chief operating instrument. The BOJ started open-market operations in government bonds in 1962, but only purchases were made to supply the necessary funds to sustain economic growth. Open-market sales began in 1972. Currently, the BOJ conducts open-market operations in several markets, including commercial bills, treasury bills, and commercial paper, in order to adjust seasonal fluctuations in funds of two or three months in duration. The BOJ still purchases outright long-term government bonds from financial institutions to control secular increases in funds. Since December 1987 these purchases have sometimes been accompanied by resale agreements.

Prior to the mid-1960s, guidance was carried out primarily through city banks that had high levels of borrowing from the BOJ. In the mid- to late 1960s, guidance was occasionally expanded from city and long-term credit banks to include trust, regional, and sogo banks. During the tight money period in early 1973, the scope of window guidance was expanded further to include virtually all of the client institutions of the BOJ, including the larger foreign banks in Japan. The broad scope of guidance during this and later episodes probably increased the impact of guidance on firm investment compared to earlier periods, by reducing the nonrestricted sources of funds. During this episode, window guidance not only applied to the overall level of loans but also restrained the lending by banks to trading companies and provided guidance on the level of securities investment (Suzuki 1987). Thus, window guidance has been used by the BOJ to influence the flow of funds to specific sectors in the economy.

In July 1977, a new formula for establishing window guidance was introduced. The voluntary lending plans of financial institutions were essentially accepted by the BOJ, though the window guidance system was maintained in order to give the BOJ the option of using guidance as a policy instrument. This option was exercised in 1979 when strict guidance similar to that of earlier periods was implemented.

After 1982 and until 1989, window guidance played an insignificant role in the conduct of monetary policy, as the lending programs of financial institutions were accepted completely. During 1990, the BOJ once again relied on window guidance in an effort to control inflation in Japan. For instance, in the last quarter of 1990, the BOJ reduced the net lending of the twelve city banks by more than 30% from a year before. For seven consecutive quarters beginning in the third quarter of 1989, the BOJ set lending growth limits lower than the results for the same period of the previous year. Moreover, the guidance for the last quarter of 1990 was more restrictive than in the past sixteen years. The announced intent of this window guidance policy was to reduce the growth in the money supply and inflationary pressures, as well as to provide encouragement for city banks to adjust toward meeting the BIS capital-level requirements (*Japan Times Weekly*, October 1990). In June 1991, the BOJ announced that it would no longer use window guidance as a policy instrument.

There is an extensive theoretical literature on the effectiveness of window guidance, most of which is in Japanese. All of the models that we are aware of analyze window guidance in economic environments with unregulated interest rates and symmetric information among participants in the loan and call markets. One of the most important papers on window guidance is by Horiuchi (1977, 1978), who argued that window guidance is completely ineffective by itself as long as the lending limits are imposed on a subset of institutions. The following argument captures the essence of Horiuchi's analysis. Suppose that there are only two types of financial institutions, city banks and regional banks, and that window guidance is imposed only on the city banks. When the BOJ tightens its window guidance, the city banks' demand for call loans falls as they reduce their loan levels. This, in turn, leads to a decrease in the equilibrium call rate, which induces the regional banks to increase their level of loans. The new equilibrium is achieved when the decrease in the city banks' lending is fully offset by lending from the regional banks.

More generally the imposition of window guidance on a subset of the creditors of manufacturing firms should lead to the substitution of loans from unrestricted sources for those from restricted banks. In the United States, an important nonbank source of funds for large corporations is the commercial paper market. A commercial paper market did not exist in Japan until November 1987, however, when notes with maturities of one to six months were introduced. Similarly, issuance of long-term corporate debt was highly restricted, and until 1977, access to the Euroyen bond markets was not available even to the largest firms in Japan. Only after 1983 did large Japanese firms issue large amounts of corporate bonds, either domestically or internationally. Consequently, a large portion of corporate liabilities consisted of loans from banks and insurance companies. Insurance companies were the primary nonbank source of loans to manufacturing firms. It follows that, if substitution of nonbank sources of funds mitigated the effects of tight monetary policy, then we should see this in the relative growth rates of loans from banks and insurance companies.

The episode of tight monetary policy that we focus on in our analysis of firm-level data is the 1979–80 period. The BOJ's *ex ante* guidance on increases in lending by city banks on a quarterly basis for the first quarter of 1978 through the second quarter of 1988 is displayed in figure 3.1. There is clearly a pronounced seasonal component to this guidance. Adjusting for this seasonality, guidance notably declines during the period of tight monetary policy in 1979 and 1980. The gaps between the *ex ante* window guidance (G) and the actual increases (A) in lending for city banks, long-term credit banks, trust banks, and regional banks are displayed in figures 3.2 through 3.5. The strict guidance during 1979 and early 1980 is reflected in the zero or negative values of $G - A$ during this period.[4] Together, figures 3.1 through 3.5 sug-

---

4. As noted previously, the period of zero gaps between 1985 and 1988 is indicative of accommodative, not restrictive, guidance.

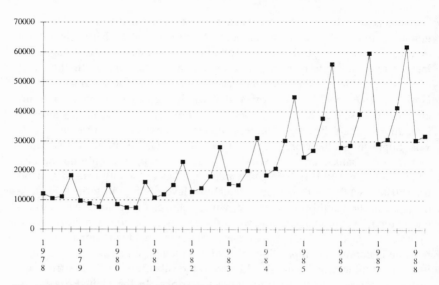

Fig. 3.1   Guidance, city banks (in 100 million yen)

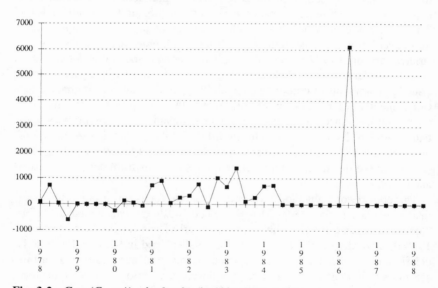

Fig. 3.2   Gap ($G - A$), city banks (in 100 million yen)

gest that window guidance hindered rather than accommodated bank lending activity during this period.

The annual growth rates of loans to corporations, individuals, and governments from city banks (GCB), trust banks (GTB), life insurance companies (GLI), and casualty insurance companies (GCI), as well as the growth of total

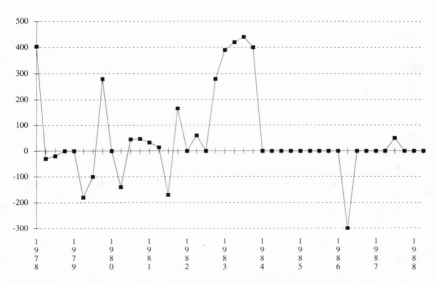

Fig. 3.3   Gap ($G - A$), long-term credit banks (in 100 million yen)

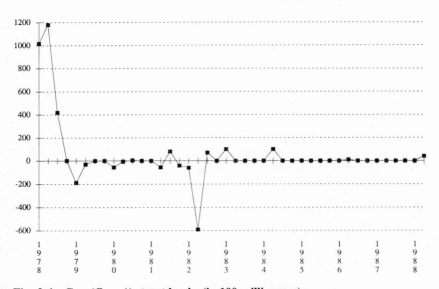

Fig. 3.4   Gap ($G - A$), trust banks (in 100 million yen)

loans from these institutions (GTOT), are displayed monthly for the period January 1978 through December 1982 in figure 3.6. The impact of the tight window guidance from late 1979 through the second quarter of 1980 is striking. GCI increases the most in late 1979 and early 1980, followed by GLI. The growth rate in loans from banks and total loans decline. The high corre-

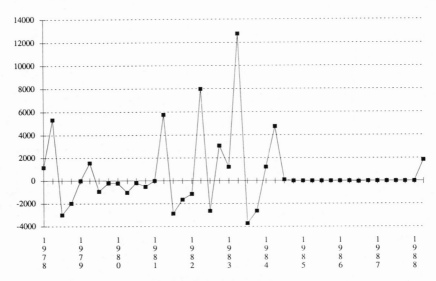

Fig. 3.5   Gap ($G - A$), regional banks (in 100 million yen)

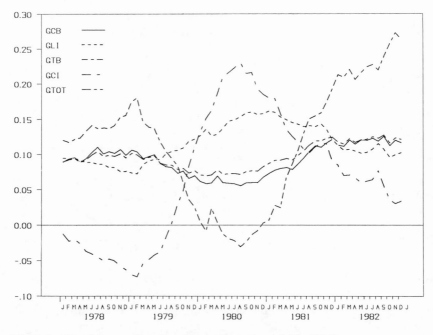

Fig. 3.6   Monthly growth rates of loans from financial institutions

lation between GCB and GTOT reflects the fact that loans from city banks were by far the largest component of total loans. The corresponding graphs of growth rates of industrial loans by city banks (GCB), trust banks (GTB), long-term credit banks (GLTCB), and insurance companies (GINS) are displayed quarterly in figure 3.7. From the middle of 1979 through the middle of 1980, GINS grew most rapidly and the growth rates of loans from the banks, especially trust banks, declined. Similar patterns of substitution are documented in Bank of Japan (1982) in its discussion of the effects of window guidance on lending by insurance companies during this period.

Growth rates for the period January 1988 through March 1990 corresponding to those in figure 3.6 are displayed in figure 3.8. Again the growth rate of loans from life insurance and casualty insurance companies increased during a period of declining growth in bank loans, especially in late 1989 and early 1990 when monetary policy, including window guidance, was relatively tight.

Horiuchi's work stimulated a large body of theoretical work on the role of window guidance in Japanese monetary policy. The earliest critique of Horiuchi's model was by Eguchi (1977, 1978). He argued that window guidance would be effective if banks' holdings of excess reserves are a decreasing function of the call rate, which is the opportunity cost of holding excess reserves. Tightening loan limits through window guidance leads to a lower call

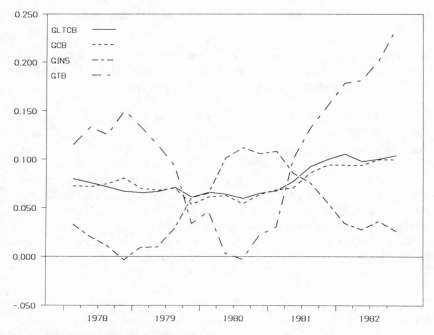

Fig. 3.7   Quarterly growth rates of loans

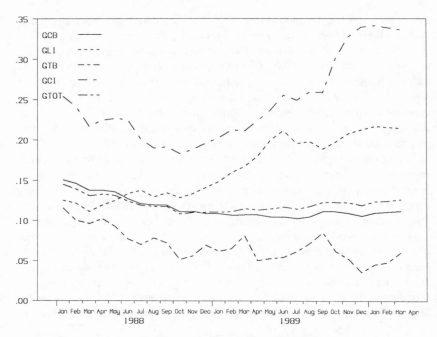

Fig. 3.8   Monthly growth rates of loans from financial institutions

rate, which induces not only more lending by regional banks but also larger holdings of excess reserves by regional and city banks. Thus, the increase in lending by regional banks does not fully offset the decrease in lending by city banks.

Teranishi (1982, chapter 10) and Shinohara and Fukuda (1982) note that another case where window guidance may be effective is when the BOJ's lending policy has a "passive" component. The BOJ has followed an accommodative lending policy under which lending has been an increasing function of the call rate. As Teranishi points out, the BOJ justified this passive component of credit in terms of its position as lender of last resort: given regulated interest rates, high call rates are indicative of excess demand in the interbank loan market, which should be at least partially fulfilled by the lender of last resort.[5] Evidence that there were in fact numerous periods of excess demand for loans in the interbank market during the postwar period and that BOJ policy was a key determinant of call rates is presented in Asako and Uchino (1987).

5. See Nihon Ginko Chosa-kyoku (1962), for example. In fact, representatives of the BOJ seemed to believe high-powered money was not controllable by the BOJ, contrary to the standard view of monetary policy. As Komiya (1988, chapter 3) has noted critically, those responsible for monetary policy in Japan seemed to take the amount of BOJ credit as *determined* by the state of the economy and as not controllable by the BOJ.

The effectiveness of window guidance under accommodative lending policies can be seen as follows. A tightening of window guidance reduces the excess demand for funds in the call market and leads to a decline in the call rate. This decrease in the call rate leads to a reduction in lending by the BOJ to private banks. Although financial institutions that are not restricted by guidance increase their loans, because of the reduced BOJ credit, the amount is not enough to offset the initial decrease in the lending by city banks. As this example makes clear, the effectiveness of window guidance cannot be evaluated without consideration of the status of the other instruments of policy used by the BOJ (see also Kuroda 1979).

There is limited empirical evidence on the effects of window guidance. Patrick (1962), in one of the earliest studies, compares the deviation of the expected level of loans by city banks from the BOJ's forecast and the deviation of the actual level of loans from the BOJ's forecast. He finds that the latter deviation was on average 83% of the former during the period of tight monetary policy in 1957–58. The corresponding number for the year preceding the start of the tight monetary policy was 153%, so he concludes that window guidance was very effective.

Horiuchi's (1977, 1980, chapter 4) findings are less supportive of the conclusion that window guidance is effective. He estimates a regression model of the growth rate of loans by private financial institutions using quarterly data for the period 1963 to 1975. The explanatory variables are the call rate, a proxy for firms' demand for funds, a proxy for firms' internal funds, and three dummy variables that are unity during the periods of tight window guidance. The coefficients on these dummy variables were not significantly negative, so he concluded that window guidance was ineffective during this period.

Furukawa (1981) reports the findings from a more indirect test. He estimated a function that determines the amount of excess reserves held by financial institutions. Included in the set of explanatory variables were the amount of required reserves and the call rate. As discussed above, a sufficient condition for window guidance to be effective is that excess reserves are sensitive to the call rate. Using monthly data from 1966 to 1978, Furukawa found that the excess reserves held by financial institutions were significantly influenced by the call rate, which indirectly supports the effectiveness of window guidance.

Subsequently, Horiuchi (1981) criticized Furukawa's results on the grounds that they were heavily influenced by a few observations during a period when the required reserve ratio was revised substantially. After dropping these observations and reestimating the regression model used by Furukawa, Horiuchi found that excess reserves were not related to the level of the call rate.

All of these studies focus on portfolio-theoretic models of the effectiveness of window guidance under the assumption of perfect capital markets. A key premise of this paper is that there are informational asymmetries in loan markets that partially explain the structure of corporate financial relationships in

Japan. One of the key ways in which Japanese firms differ from each other is the strength of their relationship to their suppliers of capital. It is common for firms to have a "main bank" that provides much of the company's debt financing, owns some of its equity (by statute no more than 5%), and may place bank executives in top management positions. For many firms, the main bank relationship is part of a larger industrial structure known as the keiretsu, which is an informally organized group of companies characterized by strong product-market ties among nonfinancial members and extensive cross-share ownership. Historically, the links have been strongest in the six largest groups—Mitsubishi, Mitsui, Sumitomo, Fuyo, Dai-ichi Kangyo, and Sanwa.

In principle, these keiretsu and main bank relationships may be helpful in promoting investment, because banks that own both large debt and equity stakes will have strong incentives to monitor the investment activities of affiliated firms. This monitoring may lower the cost of bank loans compared to the costs for companies with a weak or no main bank relationship. Indeed, Hoshi, Kashyap, and Scharfstein (1990b, 1991) find that the investments of group firms appear to be influenced less by current income than are the investments of independent, nongroup firms. While independent firms cut investment by about 50 yen in response to a 100-yen decline in cash flow, group firms cut investment by only 5 yen. They also find evidence that these financing arrangements can help firms overcome difficulties in raising capital when they are in financial distress. After the onset of financial distress, group firms and those with close main bank relationships appear to be able to invest more than independent firms.

These results suggest several reasons why group firms and those with close bank ties may respond differently to window guidance than do independent firms. First, during restrictive window guidance periods, the large city banks and trust banks that form the core of the six large groups might prefer to lend to members of their group rather than to firms outside the keiretsu. Moreover, even if the firm is not in a keiretsu but has a close main bank relationship, that bank may be more willing to lend to its main customers. This could be because they own equity in their client firms, giving them a greater incentive to lend to them when money is tight. Or it could be because the strength of their relationship allows them to better evaluate their credit; this is particularly important during periods of tight monetary policy when uncertainty is high.

Second, as our evidence in figure 3.7 suggests, during window guidance periods firms substitute away from restricted bank sources of finance to unrestricted sources, mainly insurance companies. Since the large life insurance and casualty insurance companies are members of the six major groups, they may give preferential access to funds to firms within the same group.

Finally, quite apart from these standard sources of finance, group firms may have greater access to trade credit from other nonfinancial corporations in the group with whom they have close trading and equity links. Thus, cash-rich group firms may be more prone to finance cash-poor members of the group.

Similar reasoning suggests that there will also be an aggregate effect of monetary policy in Japan on real economic activity through a credit channel of the type discussed by Bernanke and Blinder (1990) and Kashyap, Stein, and Wilcox (1991) for the U.S. economy. Window guidance will affect investment even in the absence of the use of other instruments of monetary policy in Japan, because of the imperfect substitutability of bank and nonbank loans. Window guidance may also enhance the effectiveness of the primary instruments of monetary policy. If, during periods of restrictive open-market operations and/or discount window policy, banks do not offset changes in loanable funds by selling other assets, and bank and nonbank loans are imperfect substitutes, then investment is likely to decline. In Japan, window guidance assures the imperfect substitutability of loans and other investments in the asset portfolio of banks. This credit channel is a more general phenomenon, however, and may be operative in the absence of window guidance if there are other reasons for the imperfect substitutability of bank assets.

3.3   The Mix of External Finance and Aggregate Real Growth

In this section, we explore the aggregate relations between the mix of external debt financing of corporate investment and changes in capital expenditures and inventory accumulation. Pursuant to our discussion in section 3.2, attention is focused on the proportion of loans from institutions restricted by window guidance to loans from all financial institutions, including insurance companies.[6] For the 1972–88 period examined subsequently, guidance applied generally to city banks, long-term credit banks, trust banks, and regional banks. The ratio of industrial loans from these institutions to the total of industrial loans from all banks and insurance companies is CRMIX in figure 3.9. The other series, CMIX, differs in the exclusion of regional bank loans from the numerator and denominator of this ratio. (A description of the composition of the denominator of CRMIX is presented in the appendix.) The declines in CRMIX during the periods of tight monetary policy following the first oil crisis and during the 1979–80 period, and the increases during periods of monetary ease, corroborate our interpretations of figures 3.6 through 3.8 and suggest that CRMIX is an informative indicator of the stance of monetary policy. The two series CRMIX and CMIX behave very similarly over our sample period, and so we will focus on CRMIX.

By construction, CRMIX reflects the restrictiveness of window guidance. However, changes in CRMIX may also reflect changes in the other instruments of BOJ monetary policy. For instance, the BOJ has actively used the discount rate as a policy instrument; between April 1979 and April 1980 the

---

6. Borrowings through the corporate bond market are not considered, since this was not a major source of debt financing for most of our sample period.

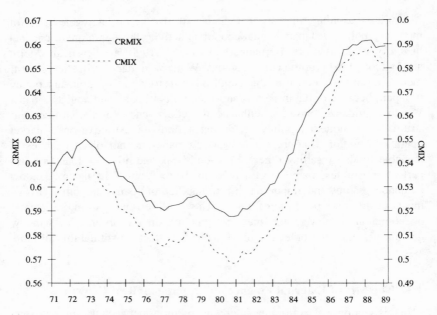

Fig. 3.9   Ratios of loans from restricted institutions to loans from all institutions

discount rate was increased 5.5 percentage points. The majority of industrial loans are issued by city banks (to large corporations) and regional banks (to small and medium-sized companies).[7] And city banks are relatively large borrowers from the discount window of the BOJ. Therefore, such discount rate increases, by disproportionately affecting loans by city banks, may have reduced CRMIX. Thus, CRMIX is not purely an indicator of window guidance. With this caveat in mind, we proceed to fit VARs to investigate the dynamic relations between monetary policy and investment.

The VARs examined are four-variable systems including the growth rate of the real capital stock, GCAP; the growth rate of inventories of corporations; the change in the ratio of industrial loans from banks subject to guidance to the total of industrial loans from financial institutions including insurance companies, $DCRMIX_t = CRMIX_t - CRMIX_{t-1}$; and the change in the call rate, DCALL. Two VAR systems were estimated using different measures of inventories: the first system used the growth rate of inventories of raw materials and stored goods (GINVR), and the second system used the growth rate of finished goods inventories (GINVF). Inventories of raw materials are related

7. In the first quarter of 1978, for instance, industrial loans from these two institutions composed just under 60% of the total. Furthermore, the rapid increase in CRMIX between 1982 and 1986 is a manifestation of the relatively rapid growth in industrial loans by city and regional banks during this period, with their share of the total being just over 63% in the fourth quarter of 1987.

to an early stage of the production process and are typically kept at minimal levels in Japan through a very efficient inventory management system. Thus, changes in this measure of inventories may reflect primarily the effects of shocks to supply. Finished goods inventories, on the other hand, may be more responsive to the decisions of final demanders and, hence, have a different response pattern to monetary policy. A complete description of the construction of these series is presented in the appendix. Four lags of each variable were included in each equation of the VAR, along with a constant term and quarterly seasonal dummies. The sample period was from the first quarter of 1971 through the first quarter of 1989.

The F-statistics for the null hypotheses that the four lags of each variable have zero coefficients in the VAR that includes raw materials inventories are presented in table 3.1, with the associated marginal significance levels in parentheses. The responses of DCRMIX, DCALL, and GCAP to innovations (one-step-ahead forecast errors) in the explanatory variables are displayed in figures 3.10 through 3.12.[8] The ordering of the variables in the VAR is given by the ordering in table 3.1. Though there is some correlation among the one-step-ahead forecast errors (see table 3.2), the qualitative features of the plots were similar for the alternative orderings we examined. We also fit this VAR for the shorter sample period of the first quarter of 1971 through the fourth quarter of 1984 to determine whether our findings were influenced substantially by the important changes in the structure of financial markets during the latter half of the 1980s. In particular, new sources of funds became available to corporations, and the BOJ introduced major reforms in the structure of money markets during the latter part of the 1980s. There were some minor differences in the test statistics, but the innovation response plots were similar for the two sample periods.

Only lagged values of DCRMIX as a group are useful for forecasting current DCRMIX at conventional significance levels, which implies that the mix of external financing is an indicator of a Granger exogenous component of monetary policy. In contrast to DCRMIX, the histories of all variables except GINVR have significant explanatory power for changes in the call rate. As expected, a positive innovation in DCRMIX (increase in the proportion of industrial loans from city, long-term credit, regional, and trust banks) leads to decreases in the call rate for about four quarters (fig. 3.11).

A positive innovation in GCAP leads to decreases in the call rate for about five quarters.[9] From the perspective of demand, the inverse negative responses of DCALL to increases in GCAP may seem surprising, since increases in GCAP are typically associated with increases in the demand for funds in the interbank market as loans to finance fixed investments are increased. However, inspection of the time series for GCAP and DCALL shows a notable

---

8. See Sims (1980) for a discussion of innovation accounting using VARs.
9. This pattern is not altered by reversing the order of DCALL and GCAP in the VAR.

Table 3.1   F-Statistics from the VAR with Raw Materials Inventories, April 1972–January 1990

Dependent Variable	DCRMIX	DCALL	GCAP	GINVR	R^2
DCRMIX	16.85	1.62	0.69	0.71	.75
	(.000)	(.184)	(.600)	(.584)	
DCALL	3.52	8.02	5.07	0.541	.63
	(.014)	(.000)	(.002)	(.706)	
GCAP	3.43	1.72	1.20	1.04	.74
	(.015)	(.162)	(.323)	(.399)	
GINVR	0.90	0.87	0.20	1.65	.21
	(.731)	(.487)	(.935)	(.177)	

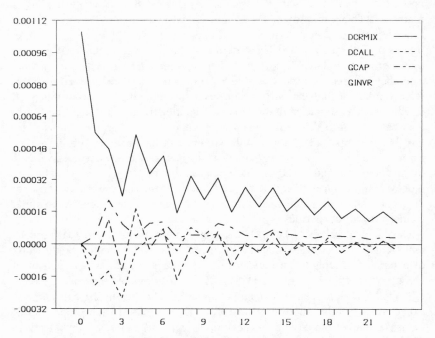

Fig. 3.10   Plot of responses of DCRMIX in VAR with GINVR

tendency for increases in GCAP to lead decreases in DCALL. This pattern may be attributable to the operating procedures of the BOJ. The BOJ operates under what is effectively a lagged reserve accounting system (Okina paper in this volume), and, hence, they must accommodate short-term demands for funds in the interbank market in order for this market to clear. This accommodation mitigates the upward pressure on rates due to an increased demand for funds. Moreover, the BOJ influences interest rates by communicating a target call rate for the end of a reserve accounting period (Okina paper in this volume), and so firms may adjust capital expenditures in anticipation of a

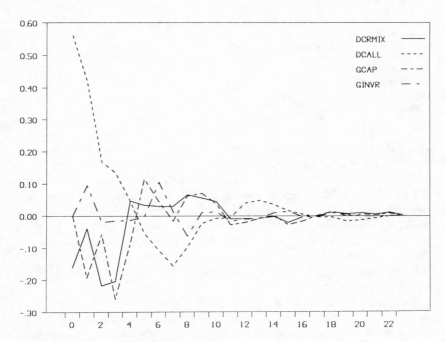

Fig. 3.11   Plot of responses of DCALL

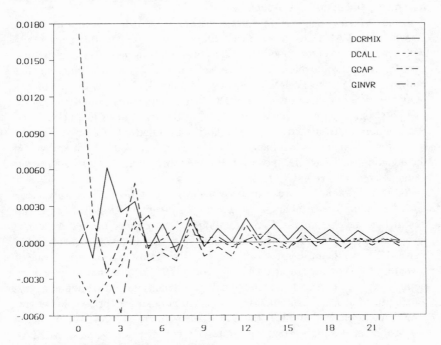

Fig. 3.12   Plot of responses of GCAP

Table 3.2   Correlations of Innovations for Table 3.1

	DCRMIX	DCALL	GCAP	GINVR
DCRMIX	1.	−.278	.150	−.000
DCALL		1.	−.183	.053
GCAP			1.	−.059
GINVR				1.

subsequent favorable movement in the call rate, based on announcements by the BOJ. These adjustments can potentially explain the patterns in figure 3.11.

The growth rate of the capital stock is significantly correlated with lagged values of DCRMIX as a group and the first lagged value of DCALL. A positive innovation in the DCRMIX is associated largely with positive increases in GCAP for about five quarters, as would be expected from the easing of monetary policy signaled by DCRMIX (figure 3.12). Unexpected increases in the call rate lead to a decline in GCAP. Together these results suggest that monetary policy, and in particular window guidance, have significant effects on capital expenditures.

The primary explanator of raw materials inventory growth is itself. However, none of the histories of explanatory variables has significant explanatory power at conventional significance levels, and the coefficient of determination is relatively low. This is consistent with our earlier remarks regarding inventory management policies in Japan.

Replacing raw material inventory growth by finished goods inventory growth in the VAR leads to somewhat different response patterns, particularly with regard to inventory shocks. Notice first of all in table 3.3 that the null hypothesis of zero coefficients on GINVF is rejected at the 4% marginal significance level in the DCRMIX equation. Figure 3.13 shows that there is a relatively weak positive response of DCRMIX to a positive shock to GINVF that persists for about eight quarters. This response suggests that unexpected accumulations of finished goods inventories are financed in part by borrowings from city and regional banks. Inventories play a relatively minor role in the equation for DCRMIX, however. For the most part, DCRMIX is Granger exogenous in this second VAR.

Another difference between the two VARs is that finished goods inventory growth is more forecastable than raw materials inventory growth. Lagged values of both DCALL and GCAP are significant at conventional significance levels. Responses of GINVF to innovations in these variables are displayed in figure 3.14. An increase in the call rate leads to increases in the growth rate of inventories for about seven quarters. Evidently, a contractionary monetary policy as reflected in increases in the call rates leads to a contraction in aggregate demand and an accumulation of finished goods inventories. This aggregate demand effect dominates the effects of the increased costs of financing inventories at the higher interbank rates. In contrast, an increase in GCAP

Table 3.3   **F-Statistics from the VAR with Finished Goods Inventories, April 1972–January 1990**

Dependent Variable	DCRMIX	DCALL	GCAP	GINVF	R^2
DCRMIX	18.8	1.54	0.34	2.73	.83
	(.000)	(.206)	(.847)	(.040)	
DCALL	2.67	6.55	5.56	0.71	.64
	(.044)	(.000)	(.000)	(.586)	
GCAP	3.17	1.61	1.12	1.49	.75
	(.022)	(.188)	(.359)	(.221)	
GINVF	0.61	3.08	5.02	0.64	.71
	(.660)	(.008)	(.002)	(.640)	

Table 3.4   **Correlations of Innovations for Table 3.3**

	DCRMIX	DCALL	GCAP	GINVF
DCRMIX	1.	−.235	.221	−.018
DCALL		1.	−.139	.034
GCAP			1.	−.221
GINVF				1.

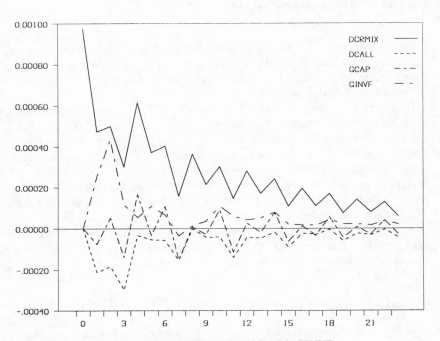

Fig. 3.13   **Plot of responses of DCRMIX in VAR with GINVF**

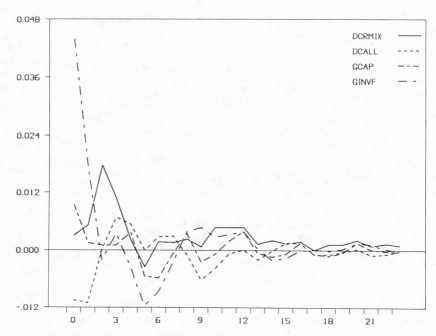

Fig. 3.14   Plot of responses of GINVF

leads to an immediate increase in GINVF followed by declines in GINVF for about three quarters. Declining inventory growth in the presence of an increase in the growth rate of capital goods is plausible during episodes of increasing aggregate demand for capital goods.

In summary, we have argued that the variable DCRMIX may be interpreted as an indicator of the stance of monetary policy, with an increase in DCRMIX reflecting an expansionary stance and a decline representing a contractionary stance. In addition, the evidence from industrial loans by city, trust, long-term credit, and regional banks and insurance companies suggests that DCRMIX also moves closely with the stance of window guidance. Therefore, we interpret the effects of DCRMIX on GCAP and GINVF as indirect evidence of the effect of window guidance on investment and inventory accumulation. Moreover, there was negligible feedback from other variables to DCRMIX, so that unexpected changes in DCRMIX are interpretable as Granger exogenous shocks to the stance of monetary policy.

3.4   Evidence from Firm-Level Panel Data

In this section, we examine the effects of window guidance on corporate investment using data on a panel of Japanese firms. We turn to microdata because the macroevidence presented above may mask potentially important differences in firms' responses to window guidance. In particular, we explore whether differences across firms in their corporate financial structures lead to different investment and borrowing activities during a tight monetary episode.

The investment behavior of group and independent firms before, during, and after the 1979–80 tight monetary regime is examined.[10] This tight monetary stance was intended to avoid an increase in inflation after the 1979 oil shock. In addition to providing relatively stringent window guidance, the BOJ increased the discount rate by 5.5 percentage points between April 1979 and April 1980. As a result of this tightening, the growth rates of high-powered money and industrial production fell substantially during 1980 and the first half of 1981.

We analyze a sample of manufacturing firms drawn from the Nikkei Financial Data tapes that were continuously listed on the Tokyo Stock Exchange from 1965 to 1988. The sample selection and data construction are described in more detail in Hoshi and Kashyap (1990). We further restricted ourselves to firms with fiscal years ending in March (by far the most common fiscal year end) because it is important to compare firms across the same period. The sample period of this study is the fiscal year ending in March 1978 to the fiscal year ending in March 1983.

We also follow Hoshi, Kashyap, and Scharfstein (1990a) in distinguishing between group and independent firms. This distinction is admittedly imprecise. Indeed, several publications (*Keiretsu no Kenkyu, Industrial Groupings in Japan,* and *Nihon no Kigyo Shudan*) attempt to classify firms according to keirestu affiliation, each resulting in somewhat different classifications. We chose *Keiretsu no Kenkyu*'s classification scheme because it focuses on the strength of a firm's relationship to the financial institutions in the group: the propensity to borrow from group banks and insurance companies and the percentage of shares held by other group firms. We use Nakatani's (1984) refinement of *Keiretsu no Kenkyu*'s classification scheme, which selects firms in the six largest groups and eliminates firms that switched groups. *Keiretsu no Kenkyu* also identifies firms that appear to be entirely independent of a keiretsu, which we use to form our sample of independent firms. Many of the firms in the sample, however, do not fit neatly into one of these two categories, and so we eliminated them from our sample. These criteria, combined with the elimination of outliers[11] in the investment data, leave us with 103 keirestu firms and 23 independent firms.[12]

We start by comparing investment in depreciable assets during fiscal years

10. For the moment, we leave aside the question of whether main bank relationships outside the keiretsu can also aid companies during this period.

11. An outlier has an investment-to-capital ratio greater than 1 or less than − 1. Nine firms were dropped from our sample using this definition.

12. The small number of independent firms in the sample is consistent with numbers for all listed companies: according to *Keirestu no Kenkyu*, as of 1981, only 83 out of 859 nonfinancial corporations listed on the Tokyo Stock Exchange were independent.

ending in March of 1979 and 1980—the years corresponding to the tight monetary episode—with investment in the remaining years. The basic question is whether independent firms were more prone than group firms to cut back on their investment during this period.

We address this question at the simplest level by comparing changes in investment over the 1978–83 period. The first column of table 3.5 reports the mean of the first difference of the investment-to-capital ratio for the entire sample of 126 firms.[13] Investment declines slightly in 1979, although the change is statistically insignificant; investment actually increases in 1980, and the change is statistically significant. The second and third columns of table 3.5 partition the sample according to whether the firm is in a group or is independent. In both 1979 and 1980 the mean change in investment is larger for group firms than for independent firms, but in neither case is the difference statistically significant at conventional levels. The only statistically significant difference is in 1981, when group firms appear to invest more than independent firms.

Of course, these statistics ignore other determinants of investment. Indeed, as discussed above, the results of Hoshi, Kashyap, and Scharfstein (1991) suggest that liquidity is an important determinant of investment. Moreover, their results indicate that current income is a more important determinant of investment for independent firms than for group firms, suggesting that independent firms have less access to short-term loans. Two natural questions arise. First, is investment particularly sensitive to liquidity when bank lending is constrained by window guidance? And second, do independent firms appear to be even more dependent than group firms on their current income for financing investment during this period?

We address these questions by estimating an investment equation along the lines of Hoshi, Kashyap, and Scharfstein (1991). The dependent variable is gross investment normalized by the capital stock and the regressors are Tobin's q for depreciable assets (the ratio of the market value of depreciable assets to their replacement cost[14]); lagged output (calculated by adding the change in finished goods inventories to total sales) normalized by the beginning of period capital stock; liquidity (as measured by income after tax plus accounting depreciation less dividend payments) normalized by the capital stock, LIQ; a dummy variable that takes the value 1 if the firm is in a group, GROUP; an interaction term, GROUP times LIQ, GROUPLIQ; and yearly dummies for 1978–82. Investment, q, lagged output, liquidity, and the interaction term are first differenced to eliminate firm-specific effects. The results are reported as model 1 of table 3.6.[15]

13. Investment in year t is measured as the changes in the value of the depreciable assets during year t plus depreciation during that year.
14. The market value of depreciable assets is measured as the market value of debt plus equity less the market value of nondepreciable assets such as land.
15. Ratios of coefficients to their estimated standard errors are reported in parentheses. These estimates are calculated using the method due to White (1984), so that they are consistent under

Table 3.5   **Mean First Differences of Investment/Capital Ratios**

	Full Sample	Group Firms	Independent Firms
1978	.0347	.0160	.118
	(.0133)	(.0130)	(.0400)
1979	−.0028	.0074	−.0408
	(.0143)	(.0132)	(.0509)
1980	.0335	.0417	−.0030
	(.0120)	(.0134)	(.0254)
1981	.0563	.0596	−.0414
	(.0157)	(.0182)	(.0282)
1982	−.0107	−.0168	.0166
	(.0190)	(.0207)	(.0492)
1983	−.0261	−.0196	−.0555
	(.0200)	(.0207)	(.0599)
Number of observations	126	103	23

Note: Standard errors are in parentheses.

Although there are slight differences in the specification and sample, the results are consistent with the findings in Hoshi, Kashyap, and Scharfstein (1991). Tobin's q measures the profitability of investment. All else equal, the firm should invest more, the greater Tobin's q is. We find no statistically significant relationship between Tobin's q and investment. This is consistent with findings in numerous studies that Tobin's q explains a surprisingly small portion of the variation in investment.

More interesting from our point of view are the coefficients of the liquidity variables, LIQ, and the interaction term, GROUPLIQ. The coefficient of LIQ measures the sensitivity of investment to liquidity for independent firms, while the sum of the coefficients of LIQ and GROUPLIQ measures the sensitivity for group firms. The positive, statistically significant coefficient of liquidity could be interpreted as evidence that independent firms are liquidity-constrained in their investment: they are more prone to invest when they have the internally generated cash to do so. One should exercise caution in jumping to such a conclusion, however. To the extent that q is mismeasured, it could be that LIQ proxies for the value of investment opportunities, and not the liquidity position of the firm.[16]

In contrast, the finding that the coefficient of GROUPLIQ is negative and statistically significant is more compelling evidence that independent firms are liquidity-constrained in their investment. Although the liquidity coefficient

---

the assumption of heteroscedasticity and first-order autocorrelation (within a firm) of the disturbance.

16. This is the well-known criticism of the important study of investment by Meyer and Kuh (1957). Recent work by Fazzari, Hubbard, and Petersen (1988) is an attempt to overcome such problems.

Table 3.6   **Group Affiliation and Investment**

Variable	Model 1	Model 2	Model 3
Tobin q	− .0047	− .0045	− .0045
	(− 0.93)	(− 0.95)	(− 0.95)
Lagged output	.076	0.76	.076
	(6.61)	(7.22)	(7.17)
LIQ	.372	.299	.299
	(2.44)	(1.77)	(1.77)
GROUPLIQ	− .347	− .222	− .222
	(− 2.18)	(− 1.23)	(− 1.23)
GROUP	.0042	− .012	− .012
	(0.39)	(− 0.69)	(− 0.69)
GROUP7980		.077	
		(2.37)	
LIQ7980		.462	
		(1.49)	
GROUPLIQ7980		− .653	
		(− 2.04)	
GROUP79			.091
			(2.04)
GROUP80			.054
			(1.83)
LIQ79			.641
			(1.57)
LIQ80			.089
			(0.33)
GROUPLIQ79			− .831
			(− 2.00)
GROUPLIQ80			− .281
			(− 0.99)
Adjusted R^2	.247	.258	.256

Notes: The dependent variable is gross investment (change in the capital stock plus depreciation) normalized by the beginning-of-period capital stock. The other variables are defined in the text. Investment, Tobin's q, output, and all liquidity variables are first differenced. The sample period is 1978–83. There are 756 observations (126 firms for six years). The numbers shown in parentheses below the coefficient estimates are t-statistics. The standard errors used to calculate t-statistics are corrected for possible heteroscedasticity and first-order autocorrelation of the error term using the method suggested by White (1984).

itself may be biased upward by measurement error in q, the difference of the coefficients of group and independent firms is less likely to be biased. Thus, the negative coefficient of GROUPLIQ indicates that independent firms do appear to be more dependent on internally generated funds than are group firms. According to the point estimates, a 100-yen decrease in liquidity leads to a 37-yen drop in investment by independent firms, but only to a 3-yen drop in investment by group firms, which is not statistically different from zero.

A key issue in our analysis is whether liquidity and group membership are more important during the 1979–80 period of window guidance. Accordingly, we next add to the basic specification three additional regressors: an interaction term between the group membership dummy and a dummy for whether the year is 1979 or 1980, GROUP7980; an interaction term between liquidity and the 1979/80 dummy, LIQ7980; and a three-way interaction of the group membership dummy, the 1979/80 dummy, and liquidity, GROUPLIQ7980.

The results are reported under model 2 of table 3.6. As in the basic regression, the coefficient of q is not different from zero and the coefficient of liquidity is positive, although statistically significant only at the 10% level. The coefficient of GROUPLIQ is negative, but not significant at conventional levels. More interestingly, the coefficient of GROUP7980 is positive and statistically significant. This variable indicates that, all else equal, group firms increase their investment more relative to the independent firms during the 1979–80 period. In all other years, however, they do not; the coefficient of GROUP is essentially zero.

The effects of liquidity also appear to be more important during the 1979–80 period. The coefficient of LIQ7980 is positive, indicating that an increase in liquidity during the credit-constrained period of 1979–80 had a larger effect on investment than an increase in liquidity in other years. Although the effect is positive, as we would predict, the coefficient is significant only at about the 15% level.

Finally, the coefficient of GROUPLIQ7980 is negative and statistically significant. As we have already noted, liquidity appears to be a more important determinant of investment for independent firms than for group firms. The coefficient on GROUPLIQ7980 measures whether liquidity is even more important for independent firms relative to group firms during 1979–80 than in the other years. The result here indicates that it indeed is, and the difference in liquidity effects between group and independent firms is substantial. The liquidity effect for independent firms during 1979–80 is given by the sum of the coefficients on LIQ and LIQ7980, which is .761. Although both LIQ and LIQ7980 are only marginally significant, the sum of the coefficients is highly significant, with t-statistics of 3.05. Thus, for a typical independent firm, a 100-yen reduction in the cash flow during the period of tight window guidance leads to a 76-yen drop of the investment. The comparable number for the group firms is obtained by adding up the coefficients on LIQ, LIQ7980, GROUPLIQ, and GROUPLIQ7980. The point estimate is −.114 and is not statistically different from zero (t-value is −0.25).

These estimates pool 1979 and 1980 under the maintained assumption that the effects on investment of tight monetary policy are the same in the two years. This is a strong assumption. Restrictive window guidance begins at the start of 1979; what we call year 1979 in our sample ends on 31 March 1979, so that the overlap is only three months. By contrast, restrictive window guidance lasts through the entire year of 1980. So, on the one hand, we would expect the effects to be stronger in 1980. On the other hand, it appears that during fiscal year 1980 guidance became less restrictive at least for one quarter (figure 3.1). To explore these possibilities, we repeat the specification of model 2 but include separate interaction terms for 1979 and 1980. The results are reported as model 3 in table 3.6.

The coefficients on GROUP79 and GROUP80 are positive, suggesting that group firms were particularly prone to invest more than independent firms in both 1979 and 1980, though their magnitudes are different. The coefficient on GROUP79 is large and significant, but the coefficient on GROUP80 is a bit smaller and significant at about the 7% level. The liquidity effects also appear to be stronger in 1979 than in 1980. The point estimate of the LIQ79 coefficient is positive with a t-statistic of 1.57, while LIQ80 has a much lower point estimate and is less precisely estimated. The three-way interaction terms, GROUPLIQ79 and GROUPLIQ80, also suggest that this effect is more pronounced in 1979 than in 1980. The coefficient on GROUPLIQ79 is large and significant; that on GROUPLIQ80 is smaller and insignificant. The more pronounced effects of liquidity in 1979 cast some doubt on whether the findings can reasonably be attributed to monetary policy. Interestingly, however, the yearly dummies, which are supposed to pick up the macroeconomic effects (including those of monetary policy) that affect all firms equally and cannot be captured by the regressors, show a similar pattern. The estimate of the coefficient of the 1979 dummy is $-.087$ with a t-value of -2.05 and that of the 1980 dummy is $-.024$ with a t-value of -0.84. Thus, 1979 seems to have been a worse year for investment than 1980. This suggests that, so far as the investment is concerned, the monetary tightening during this period had stronger effects in 1979 than in 1980.

The results above show that group affiliation mattered most during the period of tight window guidance. A related question is whether firms with relatively strong ties to their main banks behaved differently during this period. To address this question, we first need a measure of the strength of a firm's ties to its main bank. We identify such firms as those that borrow a large fraction of their funds from their largest lender. More specifically, we identify the largest lender for each firm each year during the period 1978–83. The largest lender could be one of thirty-six major private financial institutions in Japan: thirteen city banks, seven trust banks, seven life insurance companies, six casualty insurance companies, and three long-term credit banks. During the sample period, the borrowings from these thirty-six financial institutions on average account for about 85% of total borrowings from domestic private financial institutions. The remaining 15% comes from smaller financial institutions such as regional banks and credit unions. After identifying the largest lender, we calculate the proportion of the total borrowings that come from the largest lender for each firm during each year and compute the average proportion over the sample period for each firm. Finally, we create our measure of dependence on the main bank, MAIN, by assigning 1 if this average is over 22% (the median of the sample) *and* if the identity of the largest lender did not change throughout the sample period; MAIN takes 0 otherwise.[17]

There is some ambiguity in the interpretation of MAIN and its implications for investment. On the one hand, firms may have chosen not to diversify their financing sources despite the ability to do so. This interpretation leads us to expect that liquidity will not be a major determinant of investment when MAIN = 1. On the other hand, firms with MAIN = 1 may be substantially constrained by their liquidity position if the concentration of borrowing is indicative of their inability to diversify at comparable borrowing rates.

With this caveat in mind, we add our measure of main bank dependence to the basic specification. We include MAIN, an interaction between MAIN and LIQ (MAINLIQ), an interaction between MAIN and the 1979–80 dummy (MAIN7980), and an interaction among MAIN, the 1979–80 dummy, and LIQ (MAINLIQ7980).

The results in table 3.7 show that the group effects we found in table 3.6 are still present. Group firms tend to invest more during the period of tight monetary policy, and their investment is less constrained by liquidity. The difference in the sensitivity of investment to liquidity between group and independent firms is especially large during the period of tight monetary policy.

Controlling for the effects of group affiliation, a strong dependence on a main bank does not affect the change in investment before, during, or after the period of tight monetary policy. The coefficients on MAIN and MAIN7980 are both insignificant and essentially zero. The strong ties to the main bank, however, appear to change the liquidity effects. The coefficient on MAINLIQ is positive and highly significant, suggesting that, after controlling for group affiliation, the investment of a firm with higher dependence on a main bank is more constrained by the liquidity during normal times. Thus, the second interpretation of MAIN discussed above seems to emerge here: a firm with a strong main bank tends to have trouble diversifying its sources of borrowings. These firms, however, also seem to benefit from this close relation with their main banks during the period of tight monetary policy. The coefficient on MAINLIQ7980 is negative, though it is not significant, suggesting that liquidity may be less of a problem for the firms with strong ties to the main banks during this period of tight monetary policy.

3.5 Conclusions

This paper presents evidence that window guidance can have real effects on economic activity. Others have argued that window guidance need not change

---

17. Since we could not find the borrowings information broken down by the financial institutions for one firm in 1978, we could not create the MAIN variable for that firm, leaving us with 125 firms (102 group firms and 23 independent firms).

Table 3.7   Group Affiliation, Main Bank Dependence, and Investment

Variable	Coefficient Estimate
Tobin's q	−.0040
	(−0.80)
Lagged output	.080
	(7.75)
LIQ	.258
	(1.59)
GROUPLIQ	−.321
	(−1.86)
GROUP	−.013
	(−0.74)
MAINLIQ	.283
	(2.93)
MAIN	.0020
	(0.16)
GROUP7980	.076
	(2.42)
MAIN7980	−.0048
	(−0.20)
LIQ7980	.488
	(1.60)
GROUPLIQ7980	−.580
	(−1.80)
MAINLIQ7980	−.198
	(−1.24)
Adjusted R^2	.270

Notes: The dependent variable is gross investment (change in the capital stock plus depreciation) normalized by the beginning-of-period capital stock. The other variables are defined in the text. Investment, Tobin's q, output, and all liquidity variables are first differenced. The sample period is 1978–83. There are 750 observations (125 firms for six years). The numbers shown in parentheses below the coefficient estimates are t-statistics. The standard errors used to calculate t-statistics are corrected for possible heteroscedasticity and first-order autocorrelation of the error term using the method suggested by White (1984).

the total availability of credit in the economy, only the source of the credit— inducing firms to shift from constrained capital suppliers such as city banks to unconstrained suppliers such as insurance companies. Our point is that, when there are information asymmetries in particular and capital market imperfections, these financing sources are not perfect substitutes and, as a result, window guidance can have real effects. Moreover, window guidance may have distributional effects: constrained banks may be more prone to cut loans to firms with whom they do not have close ties and more prone to continue lending to those firms with whom they have close lending relationships. In addition, some firms—in particular group firms—may have better access to unrestricted sources of finance, such as from group insurance companies.

Finally, group firms may have greater access to trade credit from other member firms, which might serve as a close substitute for bank loans.

The empirical evidence from both macro- and microdata is consistent with these hypotheses. VAR results suggest that monetary policy in general and window guidance in particular have important effects on the aggregate capital stock accumulation and inventory investment. The results from firm-level regressions show that group firms tended to invest more than do independent firms during the 1979–80 period of tight window guidance. Moreover, the investment of independent firms is more sensitive to cash flow than for group firms, and this differential importance of cash flow was particularly prominent during the 1979–80 period.

In general, it is hard to distinguish the effects of window guidance per se from those of tight monetary policy. Nevertheless, in the VAR, we included the change in the call rate (DCALL) to account for the overall state of monetary policy. It is interesting to note that changes in the ratio of industrial loans from banks subject to guidance to total industrial loans (DCRMIX) has strong effects on the capital and inventory accumulation (GCAP and GINV) even when DCALL is included in the VARs. In addition, DCRMIX appears to be Granger exogenous in the VAR system. These results suggest some independent effects of window guidance.

Although this paper presents evidence on the role of window guidance, the results are far from complete. There are some obvious ways to extend our investigation of microdata. In addition to the real investment effects we have focused on so far, there are also predictions about how firms should finance this investment. Are group firms favored by group banks in the allocation of capital during the period of tight monetary policy? Are firms with close main bank ties favored by their banks? Are group firms given preferential access to financing from group insurance companies? These financing questions are left as agenda for future work.

Another important question that arises is whether the recent window guidance episode beginning in 1989 is substantially different from the 1979–80 episode. Deregulation of the financial markets in the 1980s enabled firms to supplement insurance company financing with bond financing during this period, expanding the alternatives to restricted bank financing. Thus, window guidance may have become less effective. On the other hand, the BOJ is said to be implementing window guidance, more stringently directing banks to reduce their so-called latent loans.[18] Unfortunately, the data we need to investigate this question are not yet available, and we must leave it for future work.

---

18. The biggest city banks have about 1 trillion yen each in loans outstanding, which they by various manipulative measures take off their books at the end of each quarter to make it appear they are in conformity with BOJ window guidance on loan growth. The BOJ, which has been well aware of the practice, is now telling the banks they should reduce the amount of these so-called latent loans by half as of March 1991, and completely eliminate them by the end of March 1993 (*Nihon Keizai Shimbun*, 13 November 1990).

Appendix

This appendix describes the data used in the macroeconomic analysis.

GCAP (the growth rate of capital). The capital stock for all manufacturing was collected from the *Quarterly Reports of Incorporated Enterprise Statistics,* which is based on a survey by the Ministry of Finance. The sample size for this survey changes the second quarter of every year. To adjust for these changes, a smoothed series of the number of firms in the sample was constructed by linearly interpolating the number of firms in the second quarter of each year. Then the aggregate amount of capital was divided by the actual number of firms to get the amount of capital per firm. The latter series was multiplied by the smoothed series of number of firms to get the capital stock series used in our analysis. The wholesale price index for capital goods was used to compute the real value of the capital stock, and then the first differences of the logarithms of the capital stock were computed to get growth rates.

GINV (the growth rate of inventories). The inventory levels were also collected from the *Quarterly Reports* used to compute GCAP. The same method was used to smooth the inventory levels for finished goods in manufacturing, and raw materials and stored goods in manufacturing. These smoothed series were deflated by the wholesale price index for raw materials for processing and finished goods in manufacturing, respectively; logarithms were computed; and then first differences were taken to get growth rates.

DCALL (the first difference of the call rate). The call rate is the unconditional average of daily call rates in Tokyo reported in the *Economics Statistics Monthly* by the BOJ.

DCRMIX (the first difference of the mix variable). The mix variable CRMIX was computed as the ratio of the industrial loans by banks subject to window guidance, to the total level of industrial loans from all financial institutions. The numerator included loans by city, long-term credit, trust, and regional banks. The denominator included loans from those institutions in the numerator plus the trust accounts from these institutions, sogo banks, shinkin banks, Shoko Chukin Bank, Japan Development Bank, the Export-Import Bank of Japan, the Small Business Finance Corporation, and insurance companies. The only institutions excluded from the denominator are agricultural, forestry, and fisheries financial institutions, which are not likely to be an important factor in our analysis of manufacturing. The series were obtained from the *Economics Statistics Monthly* published by the BOJ and reported in the annex table for tables 49 and 50. Industrial loans were computed by subtracting loans to local governments and individuals from total loans.

References

Asako, Kazumi, and Yuko Uchino. 1987. Bank Loan Market of Japan: A New View on the Disequilibrium Analysis. *Bank of Japan Monetary and Economic Studies* 5:169–216.

Bank of Japan. 1982. Recent Portfolio Management by Institutional Investors. Special Paper No. 97, Research and Statistics Department.

Bernanke, Ben, and Alan Blinder. 1990. The Federal Funds Rate and the Channel of Monetary Transmission. NBER Working Paper No. 3487. Cambridge, MA: National Bureau of Economic Research, October.

Eguchi, Hidekazu. 1977. Comment: Horiuchi Akiyoshi, "'Madoguchi Shido' no Yuko-sei" (Comment: Akiyoshi Horiuchi, The effectiveness of the "window guidance"). *Keizai Kenkyu* 28:242–245.

———. 1978. Tanki Kin'yu Shijo no Working ni Tsuite: Horiuchi Akiyoshi shi no Rejoinder he no Kotae mo Kanete (On the working of short-term financial markets: also answering the rejoinder by Mr. Akiyoshi Horiuchi). *Keizai Kenkyu* 29:81–84.

Fazzari, Steven M., R. Glenn Hubbard, and Bruce C. Peterson. 1988. Investment and Finance Reconsidered. *Brookings Papers on Economic Activity No. 1*, 141–95.

Furukawa, Akira. 1981. Madoguchi Kisei no Yuko-sei: Horiuchi-Eguchi Ronso o Mogutte (The effectiveness of window guidance: On Horiuchi versus Eguchi). *Keizai Kenkyu* 32:43–48.

Horiuchi, Akiyoshi. 1977. "Madoguchi Shido" no Yuko-sei (The effectiveness of window guidance). *Keizai Kenkyu* 28:204–13.

———. 1978. Eguchi Eiichi shi no Comment ni Kotaeru: Madoguchi Kisei no Yuko-sei ni Tsuite (Answering the comment by Mr. Eiichi Eguchi, on the effectiveness of the window guidance). *Keizai Kenkyu* 29:78–80.

———. 1980. *Nihon on Kin'yu Seisuku* (Japanese monetary policy). Tokyo: Toyo Keizai Shinpo-sha.

———. 1981. Ginko-Kinyu Kikan no Junbi Juyo ni Tsuite: Hamada-Iwata oyobi Furukawa no Keisoku Kekka to Sai-Kentoh (On the excess reserve holding by banks and other financial institutions: reconsidering the empirical results by Hamada-Iwata and Furukawa). *Keizai Kenkyu* 32:178–87.

Hoshi, Takeo, and Anil Kashyap. 1990. Evidence on q and Investment for Japanese Firms. *Journal of the Japanese and International Economies* 4:371–400.

Hoshi, Takeo, Anil Kashyap, and David Scharfstein. 1990a. Bank Monitoring and Investment: Evidence from the Changing Structure of Corporate Banking Relationships in Japan. In *Asymmetric Information, Corporate Finance, and Investment*, ed. R. Glenn Hubbard, 105–26. Chicago: University of Chicago Press.

———. 1990b. The Role of Banks in Reducing the Costs of Financial Distress in Japan. *Journal of Financial Economics* 27:67–88.

———. 1991. Corporate Structure, Liquidity, and Investment: Evidence from Japanese Industrial Groups. *Quarterly Journal of Economics* 106:33–60.

Kashyap, Anil, Jeremy Stein, and David Wilcox. 1991. Monetary Policy and Credit Constraints: Evidence from the Composition of External Finance. MIT, Cambridge.

Komiya, Ryutaro. 1988. *Gendai Nihon Keizai* (Contemporary Japanese economy). Tokyo: University of Tokyo Press.

Kuroda, Iwao. 1979. Madoguchi Shido o Meguru Bunseki no Sai-Kentou (Reconsidering the debates on window guidance). *Kikan Gendai Keizai* 37:141–47.

Meyer, John, and Edwin Kuh. 1957. *The Investment Decision*. Cambridge, MA: Harvard University Press.

Nakatani, Iwao. 1984. The Economic Role of Financial Corporate Grouping. In *The

Economic Analysis of the Japanese Firm, ed. Masahiko Aoki, 227–58. Amsterdam: North-Holland.

Nihon Ginko Chosa-kyoku (Bank of Japan Research Bureau). 1962. Nihon Ginko Shin'yo no Seikaku to Shin Kin'yu Chosetsu Hoshiki (The nature of the Bank of Japan credit and the new method of monetary control). *Chosa Geppo*, November.

Patrick, Hugh T. 1962. *Monetary Policy and Central Banking in Contemporary Japan: A Case Study in the Effectiveness of Central Bank Techniques of Monetary Control.* Bombay: The University of Bombay Press.

Shinohara, Soichi, and Atsuo Fukuda. 1982. Nichi-Gin Kashidashi to Madoguchi Shido no Yuko-sei (BOJ lending and the effectiveness of window guidance). *Keizai Kenkyu* 33:259–62.

Sims, Christopher A. 1980. Macroeconomics and reality. *Econometrica* 48:1–48.

Suzuki, Yoshio. 1987. *The Japanese Financial System.* Oxford: Clarendon Press.

Teranishi, Juro. 1982. *Nihon no Keizai Hatten to Kin'yu* (Economic development and the financial system in Japan). Tokyo: Iwanami Shoten.

White, Halbert. 1984. *Asymptotic Theory for Econometricians.* Orlando, FL: Academic Press.

4 The Interest Rate Process and the Term Structure of Interest Rates in Japan

John Y. Campbell and Yasushi Hamao

Macroeconomists have long been interested in the term structure of interest rates as a source of information about the transmission mechanism from monetary policy to the macroeconomy. Consider, for example, private investment decisions. These depend on the cost of capital to firms, which is not directly observable. In the United States, the cost of capital is often modeled as a weighted average of the interest rate on long-term corporate debt and the required return on equity; the long-term corporate interest rate in turn can be thought of as the sum of the yield on long-term government bonds and a "quality premium" reflecting default risk and other special features of corporate bonds. Thus, the long-term government bond yield may be a useful indicator of the unobserved cost of capital.

Of course, the long-term bond yield is very different from the short-term interest rates that are most directly influenced by the monetary authority. Thus it is important to study the mechanism by which monetary policy moves the whole yield curve while acting directly on its short end. In the U.S. markets, where a great variety of bonds of different maturities are actively traded, it is natural to model the term structure as being determined by expectations of future short rates together with risk premiums that can be modeled using general equilibrium finance theory.

John Y. Campbell is Class of 1926 Professor and professor of economics and public affairs at Princeton University and a research associate of the National Bureau of Economic Research. Yasushi Hamao is associate professor of finance at the Graduate School of Business, Columbia University.

This paper was presented at the NBER Conference on Japanese Monetary Policy, Tokyo, 18–19 April 1991. The authors thank Andrew Karolyi, Kermit Schoenholtz (the discussant), Yoshiaki Shikano, and Kenneth Singleton for useful conversations and comments, and Daiwa Securities for providing raw data. Financial support from the National Science Foundation and the Sloan Foundation (Campbell) and Batterymarch Financial Management (Hamao) is gratefully acknowledged.

Until recently this American paradigm did not seem to be applicable to the markets for Japanese fixed-income securities. Japanese corporations relied heavily on bank financing. Japanese long-term bond markets were small, il-liquid, and tightly regulated, so that quoted bond prices were not necessarily reliable reflections of market conditions, and there were no strong linkages between markets for different types of bonds. Monetary policy influenced the cost of capital to corporations as much by tightening or loosening quantity constraints as by changing bond yields, so that the long-term bond yield was a highly imperfect measure of the cost of capital. And the long-term bond market was segmented from the short-term bond market, so that relative yields did not necessarily reflect either interest rate expectations or classical notions of risk.

During the last ten years, however, bond markets have been rapidly dere-gulated and have started to play a more important role in Japanese corporate finance.[1] It may now be possible to apply the traditional American paradigm to the Japanese term structure of interest rates. In this paper we discuss the evolving relationship between long-term government bond yields and short-term interest rates in Japan.

The organization of the paper is as follows. Section 4.1 discusses the insti-tutional background and data sources. Section 4.2 lays out a framework for analysis of the term structure of interest rates. Section 4.3 studies the short end of the term structure, the gensaki market. Section 4.4 studies the market for long-term government bonds, and section 4.5 concludes.

4.1   Institutional Background and Data

In this section, we discuss the development of the Japanese money and bond markets and describe the data we use.[2]

4.1.1   Short-Term Interest Rates in Japan

Short-term government bills have existed in Japan only since 1986, so their history is too short for empirical research. As an alternative, the call money rate has often been used as the short-term interest rate in empirical studies of the Japanese economy. Only financial institutions participate in the call money market, however, so the call money rate may be a poor proxy for the short-term interest rate available to general investors. We will therefore use another short-term interest rate, the gensaki rate.

The gensaki market has existed since the early 1950s, but it grew substan-tially in volume in the 1970s and became the largest open money market in Japan. The gensaki rate is the interest rate applied to bond repurchase agree-

---

1. A number of studies have verified the impact of deregulation on the behavior of Japanese short-term interest rates (Takagi 1988; Leung, Sanders, and Unal 1991).
2. For more detailed surveys, see Bank of Japan (1986, 1988) and Takagi (1988).

ments. The agreement period varies from one month to three months, and unlike interbank markets such as those for call money and discounted bills, participants are no longer limited only to financial institutions, but also include corporations, government pension funds, and nonresidents.

Although the gensaki market has been the least regulated of Japanese money markets, there have been several institutional changes that may have influenced the behavior of gensaki rates. Leung, Sanders, and Unal (1991) study the time series process of gensaki rates over the period February 1980 through September 1989. Using a Goldfeld-Quandt switching regression technique, they identify four regime shifts in the behavior of the 1-month gensaki rate. The shifts correspond to regulatory changes in Japanese government bond and money markets, some of which are more important than others. The regulatory changes are (1) liberalization of secondary sales of government bonds by banks, and permission of banks to invest in the gensaki market (April 1981); (2) authorization for banks to sell newly issued 10-year bonds over the counter (April 1983); (3a) permission for banks to deal in government bonds (June 1985); (3b) the establishment of the bond futures market (October 1985); and (4) the establishment of the Tokyo offshore money market (January 1987). The regulatory changes in June and October 1985 bracket an apparent regime shift in the interest rate in August 1985. The deregulation in January 1987 seems comparatively unimportant for the behavior of domestic interest rates, since it made available to nonresidents a Tokyo-based equivalent of the Euroyen market but did not affect the investment opportunities of domestic residents. In addition to these changes identified by Leung, Sanders, and Unal, another change may have occurred more recently: several measures to deregulate the interbank market took effect in November 1988, and this seems to have increased interest arbitrage between the interbank and open money markets. As a result, interbank and open-market rates now appear to be more highly correlated (Bank of Japan 1990).

It is noteworthy that the shift in interest rate behavior in August 1985 occurred close to the time of the Plaza Accord in September 1985, at which leading central banks agreed to coordinate monetary policy and move toward more managed exchange rates. The change in interest rate behavior in 1985 is probably attributable to this change in monetary policy.[3]

4.1.2   Long-Term Interest Rates in Japan

The long-term bond market in Japan did not develop until the late 1970s. The first issue of long-term government bonds after World War II occurred in 1966 upon the amendment of the fiscal law that had prohibited the government from issuing debt. The bonds were underwritten by syndicates of financial institutions and were later purchased by the Bank of Japan through open-

---

3. More details on exchange rate management in this period are given in Dominguez (1990) and Funabashi (1988).

market operations. Participation in underwriting was mandatory for the financial institutions even at a low yield. The financial authorities were afraid of a drop in the price of bonds, and financial institutions were not allowed to sell government bonds in the secondary market.

Massive offerings of government bonds started in 1975 when the oil crisis caused a serious recession. In 1977, facing a rapidly increasing stock of government bonds, the Bank of Japan became unable to purchase them from the syndicates, and financial institutions were finally allowed to sell bonds 1 year after issue in the secondary market. This marked the beginning of the development of an active secondary market. In April 1981 and June 1985, secondary sales of bonds were further deregulated by reducing the required holding period after subscription. Bank dealing of government bonds was authorized for bonds with less than 2 years to maturity in June 1984, and completely liberalized in June 1985. Trading volume in government bonds in 1988 was 2,905 trillion yen, which is ten times the 1977 level. As in the United States, 97% of trading takes place over the counter. Short sales of bonds were facilitated in May 1989 by the establishment of the bond lending market.

We use yield and return data for portfolios of government bonds of different maturities. Although there are shorter-term government bonds (2–5 years to maturity at issue), 10-year government coupon bonds are most consistently and frequently issued and have the largest outstanding volume.

Our portfolios include all coupon bonds and are compiled as follows. First, all government bonds are classified according to their time to maturity: less than 1 year, 1–2 years, and so on out to 9–10 years. Then portfolio returns and yields are computed by weighting individual bond data using market values. The portfolios are rebalanced every month, since some bonds enter and leave each maturity range as their maturities shrink. Although each portfolio has a range of maturities, in our statistical analysis we take a midpoint and assume that the "less than 1 year" portfolio has a maturity of 6 months, the "1–2 year" portfolio has a maturity of 18 months, and so on.

Our sample period runs from November 1980 to August 1990 (118 observations). We split the whole sample into two subsamples, November 1980 through July 1985 (57 observations) and August 1985 through August 1990 (61 observations). The break point corresponds to the major change in the interest rate process identified by Leung, Sanders, and Unal (1991).[4] Figure 4.1 is a three-dimensional view of the term structure of interest rates in time series. To highlight the short and long ends of the yield curve as well as the midpoint, figure 4.2 plots the one-month gensaki rate and the 4–5- and 9–10-year bond portfolio yields. Both figures show a change in the character of the term structure in late 1985; before this date the short rate moves choppily

---

4. We also examined shorter subperiods as identified by Leung, Sanders, and Unal, but these results are not reported as they do not have any important effect on our conclusions.

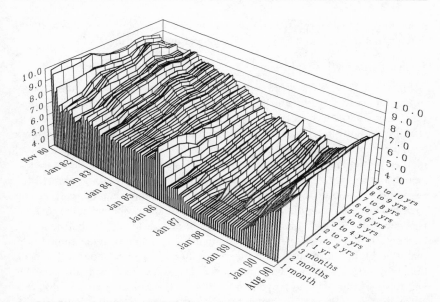

Fig. 4.1   Gensaki and Japanese government bond term structure (percent per annum)

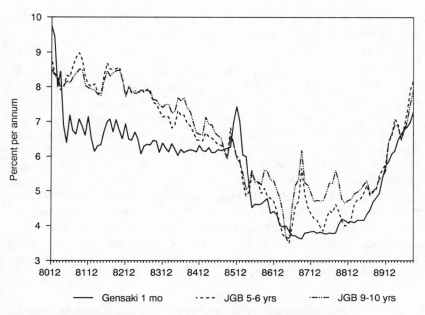

Fig. 4.2   Gensaki and Japanese government bond portfolio yields

in the range 6 to 8%, but after this date it undergoes a long, smooth movement down to below 4% and then up to 8% again at the end of the 1980s.

4.1.3 Benchmark Bond Issues

Since 1983, there has been a phenomenon known as the benchmark effect in the Japanese government bond market (Sargen, Schoenholtz, Blitz, and Elhabashi 1986). Typically, a newly issued 10-year bond with a large outstanding volume is chosen to be a benchmark and retains this status for a period of 6 months to a year. Benchmark issues are strongly preferred by bond market participants, and trading is heavily concentrated on these issues. Hence a fairly large liquidity premium is frequently observed.

Figure 4.3 shows the remaining maturity of the benchmark issue during each month of our sample period. This is almost always between 8.5 and 9.5 years, but in late 1987 and early 1988 it fell almost to 8 years before a new benchmark was chosen. This suggests that the benchmark issue should normally be highly correlated with our portfolio of 9–10-year bonds. To check this, in figures 4.4 and 4.5 we compare yields and returns of benchmark issues and the portfolio with 9–10 years to maturity. Overall the two series have a correlation of 0.986 for yields and 0.871 for returns. The unusual period in early 1988 when the benchmark issue had maturity less than 8.5 years is marked on the figures; the relation between the benchmark series and the 9–10-year series does not appear to deteriorate during this period.

4.2   An Analytical Framework for the Term Structure of Interest Rates

The study of the term structure of interest rates is greatly complicated by the nonlinearities that arise in the relation between bond prices, yields, and holding returns. When bonds do not pay coupons, these nonlinearities can be eliminated by working in logs, which is standard practice in the empirical literature on the term structure (Campbell and Shiller 1991; Fama 1984, 1990; Fama and Bliss 1987). When bonds pay coupons, however, as longer-term Japanese government bonds do, an approximation is needed to obtain a linear model relating yields and holding returns. Such a model is given in Shiller, Campbell, and Schoenholtz (1983) and elaborated in Shiller (1990). Here we briefly summarize the approximate model and indicate how we will use it.

The approximate model is accurate for coupon bonds that are close to par, that is, with yields to maturity close to their coupon rates.[5] It is obtained by taking a Taylor approximation of the nonlinear function relating holding returns to yields, around a point where the bond is selling at par. If $\bar{r}$ is the

---

5. The model as stated here assumes that coupons are paid once per period. Below we use monthly data, but Japanese government bonds pay coupons only twice a year. This makes little difference in practice.

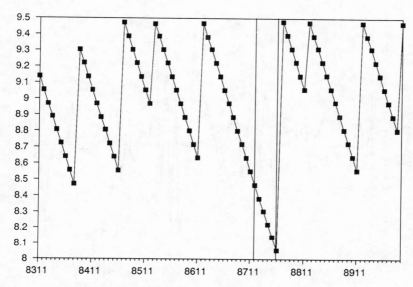

Fig. 4.3   Benchmark issues (years to maturity)

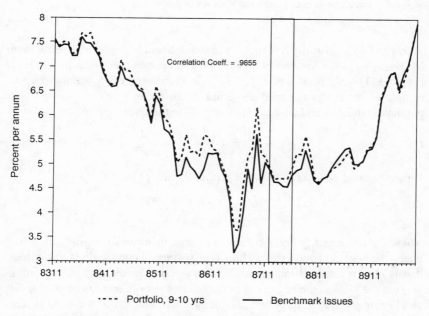

Fig. 4.4   Portfolio versus benchmark issues (yield)

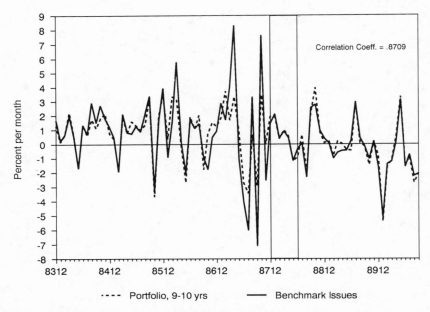

Fig. 4.5   Portfolio versus benchmark issues (return)

average yield to maturity or coupon rate of the bond, and $\gamma = 1/(1 + \bar{r})$, then Macaulay's (1938) duration of an i-period coupon bond selling at par is $D_i = (1 - \gamma^i)/(1 - \gamma)$. Now define r_t^i as the yield to maturity of an i-period coupon at time t, and $h_t^{i,j}$ as the holding-period return on an i-period coupon bond purchased at time t and held for j periods. Then the linear approximation is

$$(1) \qquad h_t^{i,j} \approx \frac{D_i r_t^i - (D_i - D_j)\, r_{t+j}^{i-j}}{D_j}.$$

When the bond is held for only one period, this simplifies to

$$(2) \qquad \begin{aligned} h_t^{i,1} &\approx D_i r_t^i - (D_i - 1)\, r_{t+1}^{i-1} \\ &\approx r_t^i - (D_i - 1)\, \Delta r_{t+1}^i, \end{aligned}$$

where the last equality holds because for large maturities i the difference between the i-period bond yield and the $(i - 1)$-period bond yield is negligible, that is $r_t^i \approx r_t^{i-1}$. Equation (2) relates the 1-period holding return on a long bond to the yield at the beginning of the holding period, and the change in the yield during the holding period. The longer the duration of the bond is, the more sensitive is its price and thus its holding return to changes in its yield.[6]

---

6. The linear approximate model thus reflects the well-known fact that duration is the elasticity of a bond's price with respect to its yield. Shiller (1990) develops this point further.

Equation (2) can be rewritten to relate the excess holding return on long bonds over short bonds to the yield spread between the two bonds and the change in the long-term yield. Subtracting the short-term interest rate r_t^1 from both sides of equation (2), we obtain

$$(3) \qquad h_t^{i,1} - r_t^1 \approx s_t^i - (D_i - 1)\,\Delta r_{t+1}^i,$$

where $s_t^i = r_t^i - r_t^1$ is the spread between the i-period and 1-period bond yields.

One appealing feature of the approximate expressions in equations (1), (2), and (3) is that they all hold exactly for zero-coupon bonds, when we replace duration D_i by maturity i and work with log returns. In section 4.3 when we study the behavior of gensaki rates, we use this exact zero-coupon version of the model.

4.2.1 The Expectations Theory of the Term Structure

The linear system stated here makes it easy to study the role of interest rate expectations in moving the term structure. If we take time t expectations of equation (3) and rearrange, we obtain

$$(4) \qquad s_t^i = E_t[h_t^{i,1} - r_t^1] - (D_i - 1)E_t\Delta r_{t+1}^i.$$

This says that the yield spread equals the expected excess return on the long bond over the short bond, less a multiple of the expected change in the long-term yield. If expected excess returns vary because risk is changing, or because long-term and short-term bond markets are segmented, then this variation should be reflected in the yield spread.

The expectations theory of the term structure is the hypothesis that, to the contrary, expected excess returns are constant through time. According to the expectations theory, excess bond returns are unpredictable, and the only force moving the yield spread is expected changes in interest rates. The expectations theory can always be tested by regressing the excess holding period return onto variables known at the beginning of the holding period. A natural variable to use as a regressor is the yield spread, since under almost any alternative model the yield spread will reflect variation in expected excess returns. The regression is then

$$(5) \qquad h_t^{i,1} - r_t^1 = \beta_0 + \beta_1 s_t^i + \varepsilon_{t+1}^i,$$

and the expectations theory implies $\beta_1 = 0$ in this regression. If exact data on holding period returns are available, this regression can be used to test the expectations theory without invoking the linear approximate framework used here.

The expectations theory can also be framed as a statement about the predictive power of the yield spread for future changes in long-term interest rates. If the expectations theory holds, then the first term on the right-hand side of equation (4) is zero. It follows that the yield spread is proportional to an optimal forecast of the change in the long-term bond yield. If we run the regression

(6) $$\Delta r^i_{t+1} = \beta_0 + \beta_1[s^i_t/(D_i - 1)] + \varepsilon^i_{t+1},$$

the coefficient β_1 should equal one. Intuitively, when the yield spread is unusually high this implies excess returns on long bonds unless the long-term yield rises to deliver offsetting capital losses. Thus if the expectations theory holds, a high yield spread must tend to be followed by rising long-term interest rates.[7]

The expectations theory of the term structure also implies that long-term interest rates forecast future short-term interest rates. According to the expectations theory,

(7) $$r^i_t = (1/D_i) \sum_{k=0}^{i-1} \gamma^k E_t r^1_{t+k},$$

or in terms of the yield spread,

(8) $$s^i_t = (1/D_i) \sum_{k=0}^{i-1} \gamma^k D_{i-k} E_t \Delta r^1_{t+k}.$$

As before, equations (7) and (8) can be applied to data on zero-coupon bonds by setting $\gamma = 1$ and $D_i = i$; they then hold exactly rather than as approximations.

An obvious way to test (8) is to regress the ex post value of the right-hand side of (8) onto the yield spread; this is the method of Fama and Bliss (1987), Fama (1990), and Mishkin (1990).[8] However, this straightforward approach is hard to apply when the maturity i of the long-term bond is large, because one loses i periods at the end of the sample period and the equation errors become highly serially correlated. Standard asymptotic corrections for equation error overlap are known to perform poorly when the degree of overlap is large relative to the sample size (Richardson and Stock 1989; Hodrick 1992).

An alternative approach, developed by Campbell and Shiller (1987, 1991), is to use a vector autoregression (VAR) to construct an empirical proxy for the multiperiod expectations in (8). In effect this method imputes the long-run dynamics of interest rates from the short-run dynamics. The yield spread itself is included in the VAR, so that if the expectations theory is true, the VAR system can match the best possible forecast of long-horizon movements in short rates by setting its forecast equal to the yield spread. If the expectations theory is false, the VAR forecast will diverge from the yield spread, and this

---

7. Recall, however, that equation (6) holds only when the maturity i is long enough that the i-period yield and the $(i - 1)$-period yield are approximately equal.

8. In fact Fama and Bliss (1987) and Fama (1990) use "forward premiums," differences between forward rates and current short rates, as their regressors. The dependent variables in the regressions are modified accordingly.

can be used to test the theory. The VAR method can be applied in much smaller samples than the direct regression method because the VAR can be estimated without losing i observations at the end of the sample. The VAR residuals are serially uncorrelated, and this helps to give the method quite good small-sample properties (Hodrick 1992).[9]

4.2.2   Approximation Accuracy

An important question in all this work is how accurate is the underlying approximation, equation (1). In our data set we can check this approximation by comparing the approximated return with the observed exact return. For our series of benchmark issues, the correlation between the approximated and the exact return exceeds .99. The correlations for our maturity-based portfolios tend to be somewhat lower, but they all exceed .96 except for the 9–10-year portfolio, where the correlation is .94. This suggests that the approximate term structure model should be applied with some caution to the long end of the Japanese government yield curve.

4.3   The Behavior of Japanese Short-Term Interest Rates

In this section, we analyze the behavior of the short end of the term structure. We begin in table 4.1 by presenting summary statistics for 1-, 2-, and 3-month gensaki rates, their first differences, and the yield spread between them. The table also reports the results of Dickey-Fuller unit root tests.

4.3.1   The Univariate Short Rate Process

In the postwar United States, the short-term interest rate has behaved much like a univariate random walk. That is, the short rate process seems to have a unit root, and there is little predictability of short rate changes from lagged short rate changes. In Germany and Switzerland, by contrast, Kugler (1988) finds considerable predictability of short rate changes. He attributes the difference to the fact that the Federal Reserve Board has pursued an interest rate smoothing policy for most of the postwar period (with the exception of 1979–82), while the monetary authorities in Germany and Switzerland have tolerated nominal interest rate variability in order to stabilize money growth.[10]

We begin our investigation of Japanese short-term interest rates by asking whether the 1-month gensaki rate follows a unit root process as the U.S. short rate appears to do. The results in table 4.1 show a striking difference between the two halves of our sample period. The unit root hypothesis for the short rate is rejected for the full sample period and the first subsample. In the second subsample, by contrast, the unit root hypothesis cannot be rejected at a con-

---

9. The VAR residuals may be conditionally heteroscedastic, but standard errors can be corrected for this in the usual way.

10. For more on shifts in U.S. interest rate behavior around the 1979–82 period, see Huizinga and Mishkin (1986).

Table 4.1   Summary Statistics, Gensaki Rates

Series	Mean	Standard Deviation	Autocorrelations				Dickey-Fuller Test
			ρ_1	ρ_2	ρ_3	ρ_4	
			Full sample (1980:11–1990:8, 118 observations)				
r_t^1	5.701	1.318	0.921	0.851	0.809	0.734	−4.32
r_t^2	5.764	1.343	0.929	0.862	0.817	0.751	−4.56
r_t^3	5.799	1.356	0.932	0.867	0.822	0.759	−4.55
Δr_t^1	−0.021	0.337	−0.018	0.026	0.392	−0.174	−55.45
Δr_t^2	−0.022	0.299	0.137	0.083	0.336	−0.124	−60.15
Δr_t^3	−0.022	0.287	0.196	0.096	0.311	−0.100	−60.18
s_t^2	0.063	0.075	0.478	0.427	0.547	0.247	−40.25
s_t^3	0.098	0.107	0.494	0.421	0.541	0.236	−38.37
			Subsample 1 (1980:11–1985:7, 57 observations)				
r_t^1	6.623	0.735	0.686	0.465	0.402	0.150	−7.56
r_t^2	6.724	0.739	0.726	0.513	0.423	0.219	−7.65
r_t^3	6.778	0.735	0.736	0.523	0.420	0.228	−8.33
Δr_t^1	−0.064	0.399	−0.239	−0.035	0.464	−0.293	−267.45
Δr_t^2	−0.065	0.335	−0.096	0.023	0.402	−0.258	−244.01
Δr_t^3	−0.065	0.317	−0.023	0.043	0.355	−0.234	−6207.23
s_t^2	0.101	0.088	0.344	0.266	0.408	−0.007	−540.40
s_t^3	0.155	0.120	0.308	0.196	0.355	−0.102	79.90
			Subsample 2 (1985:8–1990:8, 61 observations)				
r_t^1	4.839	1.148	0.923	0.833	0.728	0.605	1.80
r_t^2	4.867	1.147	0.924	0.832	0.725	0.602	1.92
r_t^3	4.884	1.150	0.924	0.833	0.726	0.603	1.81
Δr_t^1	0.018	0.265	0.402	0.128	0.225	0.055	−6.06
Δr_t^2	0.018	0.257	0.462	0.152	0.216	0.065	−5.94
Δr_t^3	0.017	0.254	0.475	0.147	0.236	0.074	−6.07
s_t^2	0.028	0.034	0.169	0.103	0.388	0.085	−18.82
s_t^3	0.045	0.054	0.342	0.251	0.445	0.200	−12.53

Notes: Dickey-Fuller test is a t-statistic from the augmented Dickey-Fuller test with six lagged changes. The Dickey-Fuller critical values are:
    50 observations: −2.60 (10%), −2.93 (5%), −3.58 (1%)
    100 observations: −2.58 (10%), −2.89 (5%), −3.51 (1%)

ventional significance level.[11] This reflects the fact that, as shown in figure 4.2, the short rate moved up and down in a narrow range during most of the early 1980s but then began to move more smoothly over a wider range in the

11. We use Dickey-Fuller regressions of the change in the gensaki rate on the lagged level and six lagged changes (the number of lagged changes was suggested by Akaike's information criterion, as discussed below). There are well-known difficulties with the interpretation of unit root tests in finite samples (see Campbell and Perron 1991 for a review). We use them here as a simple way to characterize the time series properties of the gensaki rate.

late 1980s. As discussed above, this change in behavior may be due to a change in monetary policy in the mid-1980s.

We examine the predictability of the 1-month gensaki rate by running a univariate regression of the change in the gensaki rate on lagged changes. Preliminary analysis using Akaike's information criterion suggested a lag length of 6. Thus the forecasting regression is

$$(9) \qquad \Delta r_{t+1} = b_0 + \sum_{i=1}^{6} b_i \Delta r_{t+1-i} + \varepsilon_{t+1} .$$

The results, which are tabulated in table 4.2, panel A, indicate that there is substantial univariate forecastability of the Japanese short rate process. For the full sample, the adjusted R^2 is 0.231, and the coefficients are in general significant. The forecastability is concentrated in the first subsample, where the adjusted R^2 is 0.455; in the second subsample, it drops to 0.180. This fits the pattern of the unit root tests, suggesting that the univariate interest rate process changed in the mid-1980s from a stationary, highly forecastable process to a nonstationary, less forecastable one. Looking across the two subsamples, the coefficients on lagged short rate changes switch sign from predominantly negative to predominantly positive; this again suggests a change from a mean-reverting interest rate process to a "mean-abandoning" nonstationary process.[12]

4.3.2 The Term Structure of Gensaki Rates

Our analysis of the univariate properties of the 1-month gensaki rate has suggested that this rate became harder to forecast after 1985. However, gensaki market participants may have many sources of information other than just the history of 1-month gensaki rates themselves. For example, they may know more about the likely direction of monetary policy than is revealed by the history of 1-month interest rates. This means that it is important to go beyond a univariate approach in analyzing the interest rate process.

If the expectations theory of the term structure holds, the yield spread between longer- and shorter-term gensaki rates embodies all the relevant information of market participants about the likely path of interest rates over the life of the longer-term gensaki agreement. Thus a natural next step is to examine the forecasting power of the gensaki yield spread in a regression of 1-month gensaki rate changes on this variable. Such a regression can also be used to test the expectations theory of the gensaki term structure.[13]

For 2-month rates, the regression can be written as

$$(10) \qquad (r_{t+1}^1 - r_t^1) = \alpha + \beta s_t^2 + \varepsilon_{t+1} ,$$

---

12. Variance ratio statistics for short rates confirm this casual observation. At horizon 12 months, the variance ratio is 0.81 in the first subsample, but 2.55 in the second. See Cochrane (1988) for details on the variance ratio statistic and its interpretation as a measure of persistence.

13. Similar regressions can be found in Campbell and Shiller (1991), Fama (1984), Kugler (1988), Mankiw and Miron (1986), and Shiller, Campbell, and Schoenholtz (1983).

Table 4.2   **Forecastability of Gensaki Rates**

A. Regression of Δr^1_{t+1} on Δr^1_{t+1-i} ($i = 1, \ldots, 6$)

	Full Sample (81:6–90:8)		Subsample 1 (81:6–85:7)		Subsample 2 (85:8–90:8)	
Adjusted R^2 and joint significance level	0.231 [0.000]		0.455 [0.000]		0.180 [0.000]	
	Coefficient	Standard Error	Coefficient	Standard Error	Coefficient	Standard Error
Constant	0.004	0.022	−0.025	0.027	0.011	0.029
lag 1	0.202	0.129	−0.274	0.179	0.473	0.202*
2	0.008	0.149	−0.155	0.164	−0.102	0.263
3	0.300	0.111*	0.177	0.108	0.230	0.196
4	−0.198	0.082*	−0.170	0.115	−0.073	0.127
5	−0.111	0.098	−0.172	0.093	−0.202	0.191
6	0.151	0.077	0.099	0.082	0.166	0.142

B. Regression of $(\Delta r^1_{t+2} + 2\Delta r^1_{t+1})$ on Δr^1_{t+1-i} ($i = 1, \ldots, 6$)

	Full Sample (81:6–90:8)		Subsample 1 (81:6–85:7)		Subsample 2 (85:8–90:8)	
Adjusted R^2 and joint significance level	0.162 [0.000]		0.434 [0.000]		0.129 [0.000]	
	Coefficient	Standard Error	Coefficient	Standard Error	Coefficient	Standard Error
Constant	0.008	0.054	−0.069	0.052	0.032	0.075
lag 1	0.450	0.276	−0.639	0.393	1.049	0.402*
2	0.284	0.434	−0.199	0.303	0.010	0.762
3	0.452	0.245	0.076	0.212	0.454	0.448
4	0.586	0.161*	−0.531	0.227*	−0.375	0.221
5	0.104	0.254	−0.168	0.177	−0.410	0.495
6	0.353	0.169*	0.244	0.161	0.477	0.295

C. Simple test of expectations hypothesis for 2-month gensaki rate $\Delta r^1_{t+1} = \alpha + \beta s^2_t + \varepsilon_{t+1}$

	Full Sample (80:12–90:8)		Subsample 1 (80:12–85:7)		Subsample 2 (85:8–90:8)	
Adjusted R^2 and joint significance level	0.142 [0.000]		0.233 [0.000]		0.389 [0.000]	
	Coefficient	Standard Error	Coefficient	Standard Error	Coefficient	Standard Error
α	−0.131	0.046*	−0.292	0.094*	−0.199	0.047*
β	1.733	0.477*	2.251	0.659*	4.850	1.107*
Test of expectations theory ($\beta = 2$)	[0.476]		[0.703]		[0.010]	
Standard deviation of fitted value	0.130		0.198		0.167	

Table 4.2   (continued)

D. *Simple test of expectations hypothesis for 3-month gensaki rate*
$$(\Delta r^1_{t+2} + 2\Delta r^1_{t+1}) = \gamma + \delta s^3_t + v_{t+2}$$

	Full Sample (80:12–90:8)		Subsample 1 (80:12–85:7)		Subsample 2 (85:8–90:8)	
Adjusted R^2 and	0.099		0.173		0.428	
joint significance	[0.001]		[0.002]		[0.000]	
level		Standard		Standard		Standard
	Coefficient	Error	Coefficient	Error	Coefficient	Error
γ	−0.290	0.110*	−0.638	0.215*	−0.335	0.097*
δ	2.275	0.659*	2.872	0.918*	8.197	1.317*
Test of expecta-tions theory ($\delta = 3$)	[0.272]		[0.889]		[0.000]	
Standard devia-tion of fitted value	0.245		0.351		0.448	

E. *Multiple regression of* Δr^1_{t+1} *on* Δr^1_{t+1-i} *(i = 1, . . . , 6) and* s^2_t

	Full Sample (81:6–90:8)		Subsample 1 (81:6–85:7)		Subsample 2 (85:8–90:8)	
Adjusted R^2 and	0.293		0.454		0.454	
joint significance	[0.000]		[0.000]		[0.000]	
level		Standard		Standard		Standard
	Coefficient	Error	Coefficient	Error	Coefficient	Error
s^2_t	0.995	0.420*	0.411	0.401	4.314	1.116*
Exclusion of s^2_t	[0.019]		[0.305]		[0.000]	
Test of expecta-tions theory (i.e., s_t coeffi-cient = 2 and other coeffi-cients = 0)	[0.000]		[0.000]		[0.000]	

F. *Multiple regression of* $(\Delta r^1_{t+2} + 2\Delta r^1_{t+1})$ *on* Δr^1_{t+1-i} *(i = 1, . . . , 6) and* s^3_t

	Full Sample (81:6–90:8)		Subsample 1 (81:6–85:7)		Subsample 2 (85:8–90:8)	
Adjusted R^2 and	0.856		0.423		0.453	
joint significance	[0.000]		[0.000]		[0.000]	
level		Standard		Standard		Standard
	Coefficient	Error	Coefficient	Error	Coefficient	Error
s^3_t	0.221	0.650*	0.251	0.579	7.710	1.582*
Exclusion of s^3_t	[0.019]		[0.665]		[0.000]	
Test of expecta-tions theory (i.e., s^3_t coeffi-cient = 3 and other coeffi-cients = 0)	[0.000]		[0.000]		[0.000]	

Notes: Numbers in brackets are p-values. All standard errors and p-values are corrected for heterosce-dasticity. Asterisks indicate significance at the 5% level.

where r_t^1 and r_t^2 are 1- and 2-month gensaki rates, respectively, and $s_t^2 = r_t^2 - r_t^1$. If the expectations theory holds, then we should find $\beta = 2$, while if the yield spread contains no relevant information about future short rates, we will find $\beta = 0$.

For 3-month rates, the regression can be written as

$$(11) \qquad (r_{t+2}^1 + r_{t+1}^1 - 2r_t^1) = \gamma + \delta s_t^3 + v_{t+2} ,$$

where r_t^3 is the 3-month gensaki rate and $s_t^3 = r_t^3 - r_t^1$. According to the expectations theory, $\delta = 3$, while $\delta = 0$ if there is no relevant information in the term structure of gensaki rates. In this regression the equation errors overlap, for which standard errors must be adjusted. In addition, all standard errors and hypothesis tests in this and following tables are adjusted for conditional heteroscedasticity in interest rates, although this makes little difference to our results.[14]

Table 4.2, panels C and D, report estimates of equation (10) and (11), with very similar results for the two specifications. We obtain two striking results. First, there is no decline in the forecastability of short-term rates when the yield spread is used as the forecasting variable. In fact, the R^2 statistics for regressions (10) and (11) increase after 1985, while the standard deviations of the fitted values fall very slightly in (10) and rise in (11). This illustrates the danger of relying too heavily on the univariate properties of the short rate process.

Second, regressions (10) and (11) provide no evidence against the expectations theory in the full sample or the first subsample, but they strongly reject the theory in the second subsample. In the post-1985 period, the coefficient on the yield spread is more than twice as large as it should be under the expectations theory, indicating that the yield spread was less variable than the optimal forecast of future gensaki rate changes. As shown in table 4.1, the variability of gensaki yield spreads declined considerably after 1985; regressions (10) and (11) indicate that this was not due to a decline in the forecastability of short rate changes, but to a failure of the expectations hypothesis in the post-1985 period.

As a final empirical exercise, we combine the regressors of table 4.2, panels A and B (lagged short rate changes) with those of panels C and D (yield spreads). The results are reported in panels E and F. We find that when both the history of short rates and the slope of the term structure are taken into account, there was little change in the forecastability of short rates between the early and the late 1980s. What changed was that in the early 1980s short rates could be well forecast from their own history with no marginal predictive power from the yield spread; in the late 1980s the yield spread was essential for forecasting short rates. In these regressions the expectations hypothesis is strongly rejected in the full sample and both our subsamples.

14. The adjustments can be seen as an application of Hansen's (1982) generalized method of moments.

4.4   The Long-Term Government Bond Market

In this section we extend our investigation to the longer end of the yield curve. We begin in table 4.3 by reporting summary statistics, parallel to those of table 4.1, for bond portfolios with maturities of 1–2 years (18 months), 3–4 years (42 months), 5–6 years (66 months), 7–8 years (90 months), and 9–10 years (114 months). Once again we reject the unit root hypothesis for most maturities in the full sample and first subsample, but we fail to reject it in the second subsample.

It is noteworthy that the standard deviation of the change in the bond yield (which is approximately proportional to the standard deviation of the bond return) is lower in the first subsample than in the second subsample. Also this standard deviation declines with maturity in the first subsample, whereas it increases with maturity in the second. This is what the expectations theory of the term structure would predict when there is a shift in the interest rate process from a stationary mean-reverting process to a nonstationary "mean-abandoning" one.[15]

4.4.1   Term Structure Forecasts of Long-Term Interest Rates

We now proceed to a more formal evaluation of the expectations theory of the term structure as a description of the long-term Japanese yield curve. In table 4.4, panel A, we run regressions of the form (6), with the change in the long-term bond yield as the dependent variable and the yield spread (appropriately scaled by bond duration) as the regressor. According to the expectations theory, the scaled yield spread should be the best possible forecast of the change in the long bond yield over the next period, so the coefficient on the scaled yield spread should equal one. The point estimates in table 4.4, panel A, are not very favorable to the expectations theory, at least over the full sample and the second subsample. We find that the regression coefficient on the scaled yield spread tends to be negative rather than positive, and it becomes increasingly negative as the long bond maturity increases. These results parallel those obtained for the United States by Campbell and Shiller (1991). The standard errors in this regression are very large, however, so we have no strong statistical evidence against the expectations theory. Over the first subsample the results are rather erratic and do not provide any evidence against the expectations theory.

Table 4.4, panel B, adds six lags of short rate changes to the regression of panel A. Just as in table 4.2, panels E and F, the use of lagged short rates strengthens the evidence against the expectations hypothesis. We now reject the hypothesis at the 5% level in seven out of fifteen regressions, and at the 10% level in ten out of fifteen regressions.

---

15. Chan, Karolyi, Longstaff, and Sanders (1991), Sargen, Schoenholtz, and Alcamo (1987), and Singleton (1990) discuss the changing volatility of Japanese government bond markets. Shikano (1985) and Shirakawa (1987) use the expectations theory to interpret movements in the Japanese term structure.

Table 4.3   Summary Statistics, Government Bond Yields

Series	Mean	Standard Deviation	Autocorrelations				Dickey-Fuller Test
			ρ_1	ρ_2	ρ_3	ρ_4	
Full sample (1980:11–1990:8, 118 observations)							
Level							
1–2 yrs	6.057	1.521	0.948	0.895	0.855	0.818	−5.64
3–4 yrs	6.176	1.533	0.960	0.919	0.885	0.854	−4.22
5–6 yrs	6.350	1.579	0.967	0.933	0.903	0.878	−3.61
7–8 yrs	6.468	1.544	0.963	0.926	0.891	0.858	−4.10
9–10 yrs	6.533	1.361	0.963	0.924	0.889	0.858	−4.47
Difference							
1–2 yrs	−0.015	0.299	0.168	0.110	0.002	−0.094	−77.87
3–4 yrs	−0.009	0.301	0.132	0.043	−0.003	−0.099	−92.61
5–6 yrs	−0.008	0.295	0.159	0.031	−0.005	−0.149	−94.02
7–8 yrs	−0.012	0.302	0.147	0.055	−0.055	−0.165	−90.73
9–10 yrs	−0.010	0.294	0.129	−0.012	−0.024	−0.198	−106.09
Spread with 1-month gensaki							
1–2 yrs	0.357	0.481	0.821	0.666	0.567	0.424	−21.90
3–4 yrs	0.476	0.573	0.802	0.638	0.558	0.398	−23.76
5–6 yrs	0.650	0.705	0.845	0.714	0.649	0.505	−18.00
7–8 yrs	0.768	0.695	0.828	0.664	0.553	0.384	−22.61
9–10 yrs	0.832	0.696	0.815	0.644	0.541	0.362	−23.34
Subsample 1 (1980:11–1985:7, 57 observations)							
Level							
1–2 yrs	7.221	0.886	0.866	0.726	0.637	0.553	−7.45
3–4 yrs	7.440	0.717	0.864	0.720	0.606	0.520	−6.58
5–6 yrs	7.688	0.775	0.911	0.809	0.731	0.663	−3.00
7–8 yrs	7.775	0.803	0.912	0.825	0.753	0.689	−2.30
9–10 yrs	7.747	0.577	0.874	0.756	0.652	0.578	−2.57
Difference							
1–2 yrs	−0.063	0.270	0.021	0.118	−0.056	−0.145	−40.62
3–4 yrs	−0.048	0.264	0.022	0.014	−0.130	−0.118	−46.18
5–6 yrs	−0.046	0.213	0.173	−0.078	−0.065	−0.085	−46.47
7–8 yrs	−0.050	0.199	0.082	−0.035	−0.142	−0.033	−45.48
9–10 yrs	−0.039	0.195	0.025	0.005	−0.129	−0.108	−56.31
Spread with 1-month gensaki							
1–2 yrs	0.598	0.468	0.783	0.619	0.562	0.375	−10.10
3–4 yrs	0.817	0.510	0.637	0.385	0.335	0.078	−20.33
5–6 yrs	1.065	0.668	0.745	0.571	0.541	0.333	−11.58
7–8 yrs	1.152	0.623	0.707	0.499	0.435	0.191	−14.78
9–10 yrs	1.124	0.600	0.649	0.420	0.372	0.110	−19.42
Subsample 2 (1985:8–1990:8, 61 observations)							
Level							
1–2 yrs	4.969	1.135	0.893	0.794	0.691	0.598	−0.47
3–4 yrs	4.996	1.081	0.883	0.782	0.677	0.587	−0.44

Table 4.3   (continued)

		Standard	Autocorrelations				Dickey-Fuller
Series	Mean	Deviation	ρ_1	ρ_2	ρ_3	ρ_4	Test
5–6 yrs	5.101	1.007	0.863	0.743	0.619	0.522	− 1.12
7–8 yrs	5.246	0.953	0.853	0.719	0.569	0.447	− 2.93
9–10 yrs	5.398	0.770	0.820	0.644	0.470	0.319	− 6.34
Difference							
1–2 yrs	0.028	0.319	0.233	0.083	0.032	− 0.088	− 40.62
3–4 yrs	0.025	0.329	0.178	0.041	0.053	− 0.092	− 46.18
5–6 yrs	0.026	0.352	0.139	0.052	0.001	− 0.175	− 46.47
7–8 yrs	0.021	0.370	0.151	0.064	− 0.052	− 0.214	− 45.48
9–10 yrs	0.016	0.362	0.145	− 0.032	− 0.009	− 0.232	− 56.31
Spread with 1-month gensaki							
1–2 yrs	0.131	0.374	0.692	0.406	0.163	− 0.031	− 23.49
3–4 yrs	0.157	0.429	0.719	0.432	0.213	0.002	− 23.85
5–6 yrs	0.262	0.484	0.726	0.420	0.181	− 0.075	− 25.75
7–8 yrs	0.408	0.555	0.768	0.466	0.188	− 0.049	− 25.57
9–10 yrs	0.560	0.672	0.842	0.627	0.437	0.254	− 16.19

Notes: Dickey-Fuller test is a t-statistic from the augmented Dickey-Fuller test with one lagged change. The Dickey-Fuller critical values are:
    50 observations: − 2.60 (10%), − 2.93 (5%), − 3.58 (1%)
    100 observations: − 2.58 (10%), − 2.89 (5%), − 3.51 (1%)

4.4.2 Term Structure Forecasts of Short-Term Interest Rates

In the United States, the expectations theory of the term structure is rejected statistically; nevertheless the U.S. yield curve contains useful forecasts of short-term interest rates over a long horizon, as emphasized by Fama and Bliss (1987) and Campbell and Shiller (1991). Jorion and Mishkin (1991) report that British, German, and Swiss yield curves have similar properties. We now ask whether the same is true for the Japanese yield curve.

We cannot evaluate the long-horizon forecasting power of the Japanese term structure by direct regression as we did for gensaki rates, because the regression would require shortening the sample period by the long bond's maturity (so we would have no data at all for the 9–10-year bond) and would have an equation error overlap equal to the long bond's maturity (which has very bad effects on inference in a short sample). Instead we use the indirect VAR approach proposed by Campbell and Shiller (1991). We run a VAR with four lags of the yield spread and the change in the short rate, and we calculate the unrestricted VAR forecast of the weighted sum of short rate changes given on the right-hand side of equation (8).[16] We call this the "theoretical spread."

16. We also ran VAR systems with two lags and obtained very similar results. Note that a low-order VAR system can approximate a high-order univariate process, so we do not necessarily need the VAR lag length to equal the number of lags used in the univariate regressions of section 4.3.

Table 4.4   Forecastability of Long Rate Changes

Bond Maturity i	Full Sample (80:11–90:8)	Subsample 1 (80:11–85:7)	Subsample 2 (85:8–90:8)
A. Regression of Long Rate Change on Scaled Yield Spread $\Delta r^i_{t+1} = \beta_0 + \beta_1[s^i_t/(D_i - 1)] + \varepsilon^i_{t+1}$			
18	−0.087	0.216	2.034
	(0.949)	(1.289)	(2.065)
42	−0.673	0.181	2.434
	(1.829)	(2.748)	(4.166)
66	−1.638	1.921	−3.592
	(2.304)	(2.412)	(7.177)
90	−4.231	0.514	−7.806
	(3.605)	(3.522)	(9.316)
114	−3.733	2.481	−7.377
	(4.261)	(2.973)	(8.415)

B. Test of Expectations Theory: Regression of Long Rate Change on Scaled Yield Spread and Lagged Short Rate Changes

$$\Delta r^i_{t+1} = \beta_0 + \beta_1[s^i_t/(D_i - 1)] + \sum_{j=1}^{6} \gamma_j \Delta r^1_{t+1-j} + \varepsilon^i_{t+1}$$

Significance level for H_0: $\beta_1 = 1$, and $\gamma_1 = \ldots = \gamma_6 = 0$

Bond Maturity i	Full Sample (81:6–90:8)	Subsample 1 (81:6–85:7)	Subsample 2 (85:8–90:8)
18	0.009	0.059	0.017
42	0.081	0.012	0.026
66	0.185	0.003	0.166
90	0.387	0.014	0.086
114	0.195	0.106	0.004

Notes: Numbers in parentheses are heteroscedasticity-consistent standard errors. Panel B significance levels are also heteroscedasticity-consistent.

Table 4.5 reports the estimated correlation of the theoretical and actual spreads, while table 4.6 reports the standard deviation of the theoretical spread divided by the standard deviation of the actual spread. For completeness we apply this method to the gensaki term structure as well as the term structure of bond yields.

Our results are quite similar to those of Campbell and Shiller (1991) for postwar U.S. data. We find contrasting results for the short and long ends of the term structure. At the short end the theoretical and actual yield spreads have a positive correlation of about .5 in the full sample and first subsample; this increases to almost .9 in the second subsample. The actual yield spread is somewhat less variable than the theoretical yield spread, particularly in the second subsample. This is what one would expect from our direct regression analysis in table 4.2. There we found that in the early 1980s lagged short rates contained information about future short rates that was not available from the yield spread; in the late 1980s the yield spread was the only useful forecasting

Table 4.5   **Correlation of Theoretical and Actual Yield Spreads**

Bond Maturity	Full Sample (80:11–90:8)	Subsample 1 (80:11–85:7)	Subsample 2 (85:8–90:8)
2	0.526	0.566	0.876
	(0.081)	(0.077)	(0.057)
3	0.584	0.561	0.907
	(0.128)	(0.127)	(0.043)
6	0.758	0.405	0.891
	(0.208)	(0.294)	(0.095)
18	0.842	− 0.068	0.957
	(0.247)	(0.883)	(0.067)
42	0.883	0.256	0.958
	(0.236)	(0.992)	(0.046)
66	0.493	0.130	0.883
	(1.558)	(2.013)	(0.208)
90	0.519	0.133	0.820
	(1.403)	(2.023)	(0.349)
114	0.801	0.844	0.894
	(0.707)	(0.233)	(0.271)

Notes: This table gives correlation coefficients of theoretical and actual yield spreads between long-term government bonds (including 2- and 3-month gensaki) and the 1-month gensaki rate. The theoretical spread is calculated by using a VAR model with four lags of $[\Delta r_t^1 \ s_t^i]$ to construct the weighted sum of expectations in equation (8). The first column indicates the number of months to maturity of the longer-term bond. Numbers in parentheses are heteroscedasticity-consistent standard errors.

variable for short rates, but the coefficient on this variable was larger than required by the expectations theory, indicating an insufficiently variable spread.

At the long end of the term structure, the correlations between the theoretical and actual yield spreads are also consistently positive, and highest in the late 1980s. However, the actual yield spread is now considerably more variable than the theoretical yield spread (the ratio of theoretical to actual standard deviations ranges from about one-quarter to about one-half for the two longest bond maturities). In the full sample and the first subsample the standard deviation ratios are significantly different from one at the long end of the term structure.

A visual impression of these results is given in figures 4.6 and 4.7. Figure 4.6 plots the actual and theoretical 3-month yield spreads over our full sample period, while figure 4.7 plots the actual and theoretical 9–10-year yield spreads. The figures clearly show the contrast between the short and long ends of the yield curve: at the long end, the actual yield spread is much more variable than its theoretical counterpart, while if anything the opposite is true at the short end of the yield curve.

Our VAR system can also be used to calculate a theoretical excess return, defined as the excess return that bondholders would obtain if the yield spread

Table 4.6   Standard Deviation Ratio of Theoretical and Actual Yield Spread

Bond Maturity	Full Sample (80:11–90:8)	Subsample 1 (80:11–85:7)	Subsample 2 (85:8–90:8)
2	1.331	1.328	2.769
	(0.113)	(0.107)	(0.446)
3	1.127	1.085	3.115
	(0.169)	(0.105)	(0.435)
6	0.471	0.366	1.078
	(0.139)	(0.036)	(0.241)
18	0.460	0.288	1.134
	(0.223)	(0.085)	(0.321)
42	0.416	0.314	0.983
	(0.276)	(0.040)	(0.263)
66	0.226	0.260	0.681
	(0.160)	(0.039)	(0.250)
90	0.224	0.257	0.559
	(0.151)	(0.073)	(0.262)
114	0.263	0.468	0.503
	(0.312)	(0.215)	(0.285)

Notes: This table gives the standard deviation of the theoretical yield spread divided by the standard deviation of the actual yield spread between long-term government bonds (including 2- and 3-month gensaki) and the 1-month gensaki rate. The theoretical spread is calculated by using a VAR model with four lags of $[\Delta r_t^1 \; s_t^i]$ to construct the weighted sum of expectations in equation (8). The first column indicates the number of months to maturity of the longer-term bond. Numbers in parentheses are heteroscedasticity-consistent standard errors.

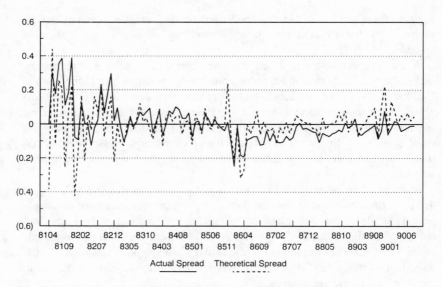

Fig. 4.6   Actual versus theoretical spread, 3-month gensaki

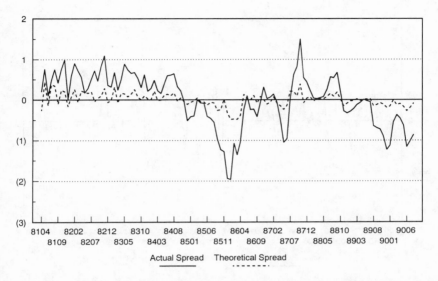

Fig. 4.7   Actual versus theoretical spread, 9–10-year Japanese government bonds

were equal to its theoretical value. Figure 4.8 plots the actual and theoretical excess returns on 9–10-year bonds over the full sample period. The figure shows that, although the Japanese yield spread is more variable than can be explained by the expectations theory, the Japanese excess bond return is not. The variability of the actual excess return is close to its theoretical counterpart, or even a little lower in 1987. According to these estimates, the increased volatility of Japanese government bond returns in the late 1980s can be explained by the changing behavior of short-term interest rates. Even though the Japanese term structure deviates from the predictions of the simple expectations theory, this deviation does not increase the volatility of returns on Japanese government bonds.

4.5   Conclusions

In this paper we have studied the behavior of short- and long-term interest rates in Japan during the 1980s. We have three main findings.

First, we find evidence that the univariate short-term interest rate process changed in Japan around 1985. Before that date the short-term rate appears to be mean-reverting, and changes in short rates are highly forecastable from their own history. In the late 1980s, changes in the Japanese short rate show no tendency to reverse themselves. The short rate behaves very much like a random walk, or even a nonstationary process that is more persistent than a

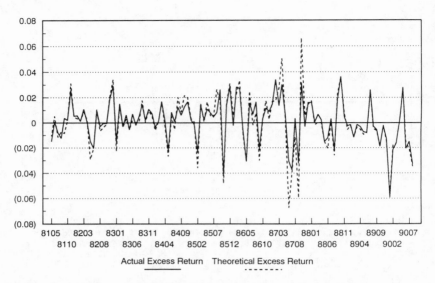

Fig. 4.8   Actual versus theoretical excess return, 9–10 year Japanese
government bonds

random walk (a "mean-abandoning" process). We suggest that this change in
interest rate behavior may be due to a shift in Japanese monetary policy
around the time of the September 1985 Plaza Accord.

Our second finding is that there has also been a shift in the ability of the
Japanese yield curve to forecast Japanese short rates. At the short end of the
term structure, we find that the yield spread between the 2- or 3-month gensaki rate and the 1-month gensaki rate had no marginal predictive power for
changes in 1-month rates in the early 1980s. In the late 1980s, by contrast,
this yield spread was a powerful forecasting variable. In fact, the decline in
the forecastability of Japanese short rates from their own past history is completely offset by the increase in forecastability of Japanese short rates from the
gensaki yield curve; the overall forecastability of short rates is roughly constant through the 1980s. At the long end of the term structure, we calculate
the correlation between the long-short yield spread and an unrestricted VAR
forecast of future short rate changes over the life of the long-term bond. We
find that this correlation increased from the early 1980s to the late 1980s; this
again suggests an increase in the ability of the term structure to forecast interest rate movements.

Our third finding is that the expectations theory of the term structure fails
to describe our data on Japanese gensaki and government bond yields. This
result may not be unexpected, given the overwhelming evidence against
the expectations theory in U.S. and European data and the earlier findings of
Shikano (1985) and Singleton (1990). We use a VAR approach to characterize

the failure of the expectations theory and argue that, at the long end of the term structure, the yield spread is consistently more variable than can be justified by rational forecasts of future movements in short-term interest rates. This result parallels the findings of Campbell and Shiller (1991) for the U.S. term structure. On the other hand, there is no excess volatility of returns, in that the volatility of returns on long-term Japanese government bonds is roughly equal to that predicted by the expectations theory of the term structure.

We leave several issues for further research. Perhaps the most important of these is the question of why the interest rate forecasting ability of the Japanese term structure has increased since the mid-1980s. One possibility is that the information available to market participants has increased over time, either because of institutional changes in the formulation of monetary policy or because of increased linkages between interest rates in different countries. A second possibility is that the efficiency of Japanese bond markets has increased with the steady deregulation of the past 10 years, so that bond prices now reveal market participants' information more effectively.

References

Bank of Japan. 1986. Structural Changes in the Secondary Market for Bonds and the Recent Changes in Yields on Long-Term Bonds. Special Paper No. 132, Research and Statistics Department.

———. 1988. Recent Developments in the Long-Term Bond Market. Special Paper No. 170, Research and Statistics Department.

———. 1990. *Chosa Geppo (Research Monthly)*, May.

Campbell, John Y., and Pierre Perron. 1991. Pitfalls and Opportunities: What Macroeconomists Should Know about Unit Roots. In *NBER Macroeconomics Annual,* ed. Olivier Blanchard and Stanley Fischer, 6:141–201. Cambridge, MA: MIT Press.

Campbell, John Y., and Robert J. Shiller. 1987. Cointegration and Tests of Present Value Models. *Journal of Political Economy* 95:1062–88.

———. 1991. Yield Spreads and Interest Rate Movements: A Bird's-Eye View. *Review of Economic Studies* 58:495–514.

Chan, K. C., G. Andrew Karolyi, Francis A. Longstaff, and Anthony B. Sanders. 1991. The Volatility of Japanese Interest Rates: A Comparison of Alternative Term Structure Models. Ohio State University.

Cochrane, John H. 1988. How Big Is the Random Walk in GNP? *Journal of Political Economy* 96:893–920.

Dominguez, Kathryn. 1990. Have Recent Central Bank Foreign Exchange Intervention Operations Influenced the Yen? Harvard University and Princeton University.

Fama, Eugene F. 1984. The Information in the Term Structure. *Journal of Financial Economics* 13:509–28.

———. 1990. Term-Structure Forecasts of Interest Rates, Inflation, and Real Returns. *Journal of Monetary Economics* 25:59–76.

Fama, Eugene F., and Robert R. Bliss. 1987. The Information in Long-Maturity Forward Rates. *American Economic Review* 77:680–92.

Funabashi, Yoichi. 1988. *Managing the Dollar: From the Plaza to the Louvre.* Washington, DC: Institute for International Economics.

Hansen, Lars P. 1982. Large Sample Properties of Generalized Method Moments Estimators. *Econometrica* 50:1029–54.

Hodrick, Robert J. 1992. Dividend Yields and Expected Stock Returns: Alternative Procedures for Inference and Measurement. *Review of Financial Studies* 5:357–86.

Huizinga, John, and Frederic S. Mishkin. 1986. Monetary Policy Regime Shifts and the Unusual Behavior of Real Interest Rates. *Carnegie-Rochester Conference Series on Public Policy* 24:231–74.

Jorion, Philippe, and Frederic S. Mishkin. 1991. A Multi-country Comparison of Term Structure Forecasts at Long Horizons. NBER Working Paper No. 3574. Cambridge, MA: National Bureau of Economic Research.

Kugler, Peter. 1988. An Empirical Note on the Term Structure and Interest Rate Stabilization Policies. *Quarterly Journal of Economics* 103:789–92.

Leung, Kwok-Wai, Anthony B. Sanders, and Haluk Unal. 1991. The Structural Behavior of the Japanese Gensaki Rate. In *Japanese Financial Market Research,* ed. William T. Ziemba, Warren Bailey, and Yasushi Hamao. Amsterdam: North-Holland.

Macaulay, Frederick R. 1938. *Some Theoretical Problems Suggested by the Movements of Interest Rates, Bond Yields, and Stock Prices in the United States since 1856.* New York: National Bureau of Economic Research.

Mankiw, N. Gregory, and Jeffrey A. Miron. 1986. The Changing Behavior of the Term Structure of Interest Rates. *Quarterly Journal of Economics* 101:211–28.

Mishkin, Frederic S. 1990. What Does the Term Structure Tell Us about Future Inflation? *Journal of Monetary Economics* 25:77–95.

Richardson, Matthew, and James H. Stock. 1989. Drawing Inferences from Statistics Based on Multiyear Asset Returns. *Journal of Financial Economics* 25:323–48.

Sargen, Nicholas, Kermit Schoenholtz, and Bernadette Alcamo. 1987. *Japanese Bond Market Volatility and International Capital Flows.* Tokyo: Salomon Brothers.

Sargen, Nicholas, Kermit Schoenholtz, Steven Blitz, and Sahar Elhabashi. 1986. *Trading Patterns in the Japanese Government Bond Market.* Tokyo: Salomon Brothers.

Shikano, Yoshiaki. 1985. Expectations Theory and Term Structure of Interest Rates. *Bank of Japan Monetary and Economic Studies* 3:47–70.

Shiller, Robert J. 1990. The Term Structure of Interest Rates. In *The Handbook of Monetary Economics,* ed. Benjamin Friedman and Frank Hahn. Amsterdam: North-Holland.

Shiller, Robert J., John Y. Campbell, and Kermit L. Schoenholtz. 1983. Forward Rates and Future Policy: Interpreting the Term Structure of Interest Rates. *Brookings Papers on Economic Activity* 1:173–217.

Shirakawa, Hiromichi. 1987. Fluctuations in Yields on Bonds: A Reassessment of the Expectations Theory Based on Japanese and U.S. Data. *Bank of Japan Monetary and Economic Studies* 5:71–117.

Singleton, Kenneth J. 1990. Interpreting Changes in the Volatility of Yields on Japanese Long-Term Bonds. *Bank of Japan Monetary and Economic Studies* 8:49–77.

Takagi, Shinji. 1988. Recent Developments in Japan's Bond and Money Markets. *Journal of the Japanese and International Economies* 2:63–91.

5 Monetary Policy and the Real Economy in Japan

Hiroshi Yoshikawa

This chapter considers the role money plays in the economy. At present, there is considerable disagreement among economists over the role of money in economic fluctuations. On the one hand, monetarists (Friedman 1968; Lucas 1972, 1977) consider unanticipated changes in the money supply exogenously caused by central banks to be the major shock driving economic fluctuations. On the other hand, real business cycle theorists argue that macroeconomic fluctuations are set off by technological shocks such as changes in total factor productivity, and that the propagation of these shocks through the economy is due to nonmonetary factors such as optimal consumption smoothing by individuals and lags in the construction of new capital. According to this theory, therefore, money does not play a major role either as a shock or as a propagation mechanism: money is nothing but a veil (King and Plosser 1984; Plosser 1990). Between these two polar views, Keynesians hold that both real demand and monetary shocks are important in business cycles. Yoshikawa and Ohtake (1987) argue that neither rational-expectations-based monetarism nor real business cycle theory can reasonably explain postwar business cycles in Japan, arguing instead that real demand shocks played the major role. This chapter focuses on money and considers its role in economic fluctuations.

To make progress toward fully understanding the role money plays in the economy, it is essential to grasp precisely how monetary policy is conducted. Irrespective of the views expressed by their authors, most macroeconomic analyses, both theoretical and empirical, assume either that the money supply is exogenous or that very simple feedback rules guide monetary policy. These

Hiroshi Yoshikawa is associate professor of economics at the University of Tokyo.

Some of the results reported here are based on ongoing research at the EPA. The author thanks M. Hori, H. Imura, and T. Watanabe for their research assistance, and the editor, professor Shoichi Royama, and other participants of the NBER Conference on Japanese Monetary Policy for their helpful comments.

121

simplifying assumptions make feasible the calculations of equilibrium that are consistent with rational expectations, but it is rarely questioned whether the assumptions made are a good approximation to how monetary policy is conducted in the real world.

This chapter argues that the money supply very often becomes endogenous, passively reflecting various shocks to the economy. The basic reason money becomes endogenous is that central banks smooth the nominal interest rate. Occasionally, however, central banks do change the money supply independently or exogenously, thus affecting the real economy ("dynamic operations" in Roosa's (1956) terminology). Monetary policy, therefore, follows *time-varying* nominal interest rate smoothing, and consists of a regime somewhere between the two polar cases of interest rate pegging and dynamic operations.

Section 5.1 demonstrates the endogeneity of the money supply using a simple model. To shed light on the role of money in economic fluctuations, section 5.2 analyzes monetary policy in seasonal fluctuations. Section 5.3 studies monetary policy at business cycle frequencies and shows that the nominal interest rate is indeed very often smoothed. This section also analyzes the proximate targets the Bank of Japan (BOJ) has pursued in its policymaking. Section 5.4 analyzes the transmission mechanism of monetary policy. The experiences of Japan over a thirty-year period are examined and then compared with those of the United States. Not surprisingly, the transmission mechanism of monetary policy is found to differ substantially over time and also across countries. Section 5.5 offers concluding remarks.

5.1 Nominal Interest Smoothing and Endogenous Money Supply

Monetarists take changes in the money supply to be exogenous. As will be observed below, however, this is not a good description of observed changes in the money supply because the BOJ very often smooths the nominal interest rate. Of course, another issue is whether nominal interest smoothing is a desirable policy, but in fact such policies have been adopted by the BOJ. When the BOJ smoothes the nominal interest rate, specifically, the call rate in the case of Japan, the money supply must endogenously change in response to real disturbances. In this case, changes in the money supply become nothing but mirror images of real shocks.

Keeping this point in mind, I first consider the relationship between the money supply and the real economy in a simple macroeconomic model. This model will form a basis for the discussion in subsequent sections.

Although the basic points I want to make in sections 5.3 and 5.4 are not model-specific, to facilitate explanation I consider a simple Taylor-type macroeconomic model (Taylor 1979, 1980). The model consists of five equations:

(1) $$Y_t = -\gamma(W_t - P_t), \gamma > 0;$$

(2) $Y_t = -a[i_t - E(P_{t+1} \mid \Omega_t) + P_t] + \bar{u}_t, \quad a > 0;$

(3) $W_t = \alpha E(P_{t+1} \mid \Omega_{t-1}) + (1 - \alpha)P_{t-1} + \bar{\eta}_t, \quad 0 < \alpha < 1;$

(4) $M_t - P_t = Y_t - \beta i_t + \bar{v}_t, \quad \beta > 0;$

(5) $M_t = d(i_t - i_t^*) + \bar{\varepsilon}_t \, .$

Y is real GNP, P is the price level, W is nominal wages, and M is the nominal money supply; all are measured in logs. $E(x \mid \Omega)$ denotes taking the expected value of x conditional on the information set Ω. $\bar{u}$, $\bar{\eta}$, $\bar{v}$, and $\bar{\varepsilon}$ are disturbances in each equation.

The BOJ is assumed to smooth the nominal interest rate i around the target rate i^*. The extent of nominal interest rate smoothing is expressed by the parameter d in (5). When d becomes large, the nominal interest rate is virtually pegged. On the other hand, when d is zero, the money supply is equal to the disturbance ε, which is supposed to reflect changes in the BOJ's policy stance, and in this case the nominal rate i becomes an endogenous variable. Note that this characterization of the BOJ's behavior implicitly assumes that the BOJ systematically reacts to income, price, or money demand shocks *within the period*.[1] In fact, the analysis of the seasonal cycle below suggests that the BOJ systematically reacts to various shocks with a lag of less than one month.

The model is otherwise standard and needs no explanation. Output Y, the price level P, the money supply M, and the nominal interest rate i in this model are determined as follows (for simplicity, i^* is taken to be zero):

(6)
$$Y_t = \frac{1}{A} [\gamma a(\phi^2 - bc)P_{t-1} - \gamma ab\bar{\eta}_t$$
$$+ \gamma a(b - 1) (\bar{\varepsilon}_t - \bar{v}_t) + \gamma \bar{u}_t];$$

(7)
$$P_t = \frac{1}{A} [\gamma c\{(b - 1)a + 1\} + a\phi^2]P_{t-1}$$
$$+ \frac{1}{A} [\gamma\{(b - 1)a + 1\}\bar{\eta}_t + (b - 1)a(\bar{\varepsilon}_t - \bar{v}_t) + \bar{u}_t];$$

(8)
$$M_t = \frac{1}{\left(1 + \dfrac{\beta}{d}\right)A} [\{cA + (\gamma + 1)a(\phi^2 - bc)\}P_{t-1}$$
$$+ \{A - (\gamma + 1)ab\}\bar{\eta}_t + (\gamma + a)\bar{v}_t$$
$$+ \{\frac{\beta A}{d} + (\gamma + 1) (b - 1)a\}\bar{\varepsilon}_t + (\gamma + 1)\bar{u}_t];$$

1. McCallum (1983) argues that in vector autoregression systems, monetary policy surprises may be more accurately represented by interest rate than by money stock innovations if the monetary authority aims to hit a money supply target but uses an interest rate instrument. His analysis, however, rests on the assumption that the monetary authority does *not* systematically react to income, price, or money demand shocks within the period.

and

(9)
$$i_t = \frac{1}{(d + \beta)A} [\{cA + (\gamma + 1)a(\phi^2 - bc)\}P_{t-1}$$
$$+ \{A - (\gamma + 1)ab\}\bar{\eta}_t + (\gamma + a)\bar{v}_t - (\gamma + a)\bar{\varepsilon}_t + (\gamma + 1)\bar{u}_t],$$

where

$$A = \gamma\left(1 + \frac{a}{\beta+d}\right) + \left(\frac{a}{\beta+d}\right) + a;$$

$$b = 1 + \frac{1}{\beta+d}, \quad b > 1; \text{ and}$$

$$c = \alpha\phi^2 + (1 - \alpha), \quad 0 < c < 1;$$

and ϕ $(0 < \phi < 1)$ is a root of the following characteristic equation of the system:

(10)
$$f(x) = \left[\frac{a}{((b - 1)a + 1)} + \gamma\alpha\right]x^2 - \left[\frac{ab}{((b - 1)a + 1)} + \gamma\right]x$$
$$+ \gamma(1 - \alpha) = 0.$$

The basic message is that in general changes in the money supply M_t contain various shocks: price shocks η, real demand shocks u, portfolio shocks v, and changes in the BOJ's policy stance ε. Monetarism takes it for granted that the ε's are by far the most dominant shocks.

Before I proceed to the empirical analysis, I will consider some special but important cases of the solutions (6)–(9).

When the BOJ smooths the nominal interest rate to a considerable degree $(d \to \infty)$, we obtain

(11)
$$Y_t = \frac{1}{(\gamma + a)} [\gamma a(\phi^2 - c)P_{t-1} - \gamma a\bar{\eta}_t + \gamma\bar{u}_t],$$

(12)
$$P_t = \frac{1}{(\gamma + a)} [(\gamma c + a\phi^2)P_{t-1} + \gamma\bar{\eta}_t + \bar{u}_t],$$

(13)
$$M_t = \frac{1}{(\gamma + a)} [\{c(\gamma + a) + (\gamma + 1)a(\phi^2 - c)\}P_{t-1}$$
$$+ \gamma(1 - a)\bar{\eta}_t + (\gamma + a)\bar{v}_t + (\gamma + 1)\bar{u}_t],$$

and

(14)
$$i_t = i^*.$$

Real output Y and the price level P become independent of portfolio shocks v, whereas the money supply responds to $\bar{v}$ one for one.

Under the same assumption that d is large, if we further assume that the marginal cost curve is fairly flat $(\gamma = \infty)$, then we obtain

$$(15) \qquad Y_t = a(\phi^2 - c)P_{t-1} - a\bar{\eta}_t + \bar{u}_t,$$

$$(16) \qquad P_t = cP_{t-1} + \bar{\eta}_t,$$

and

$$(17) \qquad M_t = \{c + a(\phi^2 - c)\}P_{t-1} + (1 - a)\bar{\eta} + \bar{v} + \bar{u}_t.$$

If a, the interest elasticity of aggregate demand, is small, output is virtually determined by the real demand shock u. On the other hand, real demand shocks do not affect price. Price is affected only by the price shock η.

We next consider the other extreme case, in which the BOJ does not attempt to smooth the nominal interest rate ($d = 0$). In this case, we obtain

$$(18) \qquad Y_t = \frac{1}{[\gamma\{(b - 1)a + 1\} + (b - 1)a + a]} [\gamma a(\phi^2 - bc)P_{t-1} - \gamma ab\bar{\eta}_t + \gamma a(b - 1)(\bar{\varepsilon}_t - \bar{v}_t) + \gamma\bar{u}_t],$$

$$(19) \qquad P_t = \frac{1}{[\gamma\{(b - 1)a + 1\} + (b - 1)a + a]} \times [\{\gamma c((b - 1)a + 1) + a\phi^2\}P_{t-1} + \gamma((b - 1)a + 1)\eta_t + (b - 1)a(\bar{\varepsilon}_t - \bar{v}_t) + \bar{u}_t],$$

$$(20) \qquad M_t = \tilde{\varepsilon}_t,$$

and

$$(21) \qquad i_t = \frac{1}{\beta A'} [\{cA' + (\gamma + 1)a(\phi^2 - b'c)\}P_{t-1} + \gamma(1 - a)\bar{\eta}_t + (\gamma + a)\bar{v}_t - (\gamma + a)\bar{\varepsilon}_t + (\gamma + 1)\bar{u}_t],$$

where $A' = \gamma(1 + a/\beta) + a/\beta + a$ and $b' = 1 + 1/\beta$. Output is affected by ε, the independent change in the money supply. This corresponds to Roosa's (1956) "dynamic" operations.

With different degrees of interest rate smoothing d, observed changes in the money supply either passively reflect various shocks to the economy (13) or embody exogenous changes in the BOJ's policy stance (20). The relative importance of the exogenous component ε in the variance of money supply M, $\sigma_\varepsilon^2/\sigma_m^2$, is

$$(22) \qquad \frac{[\frac{\beta A}{d} + (\gamma + 1)(b - 1)a]^2\sigma_\varepsilon^2}{[\{A - (\gamma + 1)ab\}^2 \sigma_\eta^2 + (\gamma + a)^2 \sigma_v^2 + \{(\frac{\beta A}{d}) + (\gamma + 1)(b - 1)a\}^2 \sigma_\varepsilon^2 + (\gamma + 1)^2 \sigma_u^2]}.$$

$\sigma_\varepsilon^2/\sigma_m^2$ approaches 1 or 0 as d vanishes or becomes infinite, respectively. With these results, I turn to the empirical analysis, in which monetary policy in both the seasonal and the business cycles is examined.

5.2   Money Supply and the Seasonal Cycle

Although seasonal cycles have long been recognized, until very recently most research on macroeconomic fluctuations used seasonally adjusted data, treating seasonal fluctuations as unworthy of study. It was against this current of research that Barsky and Miron (1989) and Yoshikawa (1989) began to study seasonal cycles in the United States and in Japan, respectively. Although the main interest here is the role of money in business cycles, much information can be obtained by studying seasonal cycles.

Fluctuations of monthly real output (in the index of industrial production [IIP] compiled by MITI) and of the money supply (M_2 + CD) in Japan are shown in figure 5.1 (in rates of change relative to the previous month). They are highly periodic and regular. This initial impression is confirmed by examining the spectrum of these variables (figs. 5.2 and 5.3): real output and the money supply indeed show very similar patterns of seasonal fluctuation. The peaks and troughs of the deterministic seasonality of the two variables, however, do not exactly coincide (table 5.1).[2] The rate of change in the money supply peaks in December, is high in March and June, and bottoms out in January and February. On the other hand, the rate of change in IIP peaks in March, is high in September, bottoms out in January, and is low in August, April, and May. This difference in the timing of fluctuations is most likely due to two facts: (1) industrial production is not equal to expenditures, and (2) there is a lag between production and other transactions on the one hand and payments on the other.[3] The money supply usually increases in December because consumption and custom payments such as interfirm settlements and wages peak during that month.

2. The seasonality measures shown in table 5.1 are the *deterministic* seasonality captured by twelve monthly dummies. The estimated coefficient for each monthly dummy can be interpreted as the average rate of change in each month. A tacit assumption is that the variance of the errors around the average is the same from January to December. Although stochastic seasonality exists, Barsky and Miron (1989) report that deterministic seasonality is quantitatively much more important than stochastic seasonality in the majority of the economic variables they examined.

3. Take the example of investment. Construction would take a year or two, and a typical payment pattern is that a quarter is paid when construction starts, another quarter in the middle, and the remaining half at the time of completion. Similarly, in the case of machinery, there is, first of all, a three-to-six-month lag between order and shipment. Payment is then made three to six months after delivery. Finally, if payment is made by a three-to-six-month bill, the lag between orders and final settlements can be at longest a year and a half. An additional point to be noted in the case of Japan is that, by custom, interfirm settlements are made at the end of March, September, or December.

So far the discussion has concerned payment made by firms that order investment goods. When firms that produce investment goods take orders and start production, it soon becomes necessary for them to pay for labor and raw materials. The lags for these payments are much shorter than those for investment orders.

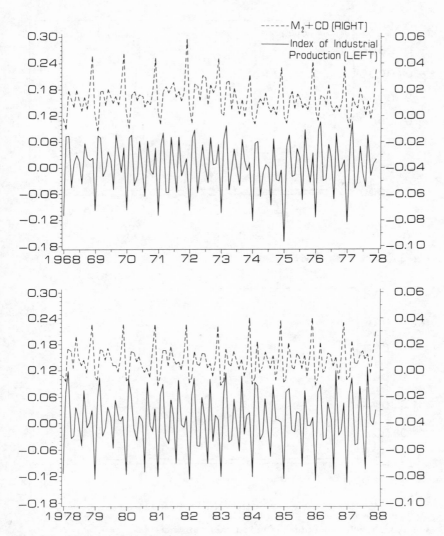

Fig. 5.1 Money and production

For reference, the deterministic seasonality in other variables is shown in tables 5.2 and 5.3. It is observed, for example, that consumption peaks in December and is high in March, whereas investment peaks in March and September. On the other hand, consumption bottoms out in January, and investment bottoms out in January, April, and October. In passing, the seasonal fluctuations in consumption, measured by the coefficient of variation (31.7), are smaller than those in machinery orders (71.3) but larger than those in shipments of capital goods (15.9). Finally, table 5.2 also shows that wage

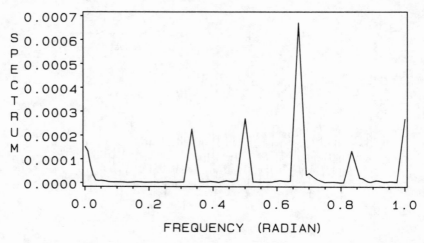

Fig. 5.2   Spectrum of M2 + CD

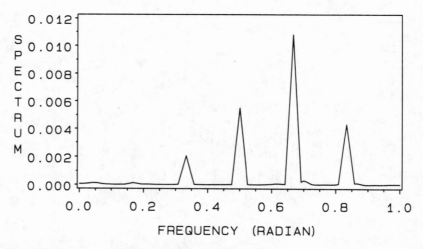

Fig. 5.3   Spectrum of index of industrial production

payments peak in December and June, a consequence of the celebrated bonus system.

Aside from a peak in consumption in December, therefore, production and expenditures tend to move concurrently over the seasonal cycle: they both increase in June and September and decrease in January.[4] A comparison of indices of production, shipments, and inventory stocks (table 5.3) in fact

---

4. Indices of industrial production in all industries except for food peak in March and September. Production in the food industry peaks in December.

Table 5.1   **The Deterministic Seasonality of Money and Output**

	(1) Mean (× 10)	(2) S.D. (× 10)	(3) (2)/(1)	(4) S.E.	Jan	Feb	Mar	Apr	May
I I P	0.05	0.62	12.40	0.18	−1.20 (−30.29)	0.66 (17.08)	0.90 (23.32)	−0.41 (−10.63)	−0.24 (−6.26)
M2 + CD	0.10	0.13	1.30	0.06	−0.04 (−3.43)	−0.07 (−5.45)	0.18 (14.66)	0.12 (10.21)	0.06 (4.57)

Jun	Jul	Aug	Sep	Oct	Nov	Dec	Sample
0.46 (11.89)	0.08 (2.11)	−0.68 (−17.68)	0.81 (21.12)	−0.05 (−1.21)	−0.02 (−0.63)	0.25 (6.43)	67.2 ~87.12
0.18 (14.77)	0.12 (9.71)	0.04 (3.44)	0.10 (8.56)	0.01 (1.23)	0.13 (10.99)	0.39 (32.46)	67.2 ~88.1

Note: t = values in parentheses.

Table 5.2   **The Deterministic Seasonality of Household Income and Consumption**

	(1) Mean (× 10)	(2) S.D. (× 10)	(3) (2)/(1)	(4) S.E.	Jan	Feb	Mar	Apr	May
Household income	0.07	4.44	63.43	0.30	−10.17 (−155.54)	0.12 (0.89)	1.37 (21.01)	−0.72 (−10.98)	0.03 (0.52)
Consumption	0.06	1.90	31.67	0.24	−4.13 (−73.93)	−0.58 (−10.02)	1.99 (34.71)	−0.44 (−7.65)	−0.48 (−8.39)

Jun	Jul	Aug	Sep	Oct	Nov	Dec	Sample
4.81 (73.57)	−0.89 (−13.59)	−2.92 (−44.64)	−0.87 (−13.34)	0.18 (2.73)	0.13 (1.97)	9.80 (149.83)	67.2 ~88.1
0.26 (4.52)	0.75 (13.07)	−0.46 (−8.00)	−0.75 (−13.08)	0.59 (10.63)	−0.19 (−3.38)	4.19 (74.99)	69.10 ~88.1

Note: t = values in parentheses.

shows that there is little production smoothing. The variance of shipments (0.76) is slightly greater than that of production (0.62), but the difference is rather marginal. As a result, seasonal fluctuation in inventory stocks is small. Substantial production smoothing is observed only in December: the high consumption in December is met by a decumulation of inventory stocks. The fact that production and expenditures broadly move together contradicts the notion of an increasing short-run marginal cost curve and suggests a flat marginal cost curve. This case is also strengthened by the fact that seasonal fluctuations in expenditures are largely anticipated by producers.

Aside from timing, money and real output show very similar seasonal fluctuations. As noted at the beginning of this chapter, it is a matter of much dispute whether the high correlation between money and real output over the

Table 5.3   **The Deterministic Seasonality of Investment**

	(1) Mean ($\times 10$)	(2) S.D. ($\times 10$)	(3) (2)/(1)	(4) S.E.	Jan	Feb	Mar	Apr	May
Orders of machinery	0.04	2.85	71.25	1.21	-2.90 (-10.48)	1.34 (4.71)	4.80 (16.89)	-3.78 (-13.29)	-0.40 (-1.43)
Shipment of capital goods	0.08	1.27	15.88	0.43	-1.28 (-13.26)	1.14 (12.13)	2.32 (24.68)	-1.77 (-18.84)	-0.55 (-5.80)

Jun	Jul	Aug	Sep	Oct	Nov	Dec	Sample
0.81 (2.94)	-0.92 (-3.32)	-0.08 (-0.28)	4.18 (15.11)	-3.50 (-12.67)	-0.58 (-2.11)	1.61 (5.81)	69.5 ~88.1
0.69 (7.30)	0.06 (0.69)	-0.27 (-2.89)	1.63 (17.32)	-1.39 (-14.79)	-0.17 (-1.86)	0.46 (4.87)	67.2 ~87.12

Note: t = values in parentheses

business cycle reflects a causal mechanism running from money to output or the other way around. In contrast to the case of business cycles, however, it is absurd to argue that seasonal fluctuations in real activities are caused by similar fluctuations in money: they clearly reflect real factors such as weather or customs (for example, New Year's Day in Japan or Christmas in the United States). In other words, there is an "identifying restriction" that fluctuations in real output are independent of money in the case of seasonal cycles.

It is theoretically possible, in the context of models in which agents are solving intertemporal optimization problems, that seasonal power in output is due in part to a white-noise monetary shock. This possible effect is not very important, however, because real variables such as outputs in various industries, consumption, and investment have similar spectral patterns but different seasonal patterns of peaks and troughs (tables 5.1–5.3). To the extent that (as a first approximation) all the agents are subject to the same monetary shocks, it is difficult to understand that optimum responses of the agents to a *common* monetary shock produce changes in real variables which have similar spectral patterns but at the same time different seasonal patterns of peaks and troughs. It is more reasonable to consider that tastes and technology show their own idiosyncratic seasonal fluctuations, which are conditioned by weather and custom. Therefore, I argue that the "identifying restriction" that fluctuations in real variables are independent of money in the case of seasonal cycles is, if not definite, at least quite reasonable.

The reason money fluctuates similarly to real variables is that the money supply responds endogenously to seasonal fluctuations in real activities. If the money supply did not respond endogenously to seasonal real shocks, then interest rates would show seasonal fluctuations. In fact, the BOJ intentionally responds to real shocks in order to smooth the nominal interest rate.[5] It can be observed that changes in the money supply broadly coincide with changes in high-powered money and BOJ lending rather than with changes in the reserve ratio or the currency/deposit ratio (table 5.4). They all peak in December and are high in March and June, bottoming out in January and February.

Cash moves slightly differently from money. It peaks in December but is also high in July. The high in July coincides with high consumption and confirms that cash is used mostly by consumers rather than by firms. As a digression, it would be interesting to examine the other component of money—bank deposits—as well. As of December 1988 cash amounted to only 31.5 billion yen of M_2 + CD, which totaled 409.3 billion yen. Demand deposits and time deposits were 80.3 and 297.5 billion yen, respectively. Table 5.4 shows the seasonal cycles of the demand and time deposits of individuals and firms. Time deposits do not exhibit any clear seasonal movements, but demand deposits do. Demand deposits of individuals and firms, however, show quite different seasonal patterns. For individuals, they are high in the second and fourth quarters. Evidently they reflect bonus payments (table 5.2). In contrast, the demand deposits of firms peak in the third quarter and reach a trough in the second quarter. This seasonal pattern is broadly consistent with that of production.

Coming back to the main argument, we see that as a result of the BOJ's actions seasonal fluctuations in the nominal interest rate are substantially weakened. Indeed, the spectrum of the call rate does not show any significant seasonality (figure 5.4).

Interest rate smoothing or money supply accommodation would make changes in real output greater than otherwise, which is not a fault of this policy in the case of the seasonal cycle, since seasonal fluctuations of real activities are mostly desirable. As argued above, agents' intertemporal optimization that produces smoothing of consumption or production makes much less sense over the seasonal cycle than over the business cycle or the life cycle of an individual. Tastes and technology, which are usually taken as stable in intertemporal optimization models, fluctuate during the seasonal cycle. As the example of a fall in construction activities during the rainy season shows, seasonal fluctuations in real activities are mostly desirable. Seasonal fluctuations in interest rates, on the other hand, can be a disturbance to the real economy. Miron (1986), for example, argues that in the United States prior to the foundation of the Fed in 1914, seasonal fluctuations in the nominal interest rate often created financial panic, whereas the number of financial panics substantially decreased after 1914 when the Fed started smoothing the nominal inter-

---

5. In the United States, the Federal Reserve also smooths the nominal interest rate at seasonal frequencies. Indeed, one of the major objectives of the Federal Reserve System since its establishment in 1914 has been to smooth the nominal interest rate. See, for example, Shiller (1980) and Miron (1986).

Table 5.4   **The Deterministic Seasonality of Monetary Aggregates**

	(1) Mean (×10)	(2) S.D. (×10)	(3) (2)/(1)	(4) S.E.	Jan	Feb	Mar	Apr	May
M2 + CD	0.10	0.13	1.30	0.06	−0.04	−0.07	0.18	0.12	0.06
					(−3.43)	(−5.45)	(14.66)	(10.21)	(4.57)
High-powered money	0.09	0.70	7.78	0.18	−1.42	0.17	0.43	−0.09	−0.29
					(−34.40)	(4.07)	(10.13)	(−2.18)	(−6.81)
Cash	0.09	0.75	8.33	0.14	−0.94	−0.76	0.40	−0.01	−0.12
					(−30.70)	(−24.81)	(12.96)	(−0.40)	(−4.00)
Reserves	0.12	0.58	4.83	0.54	0.10	−0.29	0.55	0.12	−0.01
					(0.82)	(−2.45)	(4.72)	(1.06)	(−0.08)
BOJ's lending	0.08	3.29	41.13	2.72	0.52	−0.16	0.31	−3.55	−1.93
					(0.82)	(−0.25)	(0.49)	(−5.69)	(−3.09)

Jun	Jul	Aug	Sep	Oct	Nov	Dec	Sample
0.18	0.12	0.04	0.10	0.01	0.13	0.39	67.2
(14.77)	(9.71)	(3.44)	(8.56)	(1.23)	(10.99)	(32.46)	~88.1
0.62	−0.12	−0.17	0.13	−0.13	0.35	1.60	69.10
(14.62)	(−2.93)	(−3.93)	(3.19)	(−3.18)	(8.58)	(38.88)	~88.1
0.62	−0.12	−0.17	−0.38	0.07	0.10	2.14	67.2
(7.70)	(15.82)	(−2.94)	(−12.48)	(2.13)	(3.29)	(70.01)	~88.1
0.28	−0.09	0.05	0.44	−0.24	0.14	0.42	67.2
(2.39)	(−0.76)	(0.41)	(3.75)	(−2.04)	(1.18)	(3.58)	~88.1
1.55	0.63	−0.27	2.18	−0.56	−1.87	4.16	66.10
(2.48)	(1.01)	(−0.43)	(3.50)	(−0.90)	(−3.00)	(6.67)	~87.12

Note: t = values in parentheses.

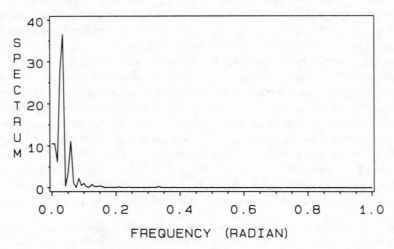

Fig. 5.4   Spectrum of call rate

est rate at seasonal frequencies. This is a standard argument for seasonal nominal interest smoothing.

In terms of the model in section 5.1, therefore, the BOJ's behavior at seasonal frequencies corresponds to $d \cong \infty$. The call rate does not fluctuate much, but the money supply does. Then to what shocks does the money supply respond? First, it is also observed here that price movements do not show any significant seasonality (fig. 5.5). Output fluctuates, but price does not. Comparing equations (11) and (12) to (15) and (16), one can conclude that the marginal cost curve is fairly flat ($\gamma = \infty$) and that price shocks are not significant ($\eta = 0$) at seasonal frequencies. As noted above, a comparison of the seasonal cycles of production and shipments also indicates that the marginal cost curve is flat. From equation (17), therefore, it becomes apparent that seasonal changes in the money supply simply reflect portfolio shocks v (such as sharp increases in the demand for cash in December), and real demand shocks u, one for one. There is little exogenous component (ε) in money. Monetarism both old and new, therefore, makes no sense in explaining seasonal cycles.

Barsky and Miron (1989) obtain similar results for the U.S. economy and make the following argument. If it is accepted that the seasonal comovements of money and output reflect the endogeneity of money, does this allow one, by analogy, to draw any inference about similar high correlations associated with the conventional business cycle? Application of the principle of parsimony suggests, they argue, that money is endogenous rather than causal with respect to the business cycle as well as the seasonal cycle. Of course, one might take the position that two different mechanisms are operative in gener-

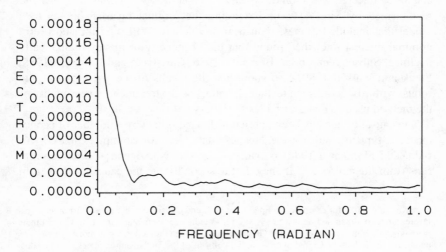

Fig. 5.5   Spectrum of price inflation (WPI)

ating the observed correlations over seasonal and business cycles. Nonetheless, the similar comovement of money and output at the two sets of frequencies is at the very least suggestive of an endogenous money supply.

5.3   Money Supply and the Business Cycle

It was found that in the seasonal cycle the money supply endogenously responds to portfolio and real demand shocks. This section examines the relation between money and output over the business cycle.

A fairly high correlation between the money supply and GNP is observed over the business cycle, though it is not as high as in the seasonal cycle. Monetarists (Friedman and Schwartz 1963) contend that changes in the money supply have been "exogenous" and largely determined by autonomous policy decisions of the central bank. They also find that the velocity of money or the money demand function is stable, and accordingly argue that money is the causal factor in explaining economic activities.

Economists such as Kaldor (1970) argue the story the other way round. The money supply "accommodates itself" to the needs of trade, rising in response to an expansion and vice versa, just as in a seasonal cycle. According to their view, the relative stability in the demand for money is merely a reflection of the instability in its supply: if the supply of money had been kept more stable, the velocity of money would have been more unstable.[6] In short, income causes endogenous changes in money.

The issue has been analyzed using a causality test (Granger 1969; Sims 1972). Sims's original finding that causality running from money to income cannot be rejected was soon discovered to be not robust by Mehra (1978) and reconfirmed by Sims (1980). Extending the original bivariate model to a model that included money, industrial production, WPI, and the short-term nominal interest rate, they found that the exogeneity of money dramatically declines. Subsequent works (Bernanke 1986; Christiano and Ljungvist 1988; Stock and Watson 1989) also show that the results of the test are not quite robust with respect to such technical matters as the treatment of seasonality or the method used to make variables stationary.

The causality test has been applied to Japanese data by a number of economists. A typical result for the Japanese data (see, for example, Suzuki, Kuroda, and Shirakawa 1988) is that the call rate is exogenous, and causality runs from the call rate to money. In the second stage the causality runs from

6. Kaldor (1970), for example, compares the U.S. and Canadian experiences during the Great Depression (Friedman and Schwartz 1963, 352) as evidence for this argument. In Canada there were no bank failures at all during the Great Depression; the contraction in the money supply was much smaller than in the United States—only two-fifths of that in the United States, or 13 against 33%—yet the contraction in nominal GNP was nearly the same. The difference in the change in the money supply was largely offset by differences in the decline in the velocity of money: in the United States it fell by 29%, in Canada by 41%.

money to high-powered money and output. This result is taken by some BOJ officials as being consistent with the view that changes in high-powered money are the result rather than the cause of changes in more broadly defined monetary aggregates such as M_2 + CD, and that the BOJ cannot control the money supply by simply controlling high-powered money. In addition, the finding of causality running from money to income is often taken as evidence in support of the monetarist view that the stability of the money supply necessarily contributes to the stability of output.

Aside from a lack of robustness in the test with respect to the sample period or such technical matters mentioned above, the most serious problem of the causality test is that it can falsely indicate causality in certain cases. For example, suppose that stock prices are determined by the present value of future profits. If expectations of future profits embodied in the price of stock contain more information than is contained in the series of past profits, then the stock price would Granger-cause profits even though the truth is in fact the opposite. Yoshikawa (1989) provides a model that produces spurious causality in the money-output relation. Since the demand for loans depends on the future interest rate as well as on the current interest rate, the quantity of money depends on expectations of future output. One must, therefore, be cautious in interpreting the results of causality tests.

Given these considerations, how does one approach the money-output relationship in the business cycle? Our prior view is that the BOJ often smooths the nominal interest rate over the business cycle just as it does over the seasonal cycle, and therefore the money supply is endogenous during those interest-smoothing periods. There is an important difference between the two cycles, however. In the case of the business cycle, the BOJ does not always smooth the nominal rate, and as a result the money supply often reflects exogenous changes in the BOJ's policy stance (nonzero ε). The basic problem is that there is no simple feedback rule that governs the money supply, but rather one that involves *a shift in regime:* the BOJ often accommodates various shocks to smooth the nominal interest rate, but at other times it does not. This makes it extremely difficult to productively use conventional econometric methods including vector autoregressions (VARs), which "flatten" shifts in regime and see only the averages. Still, it is desirable to identify the circumstances under which the BOJ either smooths the nominal interest rate or actively changes the money supply. As a first step, I have simply plotted the data. By plotting monthly data on money, output, and the nominal interest rate, we can at least identify when the BOJ smoothed the nominal rate, making changes in the money supply largely endogenous as in the seasonal cycle, and we can also determine what kinds of shocks drove the money supply in each period.

In figure 5.6, monthly rates of change in money, output, and inflation are plotted against the level of the nominal interest rate (only a few examples are shown here). The measures of money, output, inflation, and the nominal inter-

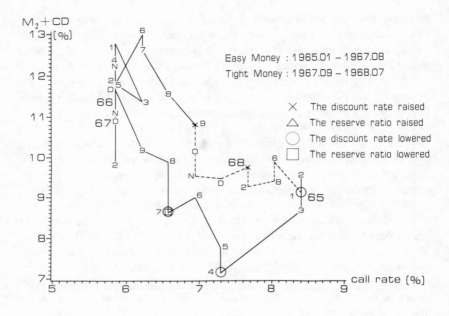

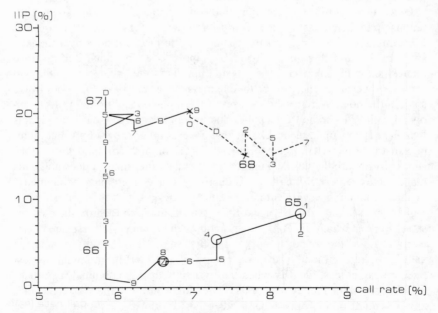

Fig. 5.6   Chronology of monetary policy

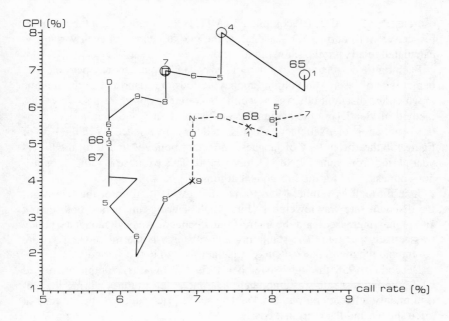

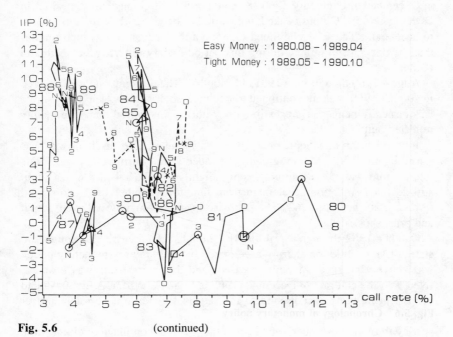

Easy Money : 1980.08 – 1989.04
Tight Money : 1989.05 – 1990.10

Fig. 5.6   (continued)

est rate are M_2 + CD, IIP compiled by MITI, CPI inflation, and the call rate, respectively. To correct for seasonality, the rate of change of each variable is calculated relative to the same month of the previous year.

Each figure corresponds to a pair of "easy" and "tight" money periods. The beginnings of "easy" and "tight" money periods are identified as the months in which the discount rate was *first* either lowered or raised, respectively. This method of identifying the beginnings and ends of easy and tight money periods is not altogether satisfactory but is used for convenience. With the help of figure 5.6 the chronology of Japanese monetary policy is traced for the thirty-year period from June 1958 to October 1990. This exercise is rather monotonous but essential for the subsequent argument.

June through November 1958 (6 months): At the bottom of the recession, the discount rate was lowered in June 1958. During this period both output and money increased, and the interest rate declined. An easy monetary policy was actively pursued. The stable price level suggests that price shocks were absent and the marginal cost curve was flat ($\gamma = \infty$) in this period.

December 1958 through November 1959 (12 months): Output increased while the interest rate was smoothed. The increase in money during this period mainly reflected output shocks. The stable price suggests the absence of price shocks and flat marginal costs.

December through July 1960 (8 months): The discount rate was raised in December 1959. Output peaked and started to decline, while inflation began to accelerate. The BOJ continued to smooth the interest rate, which implies that the decrease in money during this period mainly reflected the decline in output.

August 1960 though June 1961 (11 months): The discount rate was lowered in August 1960. Output continued to decline, albeit slightly. The interest rate was basically pegged: changes in money during this period therefore mainly reflected output shocks.

July 1961 through September 1962 (15 months): The discount rate was raised in July 1961. Money growth continued to fall during this period. The interest rate was raised, although only slightly—from 8.4 to 8.8%. Output still declined. Inflation accelerated from June to December 1961 and started to decelerate in May 1962. The decrease in money mainly reflected output and price shocks.

October 1962 through April 1963 (7 months): Output hit the trough and started rising. Inflation sharply accelerated but still an easy monetary policy was actively pursued: money increased, and the interest rate was lowered. (Note that the call rate in December 1962 is clearly abnormal, perhaps due to the BOJ's failure to accommodate the seasonal increase in the demand for money.)

May through November 1963 (7 months): Output continued to climb while inflation stayed high. The interest rate was virtually pegged. Changes in money during this period therefore mainly reflected output and price shocks.

December 1963 through June 1964 (7 months): Output stayed high while inflation decreased. A tight monetary policy was actively pursued, which drove the interest rate up.

July through December 1964 (6 months): Output fell while inflation accelerated. The interest rate was pegged. The decrease in money during this period mainly reflected output and price shocks.

January through October 1965 (10 months): The discount rate was lowered in January 1965. Output growth kept decelerated while inflation stayed high. The interest rate was sharply lowered. The increase in money during this period suggests that an easy monetary policy was actively pursued.

November 1965 through May 1967 (19 months): Output kept rising while inflation kept decelerating. The interest rate was pegged. Therefore, changes in money basically reflected output and price shocks.

June 1967 through July 1968 (14 months): Output started to decrease while inflation accelerated. The money supply was actively lowered, raising the interest rate.

August through December 1968 (5 months): Output kept decreasing while inflation also decelerated. The interest rate was actively lowered.

January through June 1969 (6 months): Output began to increase while inflation also accelerated. The interest rate was smoothed.

July through September 1969 (3 months): Both output and inflation stayed high. The growth rate of the money supply was kept stable, allowing the interest rate to rise. In September the discount rate was also raised.

October 1969 through September 1970 (12 months): The interest rate was basically pegged. During the first six months (October 1969 through March 1970), output stayed high and inflation sharply accelerated. Afterward (April 1970 through September 1970), output fell, and inflation also decelerated. Changes in money during this period basically reflected output and price shocks.

October 1970 through July 1972 (22 months): During this period, the interest rate was sharply lowered by allowing the money supply to grow. Until January 1972 output fell, but it hit its trough at December 1971, and a recovery began. Inflation continued to decelerate.

August through December 1972 (5 months): The interest rate was pegged. Output kept growing while inflation was stable at the 5% level.

January 1973 through October 1974 (22 months): The interest rate was sharply raised from below 5% to above 12% by reducing the money supply: inflation accelerated from 6% (January 1973) to the unprecedented level of 26% (February 1974) and finally started to decelerate (October 1974). Output stayed high for most of 1973, then sharply declined from 14% (November 1973) to − 11% (October 1974).

November 1974 through March 1975 (5 months): The interest rate was basically pegged. Inflation kept decelerating from 25% to 14%. Output also decelerated from − 13% to − 18%.

April 1975 through January 1976 (10 months): The interest rate was actively lowered by increasing the money supply. During this period inflation decelerated from 13% to 9%, while output was steadily rising from −14% to 6%.

February 1976 through February 1977 (13 months): The interest rate was basically pegged. Output stayed high at the level of 12% and then started decelerating in November 1976, while inflation also stayed high at 9%. Changes in the money supply reflected output shocks.

March 1977 through March 1978 (13 months): The interest rate was actively lowered from 7% to 4.5%. Output continued to fall, while inflation started decelerating from 9.5% to 5%.

April 1978 through March 1979 (12 months): The interest rate was basically pegged. During this period, output stayed high at 7% while inflation continued to decelerate from 5% to below 3%.

April 1979 through July 1980 (16 months): The interest rate was actively raised from 5% to 12.5% by reducing the money supply. Output was fairly stable around 10% and started to decelerate in April 1980. On the other hand, inflation was stable during the first six months of this period, then accelerated from 4% (October 1979) to 7.5% (February 1980) and stayed at that level afterward.

August 1980 through April 1981 (9 months): The interest rate was actively lowered from 12% to 5% by increasing the money supply. Output continued to decline below zero while inflation decelerated from 8% to 5%.

May 1981 through December 1985 (56 months): The interest rate was kept stable at around 6–7%. Output first recovered from −4% (May 1981) to 5% (November 1981) but then declined from 5% (November 1981) to −5% (October 1982). Afterward (November 1982 through October 1984) it rose from −5% to 12% and declined again from 10% (October 1984) to zero (December 1985). In the same period, inflation continued to decline from 5% (May 1981) to 2% (November 1982) and remained at about that level afterward. The growth of the money supply changed irregularly, reflecting output and price shocks.

January 1986 through April 1987 (16 months): The interest rate was actively lowered. The yen sharply appreciated in real terms after the Plaza Accord in September 1985, and the subsequent decline in exports caused a recession in 1986. Output growth continued to decline below zero. The bottom of this recession occurred in December 1986. Inflation declined, due partly to the sharp appreciation of the yen.

May 1987 through March 1989 (23 months): The interest rate was basically pegged at 3%. Output growth recovered from −1% (May 1987) to 11% (March 1988) and stayed high afterward. Throughout this period inflation was very stable. Changes in the money supply therefore mainly reflected output shocks.

April 1989 through October 1990 (19 months): The interest rate was actively raised. Output growth declined from 7% (May 1989) to zero (March 1990) but recovered to 8% (October 1990) again. Inflation was stable at 3% during this period.

These findings are summarized as follows.

First of all, in 195 out of 389 months in the sample period from June 1958 to October 1990, the interest rate was either pegged or tightly smoothed. During those periods in which the interest rate was substantially smoothed, money, output, and inflation all widely fluctuated. It is very unlikely that real output and inflation respond within a month to exogenous changes in the money supply in such a way as to keep the interest rate unchanged. In contrast, it is known from the study of the seasonal cycle that the BOJ can accommodate output, price, and portfolio shocks to wipe out monthly movements in the interest rate. The conclusion, therefore, is that in about half of the thirty-year period, changes in the money supply were endogenous and simply reflected output, inflation and/or portfolio shocks just as it does over the seasonal cycle. This fact alone implies that monetarism, both new and old, is very misleading in interpreting the observed changes in money supply and therefore in explaining the business cycle.

This fact also means that monetary models that emphasize nominal rigidities due to temporary wage and price stickiness (Taylor 1989; Fischer 1977) are likewise untenable to the extent that they take exogenous money supply shocks to be the major impulses behind economic fluctuations. The literature on monetary models with nominal rigidities, however, which is sometimes referred to as "Keynesian," flourishes. In theory, attempts to explain nominal price rigidities are clearly motivated by the premise that exogenous money supply shocks are the major disturbances to the economy. Empirical works also abound. Blanchard and Quah (1989), for example, assume the existence of a "demand shock" that has no permanent effect on real variables in their VAR analysis. They use this assumption as an identifying restriction and then interpret "demand shocks" as money supply innovations. Taylor (1989) also assumes that money supply shocks are the major disturbances in the economy, and he emphasizes differences in price/wage flexibility (specifically, the synchronized wage setting known as *Shunto*) as the key factor in explaining the difference in output variability between Japan and the United States. He argues that, thanks to the Shunto, nominal wages are much more flexible in Japan than in the United States, and therefore that nominal money supply shocks do not translate into real shocks, thereby making real output in Japan more stable than is the case in the United States.

A brief review of the postwar record of monetary policy in Japan reveals, however, that the interest rate was very often (half the period) either pegged or substantially smoothed, suggesting therefore that money supply innovations during those periods simply reflect output, price, and portfolio shocks. The fact that changes in output fluctuate considerably during periods of interest smoothing suggests the importance of real shocks in explaining the business cycle. Whether these real shocks are the supply (productivity) shocks emphasized by the real business cycle theorists or the real demand shocks emphasized by the Keynesians is, of course, another issue. Yoshikawa and Ohtake (1987) argue that for the postwar business cycle in Japan, real demand shocks were the major disturbance.

The BOJ's ability to peg or smooth the interest rate from month to month over the business cycle as well as the seasonal cycle necessarily implies that changes in the interest rate reflect the BOJ's policy stance. This is the case whether the BOJ actively changes the interest rate in the absence of other shocks or allows the interest rate to change when the shocks do not originate in the actions of the BOJ. Bernanke and Blinder (1992) also attempt to show that changes in the federal funds rate reflect the Federal Reserve's policy stance, by estimating the interest elasticity of the reserve supply function. The point of their estimation is to find a proper instrument to identify the supply function. I make a similar argument by showing that the call rate was very often pegged or tightly smoothed from month to month by the BOJ.

When the interest rate changes consistently and substantially between months, it reflects the BOJ's policy stance. In this sample, in 96 out of 389 months, the interest rate was raised, whereas it was lowered in 98 months. The question is whether there is any systematic feedback rule guiding the BOJ's choice either to smooth or to change the interest rate. Since the data contain many zeros or close to zero values for the rate of change of the interest rate, one would have to resort to an estimation method involving probit to take into account a regime shift in monetary policy. In what follows, however, as a preliminary exercise a VAR is used simply to explore the policy reaction function of the BOJ.

For the United States, Papell (1989) argues that a rule that stabilizes the rate of growth of nominal GNP provides a good description of monetary policy since 1973. Bernanke and Blinder (1992) also estimate a VAR with three variables and show that the federal funds rate responds positively to an inflation shock and negatively to an unemployment shock (during the pre–October 1979 period). This result is broadly consistent with Papell (1989). In the United States, monetary policy appears to have been conducted as a standard stabilization policy.[7]

In Japan the case is not as simple. A previous review of the records, for example, shows that in the period from October 1962 to April 1963, the interest rate was successively lowered while output was rising and inflation was rapidly accelerating to 9%. During this period (particularly March and April 1963), the BOJ explicitly stated that the purpose of the reduction of the discount rate was not stabilization, but rather to strengthen the international com-

---

7. Examination of Federal Reserve records (Romer and Romer 1989) also confirms that during the postwar era the Federal Reserve appears to have made deliberate decisions to sacrifice real output to lower inflation (in October 1947, September 1955, December 1968, April 1974, August 1978, and October 1979).

petitiveness of Japanese industry by encouraging investment (BOJ 1986). Anticipating the liberalization of capital import regulations in April 1964 when Japan became a member of OECD, policymakers as well as business people in those days regarded international competitiveness as one of the most important policy targets.

In the 1980s the interest rate was substantially lowered between December 1985 and May 1986. Although 1986 was a recession year, it is widely believed that these reductions in the interest rate were aimed mainly at assisting the smooth appreciation of the yen, which the G5 countries agreed upon at the Plaza in September 1985. These examples and my previous discussion both suggest that the BOJ's policy objective is not simply stabilized output, but rather multivalued.

Within the confines of stabilization, the nominal interest rate smoothing often pursued by the BOJ complicates matters. Consider for example the following feedback rule:

$$(23) \qquad M_t = -\alpha Y_t - \beta P_t + \varepsilon_t.$$

If the authority attempts to stabilize Y and P, we would expect α and β in (23) to be positive. As mentioned above, this seems to be the kind of rule that the Federal Reserve pursues. When the BOJ smooths the interest rate, however, α and β are negative in (23). Since the BOJ does in fact attempt to stabilize the interest rate at times, even the signs of α and β are time-varying in the BOJ's policy reaction function.

How can we characterize the BOJ's policy reaction governing nominal interest rate smoothing? To answer this question, I confine the discussion to real output Y. Let the "natural," "potential," "non-inflation-accelerating," or "full-employment" output be denoted by Y^*. The BOJ seems to pursue the following rules: raise the interest rate if $Y_t > Y_t^* - \varepsilon$; smooth or peg the interest rate if $Y_t^* - \varepsilon \geq Y_t \geq Y_t^* - \delta$; lower the interest rate if $Y_t^* - \delta > Y_t (\delta > \varepsilon > 0)$.

The important point is that Y_t^* cannot be found by mechanical methods such as estimating a time trend. Indeed, it would not be an exaggeration to say that one of the major tasks of the BOJ is to grasp current Y^* as soon and as accurately as possible. No monetary authority would attempt to curb economic growth simply because output exceeded its trend line. Rather, growth would be always welcomed and accommodated, just as are seasonal cycles, provided that it did not fuel inflation or conflict with other important policy objectives such as exchange rate or balance of payment targets. The point is that Y_t^* cannot be measured accurately enough using past data to make it feasible for monetary policy to be described as a stable, time-invariant feedback rule. Given this caveat, I will nevertheless check the response functions of the call rate based on VARs.

For this purpose, I first estimated a four-variable VAR with the call rate, the rate of change in IIP, CPI inflation, and a net export variable. The last variable is defined as nominal net exports divided by CPI × IIP. The whole sample period is July 1958 through November 1990, but I also estimated VARs for two subsample periods: July 1958 through December 1972 and January 1973 through November 1990. In table 5.5 the impulse response functions of the call rate to shocks to other variables are shown (see column 1).

The results look like plausible response functions. Output shocks drive up the call rate, with the peak effect coming after fifteen months and then decaying very slowly. Inflation shocks also drive up the call rate in a very similar fashion for the January 1973 through November 1990 period, but push it in the opposite direction for the July 1958 through December 1972 period. Judging from this result, we can conclude that the anti-inflation stance of the BOJ was much stronger in the post–oil shock period than in the 1950s and 1960s. Finally, for the entire period the call rate responds negatively to an increase in the trade balance. The response of the call rate to net export shocks is more substantial than its response to output and inflation shocks, and the peak effect comes after twenty months. In Japan the trade balance or current account has always been one of the main targets of monetary policy. Put differently, Japan's "potential" output has been effectively constrained by the supply of raw materials, which constitute the bulk of Japan's imports.

Irrespective of its objectives, when the BOJ changes its policy stance, how does this affect the economy? Table 5.5 shows that innovations in the call rate very strongly drive down output, with the peak effect coming after twelve to fifteen months. Since it has already been observed that innovations in the call rate mainly reflect changes in the BOJ's policy stance, one can conclude that monetary policy does affect real output.[8] Accordingly, it is possible to reject the real business cycle theorist's view, which holds that money is always nothing but a mirror image of real shocks and plays no role in the business cycle (King and Plosser 1984; Plosser 1990). This point can also be confirmed, though more casually, just by looking at figure 5.6. Inflation also negatively responds to call rate shocks, but its response is much weaker than the response of output, and the lags are longer.

By focusing on the periods of interest rate smoothing, I have argued that real shocks are important in the business cycle. When the BOJ changes its policy stance, however, it also affects the real economy.

5.4   The Transmission of Monetary Policy

Monetary policy affects the real economy. What is the transmission mechanism of monetary policy? As a preliminary step to answering this question, table 5.6 summarizes, for the postwar business cycle, the extent to which

---

8. Romer and Romer (1989) put a dummy variable (which identifies the six months when the Federal Reserve made the decision to seek to induce a recession in order to reduce inflation) into the univariate autoregressive equation for industrial production. They found that this dummy variable has a significantly negative effect on industrial production. The dummy variable constructed from Federal Reserve records, however, does not indicate the length of the shocks caused by the Fed, nor does it differentiate the shocks by size. I believe that changes in the call rate identify the timing and size of changes in the BOJ's policy stance.

Table 5.5   **Responses to One Standard Deviation Shock**

Entry	Call	IIP	CPI	NEX
		1958:7–1990:11		
		Call		
1	.451915	− .251948E-01	− .261513E-01	.348897
2	.390639	− .174553	.463459E-01	− .306428
3	.403578	− .277046	.127254	.115980E-01
4	.472020	− .494240	.199149	.463057E-01
5	.446735	− .508574	.227798	.705311E-01
6	.432520	− .671324	.222736	− .188166
7	.410158	− .719435	.214346	.539650E-01
8	.386531	− .714655	.190505	.399531E-01
9	.340379	− .769521	.162276	− .485095E-01
10	.302258	− .744029	.134719	.656681E-01
11	.263490	− .711218	.983827E-01	.569025E-01
12	.219125	− .675445	.577705E-01	.564377E-01
13	.179454	− .610880	.207843E-01	.842084E-01
14	.141253	− .541397	− .164786E-01	.102610
15	.104908	− .465697	− .523441E-01	.107114
16	.713187E-01	− .382622	− .843619E-01	.117829
17	.414448E-01	− .298199	− .113807	.131045
18	.146865E-01	− .213365	− .140072	.133669
19	− .892036E-02	− .130393	− .162467	.138640
20	− .289494E-01	− .509359E-01	− .181221	.142830
21	− .458361E-01	.239390E-01	− .196503	.143427
22	− .597504E-01	.925754E-01	− .208267	.143235
23	− .707750E-01	.154704	− .216755	.142219
24	− .791732E-01	.209643	− .222275	.139862
		IIP		
1	.000000	1.93870	− .404968	− .174424
2	− .719107E-03	1.45175	− .361983	.276811E-01
3	− .741255E-02	1.49619	− .325161	.271821E-03
4	.182094E-01	1.95114	− .316685	− .110917
5	− .165459E-01	1.74494	− .273859	− .115514
6	.311224E-02	1.84962	− .275887	− .849986E-01
7	.167063E-01	1.80767	− .252514	− .122911
8	.936477E-02	1.70544	− .225727	− .123965
9	.253457E-01	1.65916	− .203541	− .146173
10	.313907E-01	1.53202	− .174542	− .114822
11	.378390E-01	1.42451	− .152298	− .140559
12	.463838E-01	1.30670	− .129983	− .146584
13	.527668E-01	1.17971	− .107660	− .122549
14	.593096E-01	1.06187	− .891609E-01	− .139172
15	.640610E-01	.939334	− .711475E-01	− .131411
16	.683418E-01	.826103	− .549967E-01	− .122894
17	.716155E-01	.718813	− .416513E-01	− .123838
18	.734911E-01	.617120	− .297332E-01	− .116448
19	.746518E-01	.526084	− .197923E-01	− .110994
20	.748184E-01	.442428	− .118207E-01	− .105699
21	.740112E-01	.367823	− .535052E-02	− .995787E-01
22	.725173E-01	.302483	− .460963E-03	− .937104E-01

(continued)

Table 5.5   (continued)

Entry	Call	IIP	CPI	NEX
23	.703327E-01	.245195	.305770E-02	−.875551E-01
24	.675603E-01	.196399	.539831E-02	−.818328E-01

CPI

1	.000000	.000000	.807994	−.301015E-01
2	.246178E-01	−.220914	.900214	−.471669E-01
3	.446420E-01	−.142202	.901251	−.128321
4	.599440E-01	−.144987	.885858	−.239186
5	.109790	−.255200	.840905	−.128907
6	.134779	−.317590	.861784	−.192851
7	.146244	−.471135	.864394	−.215257
8	.164498	−.606159	.858800	−.187376
9	.176348	−.720153	.845387	−.195476
10	.183705	−.861891	.823085	−.208762
11	.189032	−.973177	.802277	−.193269
12	.191293	−1.07546	.778606	−.180609
13	.189401	−1.16999	.752247	−.179483
14	.185650	−1.24075	.724205	−.166131
15	.180028	−1.29809	.693791	−.153202
16	.172312	−1.33788	.661660	−.144332
17	.163337	−1.36066	.628850	−.132507
18	.153265	−1.36894	.595539	−.120042
19	.142446	−1.36246	.561908	−.109881
20	.131103	−1.34368	.528513	−.995305E-01
21	.119580	−1.31367	.495576	−.893083E-01
22	.108109	−1.27409	.463344	−.805144E-01
23	.968169E-01	−1.22684	.432149	−.722240E-01
24	.859424E-01	−1.17324	.402165	−.646859E-01

Net Exports

1	.000000	.000000	.000000	2.02431
2	−.587840E-01	.124346E-01	.878078E-02	.233568
3	−.861485E-01	−.168360	−.160674E-01	.649400
4	−.474438E-01	−.213482	−.489064E-01	1.00044
5	−.818597E-01	−.227968	−.120922	.546051
6	−.108454	−.358756	−.146262	.677360
7	−.123530	−.369464	−.152667	.759102
8	−.142656	−.413756	−.187364	.677630
9	−.168890	−.464972	−.212614	.645373
10	−.186441	−.449452	−.238842	.687676
11	−.201860	−.456929	−.267572	.664819
12	−.220897	−.444802	−.290309	.643405
13	−.234655	−.417372	−.310508	.646648
14	−.246967	−.389299	−.329377	.637699
15	−.257960	−.349251	−346223	.620754
16	−.266657	−.307440	−.360011	.610413
17	−.273219	−.261140	−.371428	−.601013
18	−.277966	−.212757	−.380533	.584513
19	−.281153	−.165172	−.386955	.571008

Table 5.5 (continued)

Entry	Call	IIP	CPI	NEX
20	− .282385	− .117048	− .391156	.557342
21	− .282140	− .710436E-01	− .393295	.541400
22	− .280552	− .275637E-01	− .393374	.525994
23	− .277602	− .132165E-01	− .391630	.510394
24	− .273552	.502881E-01	− .388265	.494504

1958:7–1972:12

Call

1	.463816	.154725	− .129125	.268250
2	.235975	.887188E-01	− .617366E-01	− .169161
3	.265744	− .356279E-01	.353317E-01	.512376E-02
4	.341445	− .190919	.708389E-01	.625894E-01
5	.255041	.947892E-01	.430471E-01	− .209170E-01
6	.223765	− .778355E-01	.306688E-02	− .834157E-01
7	.217228	− .152236	.450199E-01	− .294483E-01
8	.193465	− .143778	.307972E-01	− .254329E-01
9	.144985	− .290790	.356738E-01	− .756735E-01
10	.138428	− .349881	.630513E-01	− .534878E-01
11	.123604	− .399172	.622603E-01	− .455309E-01
12	.948564E-01	− .456257	.627437E-01	− .491060E-01
13	.869052E-01	− .504200	.687061E-01	− .473857E-01
14	.747465E-01	− .522382	.682926E-01	− .378897E-01
15	.606252E-01	− .531811	.634109E-01	− .300621E-01
16	.526266E-01	− .552265	.628454E-01	− .259016E-01
17	.448870E-01	− .545410	.609817E-01	− .195882E-01
18	.362380E-01	− .532505	.561452E-01	− .137695E-01
19	.297233E-01	− .523928	.537104E-01	− .740348E-02
20	.241575E-01	− .502043	.505111E-01	− .348843E-02
21	.176786E-01	− .476048	.462929E-01	− .377441E-03
22	.123580E-01	− .450362	.429800E-01	.394644E-02
23	.786032E-02	− .420751	.396008E-01	.670167E-02
24	.294365E-02	− .389142	.359865E-01	.819396E-02

IIP

1	.000000	2.02244	− .514355	− .134834
2	.393852E-01	1.60244	− .394727	− .857447E-01
3	.504268E-01	1.34394	− .329176	− .439390E-03
4	.962156E-01	1.76283	− .306749	− .137799
5	.726187E-01	1.50776	− .207829	− .119309
6	.119329	1.60323	− .179729	− .849393E-01
7	.130386	1.57640	− .169717	− .130615
8	.119192	1.47825	− .145454	− .143366
9	.141387	1.45684	− .137533	− .138143
10	.148468	1.32492	− .114989	− .131499
11	.148927	1.21368	− .101715	− .141715
12	.160013	1.08473	− .823503E-01	− .143263
13	.165089	.942478	− .625884E-01	− .131534
14	.168117	.816103	− .511506E-01	− .130465
15	.170653	.671366	− .361767E-01	− .127861
16	.171983	.543799	− .238889E-01	− .119909

(continued)

Table 5.5   (continued)

Entry	Call	IIP	CPI	NEX
17	.171271	.420757	−.151552E-01	−.113035
18	.168861	.295410	−.517689E-02	−.106245
19	.165839	.185203	.301902E-02	−.994921E-01
20	.160963	.816758E-01	.100145E-01	−.917810E-01
21	.155003	−.144939E-01	.165168E-01	−.837865E-01
22	.148399	−.995036E-01	.219774E-01	−.767762E-01
23	.140504	−.174712	.265715E-01	−.696628E-01
24	.132090	−.240101	.303423E-01	−.623115E-01

CPI

Entry	Call	IIP	CPI	NEX
1	.000000	.000000	.727932	.692156E-01
2	−.611066E-01	−.210813	.726385	−.523411E-01
3	−.644215E-01	.144553	.632892	−.583901E-01
4	−.385368E-01	.174354	.569543	−.495216E-01
5	−.703329E-01	.169784	.448898	−.978552E-01
6	−.828531E-01	.138884	.406792	−.899858E-01
7	−.501309E-01	−.104655	.401509	−.504198E-01
8	−.446885E-01	−.203637	.368807	−.530313E-01
9	−.349783E-01	−.353044	.351953	−.555566E-01
10	−.167156E-01	−.529760	.339718	−.263476E-01
11	−.597528E-02	−.605113	.311745	−.126225E-01
12	−.398661E-02	−.715755	.284744	−.760553E-02
13	.154712E-02	−.801617	.262863	.866628E-02
14	.481747E-02	−.855074	.238337	.219776E-01
15	.980013E-03	−.913187	.216745	.305345E-01
16	−.157717E-02	−.949302	.198593	.388319E-01
17	−.570577E-02	−.969120	.181533	.468921E-01
18	−.133162E-01	−.975717	.164844	.532465E-01
19	−.205402E-01	−.969565	.149742	.576458E-01
20	−.284744E-01	−.950769	.135803	.614965E-01
21	−.372512E-01	−.918928	.121944	.644094E-01
22	−.455415E-01	−.880119	.109314	.664468E-01
23	−.533962E-01	−.832504	.976385E-01	.676738E-01
24	−.608669E-01	−.777076	.863228E-01	.680235E-01

Net Exports

Entry	Call	IIP	CPI	NEX
1	.000000	.000000	.000000	1.11223
2	−.497889E-01	−.965139E-01	.396278E-01	.213031
3	−.743544E-01	−.229250	−.204372E-01	.342844
4	−.406194E-01	−.183668	−.194451E-01	.470098
5	−.928896E-01	−.462482	−.320531E-01	.441305
6	−.133481	−.616518	−.527506E-02	.275186
7	−.181845	−.494707	−.531743E-02	.242348
8	−.187594	−.584694	−.962022E-02	.325647
9	−.229062	−.600060	−.237193E-01	.242996
10	−.251499	−.525763	−.265802E-01	.187954
11	−.265562	−.480013	−.318457E-01	.201723
12	−.271219	−.389776	−.402269E-01	.205579
13	−.277078	−.321000	−.484172E-01	.169139

Table 5.5   (continued)

Entry	Call	IIP	CPI	NEX
14	−.279292	−.204199	−.534016E-01	.152805
15	−.270581	−.848766E-01	−.616230E-01	.157815
16	−.263603	.165947E-01	−.687443E-01	.146958
17	−.254542	.135710	−.754149E-01	.128885
18	−.241697	.247423	−.806925E-01	.120610
19	−.227779	.350651	−.854246E-01	.115726
20	−.213229	.444307	−.896696E-01	.103038
21	−.198507	.528040	−.919035E-01	.906959E-01
22	−.182631	.603152	−.935124E-01	.824911E-01
23	−.166812	.663012	−.943535E-01	.732438E-01
24	−.151451	.711039	−.940334E-01	.623556E-01

1973:1–1990:11

Call

1	.345314	−.521271E-01	.358766E-02	.643173
2	.430163	−.244549	.764083E-01	−.483027
3	.438019	−.327619	.115689	.655225E-01
4	.441549	−.331405	.144017	−.762214E-01
5	.422529	−.606613	.170416	.262974
6	.417857	−.708228	.191912	−.300318
7	.405033	−.751015	.181749	−.101941
8	.392066	−.833962	.140724	.109706
9	.347660	−.781982	.972191E-01	−.810666E-01
10	.307137	−.808896	.656081E-01	.176427
11	.267147	−.775428	.284819E-01	.155407
12	.222534	−.704136	−.247099E-01	.139488
13	.180585	−.659767	−.770748E-01	.211247
14	.138194	−.557412	−.134020	.245367
15	.955394E-01	−.457188	−.189025	.270406
16	.522549E-01	−.359419	−.237836	.297365
17	.127891E-01	−.245657	−.284997	.327480
18	−.247366E-01	−.135112	−.329287	.335237
19	−.596628E-01	−.254738E-01	−.370063	.349588
20	−.906605E-01	.847574E-01	−.406071	.362119
21	−.118816	.188853	−.436915	.371074
22	−.143685	.286277	−.462200	.373520
23	−.165011	.376025	−.481849	.376195
24	−.182709	.456068	−.496425	.376888

IIP

1	.000000	1.57782	−.257672	−.124713
2	−.668887E-02	.834421	−.204889	.709747E-01
3	−.992714E-02	1.01760	−.104790	.867949E-01
4	.648149E-02	1.27487	−.175380E-01	−.450686E-01
5	−.351863E-01	.947907	.393420E-01	−.133210
6	−.218546E-01	.940310	.727841E-01	−.212827E-01
7	−.505374E-02	.832118	.131935	−.201965E-02
8	−.349703E-03	.651661	.175440	−.156930E-01

(continued)

Table 5.5   (continued)

Entry	Call	IIP	CPI	NEX
9	.114719E-01	.554080	.223555	−.626642E-01
10	.217078E-01	.365298	.270992	.114335
11	.313481E-01	.217277	.303804	.201918E-01
12	.391063E-01	.798225E-01	.332629	.987168E-02
13	.511784E-01	−.848074E-01	.354301	.990174E-01
14	.591249E-01	−.190821	.364297	.366230E-01
15	.637336E-01	−.307999	.370328	.644456E-01
16	.676416E-01	−.410498	.371557	.831050E-01
17	.689509E-01	−.478718	.364303	.683073E-01
18	.680475E-01	−.546494	.352609	.731334E-01
19	.656954E-01	−.589107	.335643	.730029E-01
20	.619555E-01	−.612374	.313867	.715058E-01
21	.560879E-01	−.624883	.289447	.681586E-01
22	.491835E-01	−.619441	.262670	.654898E-01
23	.414553E-01	−.601935	.234396	.624247E-01
24	.328702E-01	−.573943	.205206	.565270E-01

CPI

1	.000000	.000000	.807020	−.410476E-01
2	.673291E-01	−.821613E-01	.915074	−.631172E-01
3	.111601	−.260953	.944603	−.796559E-01
4	.105739	−.235262	.908378	−.363744
5	.192335	−.353933	.874586	−.138283
6	.232553	−.395178	.906294	−.192817
7	.246533	−.574410	.950325	−.282032
8	.252260	−.703436	.988558	−.304969
9	.258885	−.863333	1.00479	−.142415
10	.262989	−.999266	1.00073	−.358269
11	.268271	−1.10463	.988139	−.296260
12	.275344	−1.20465	.969256	−.224240
13	.270114	−1.25324	.941028	−.289692
14	.262668	−1.31378	.913144	−.234901
15	.254426	−1.34649	.880573	−.225515
16	.244270	−1.34943	.838561	−.243400
17	.232683	−1.34761	.794052	−.238564
18	.220316	−1.31887	.746325	−.225739
19	.206566	−1.27434	.697249	−.226662
20	.191098	−1.22232	.649195	−.225056
21	.176012	−1.15732	.601707	−.220878
22	.161031	−1.08407	.555039	−.223167
23	.146327	−1.00607	.509976	−.224709
24	.132492	−.923065	.467457	−.225515

Net Exports

1	.000000	.000000	.000000	2.32720
2	−.865343E-01	.711964E-01	−.139190E-01	.311834
3	−.135694	−.752655E-01	−.308229E-01	.701730
4	−.883904E-01	−.207102	−.580918E-01	1.23770
5	−.115579	−.504608E-01	−.139423	.414948

Table 5.5   (continued)

Entry	Call	IIP	CPI	NEX
6	−.145850	−.145090	−.181230	.756236
7	−.168843	−.144832	−.191985	.939649
8	−.199989	−.739442E-01	−.230280	.767357
9	−.230690	−.112180	−.256277	.682070
10	−.247004	−.698565E-01	−.292984	.774259
11	−.259240	.586466E-02	−.341853	.707556
12	−.280053	.566298E-01	−.381175	.659603
13	−.293665	.123205	−.411597	.696789
14	−.305525	.201987	−.439251	.656171
15	−.317145	.267430	−.464475	.611368
16	−.323959	.337496	−.485212	.583736
17	−.327311	.410010	−.503360	.565395
18	−.329195	.476209	−.516911	.522976
19	−.329002	.537379	−.524176	.493730
20	−.325686	.591070	−.526417	.472400
21	−.320595	.638540	−.524594	.433319
22	−.313327	.676171	−.518447	.403288
23	−.303681	.705494	−.508323	.376830
24	−.292434	.727257	−.494887	.346518

different demand components have accounted for different shares of the change in GNP.

Since the Japanese economy has been growing rapidly, almost all variables increase in absolute terms even in recessions. I therefore first calculated the change in each variable measured from trough to peak in case of a recovery, and from peak to trough in case of a growth recession. I then subtracted the latter from the former to obtain the difference. Table 5.6 reports the relative contribution of each demand component, for each postwar cycle, to this cyclical difference in the change in real GNP. Friedman (1990) presents a similar but slightly different table for postwar U.S. recessions. For the sake of comparison, I present results for the United States based on the method described above (table 5.7).

In Japan throughout the whole period, the relative contribution of fixed investment has been the greatest of all the demand components: 60% of GNP on average. In contrast, in the United States fixed investment accounts for only 25% on average of the change in real GNP. The relative contribution of inventory and housing investments is greater in the United States than in Japan. Changes in housing investment in Japan are not really systematic over the business cycle. On the other hand, until the mid-1960s, inventory investment had a large impact on Japanese business cycle: a 60–70% contribution. A substantial portion of the inventory investment was, however, raw materials— which were also imports. Therefore, the contribution of inventory investment and imports almost canceled each other. As a result, fixed investment retained

Table 5.6   The Relative Contribution of Demand Components to the Business Cycle, Japan

Peak	Trough	Peak	GNP	II	D	IH	IF	C
								%
5702	5802	6104	100	60.955	39.045	2.8816	56.7851	47.9378
6104	6204	6404	100	71.822	78.178	14.9896	46.1396	45.3235
6404	6504	7003	100	5.270	94.730	1.6540	62.5451	35.8547
7003	7104	7304	100	-10.643	110.643	27.2298	77.9559	90.6800
7304	7501	7701	100	6.754	93.246	41.2309	29.2053	37.8202
7701	7704	8001	100	30.916	69.084	-9.1070	81.1159	74.5326
8001	8301	8502	100	22.322	77.678	1.3227	73.6131	8.9868
8502	8604	9003	100	12.840	87.160	11.8504	67.5603	35.8865
Average %			100	15.7818	84.218	16.6272	58.237	45.0169

Peak	Trough	Peak	CD	CND	NEX	EX	IM	G
5702	5802	6104	.	.	-62.257	7.492	-69.75	-6.302
6104	6204	6404	.	.	-45.338	6.863	-52.20	-32.937
6404	6504	7003	.	.	-11.176	10.953	-22.13	5.851
7003	7104	7304	8.8544	81.8256	-82.482	-5.144	-77.34	-2.741
7304	7501	7701	15.4472	22.3729	-21.105	2.321	-23.43	6.095
7701	7704	8001	44.6072	29.9255	2.901	60.069	-57.17	-80.357
8001	8301	8502	14.0854	-5.0986	10.281	63.956	-53.67	-16.525
8502	8604	9003	10.6049	26.5199	-5.124	87.435	-92.56	-23.013
Average %			18.0807	35.8718	-24.065	27.780	-51.845	-11.598

Table 5.7 The Relative Contribution of Demand Components to the Business Cycle, United States

Peak	Trough	Peak	GNP	II	D	IH	IF	C
						%		
5703	5801	6001	100	34.0739	65.9261	8.5508	17.0499	27.1248
6001	6004	6903	100	52.5561	47.4439	15.7570	15.9706	33.2836
6903	7002	7304	100	28.2595	71.7405	24.4541	21.9450	13.9530
7304	7501	8001	100	31.5844	68.4156	21.5106	25.4131	35.2068
8001	8002	8103	100	8.6601	91.3399	31.0866	31.4134	53.9011
8103	8203	9003	100	19.7589	80.2411	13.2042	27.2770	25.5607
Average %								
			100	24.2747	75.7253	20.7552	25.1305	35.4643

Peak	Trough	Peak	CD	CND	NEX	EX	IM	G
5703	5801	6001	7.7241	19.4007	15.397	15.9907	-0.465	-2.2991
6001	6004	6903	7.8344	25.4492	-18.225	0.5729	-18.679	0.6577
6903	7002	7304	11.9637	1.9893	-7.534	4.5817	-12.116	18.9436
7304	7501	8001	13.8456	21.3612	-12.426	10.7646	-23.191	-1.2044
8001	8002	8103	34.1299	19.7712	-18.791	5.5147	-24.306	-6.4134
8103	8203	9003	10.8982	14.6625	9.814	27.3771	-17.463	4.2434
Average %								
			17.8298	17.6345	-6.059	11.4677	-17.496	0.36471

its importance. As a long-term trend, the role of inventory investment in the business cycle seems to have diminished in both Japan and the United States.

Net exports have been countercyclical in Japan's business cycle except for the years 1977–85, in which economic growth was export-led. In particular, imports have been very countercyclical: the fraction of output was −52% on average, compared to −17% in the United States. Until very recently, the bulk of Japanese imports consisted of raw materials and therefore moved very mechanically in parallel with the level of aggregate economic activity.

The contribution of consumption to GNP seems to be in large part similar in the two countries, although the contribution of nondurables is substantially higher in Japan. As for government expenditures, we find them countercyclical for Japan (−12% of GNP on average) but neutral (0.4%) for the United States.

In sum, the major differences between Japan and the United States lie in the facts that fixed investment plays a much larger role in the business cycle in Japan than in the United States, and that net exports and government expenditures are much more countercyclical in Japan. These findings help us identify the important components in the Japanese business cycle. Yet it remains to be seen how they are related to monetary policy. To see these relations, I ran a set of bivariate VARs using the call rate and each component of expenditures. (All the variables except for inventory investment are log differenced. Inventory investment is differenced.) One can see from figures 5.7–5.12 that investment and imports are the components that respond substantially to innovations in the call rate. There are lags of two to three quarters before changes in the call rate have an impact on these variables.

Summing up the findings in this section, I conclude that monetary policy, represented by changes in the call rate, exerts substantial effects on real output in Japan mainly through its effect on fixed investment and imports. Since imports were almost identical to inventory investment in the 1950s and 1960s,

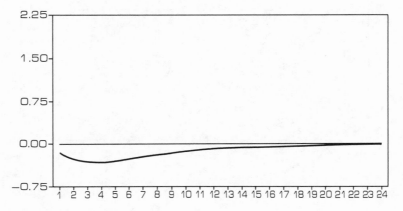

Fig. 5.7   Responses of consumption

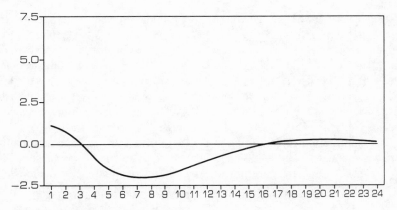

Fig. 5.8   Responses of fixed investment

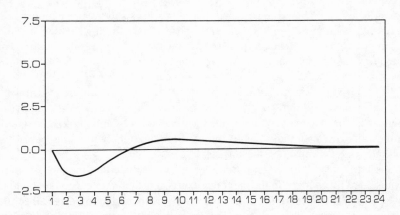

Fig. 5.9   Responses of housing investment

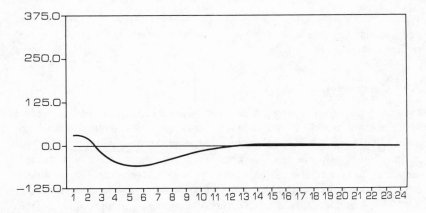

Fig. 5.10   Responses of inventory investment

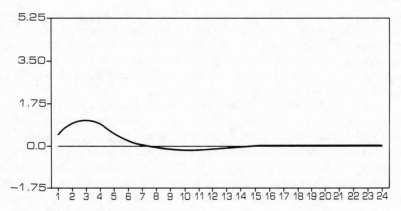

Fig. 5.11   Responses of exports

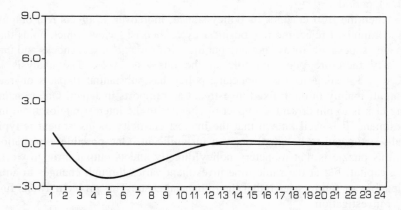

Fig. 5.12   Responses of imports

one can also say that inventory investment was a major channel of monetary policy in those days.

5.5   Conclusion

Economists often assume an exogenous money supply in both theoretical and empirical works. In this chapter, I show that this assumption is highly misleading. Over the seasonal cycle, changes in the money supply are actually nothing but mirror images of the changes in real output and/or portfolio preferences. This is because the BOJ either pegs or smooths the nominal interest rate. The same observation also applies to the business cycle as well—even in the 1980s—and leads us to reject an array of monetary models of the business cycle such as monetarism both new and old, and monetary models with nominal rigidities. To the extent that the money supply responds endogenously to real output through interest rate smoothing, it is not at all surprising that nominal money and real output are highly correlated. From this viewpoint, we find that the distinction between anticipated and unanticipated changes in the money supply (Barro 1977) is not very important.

There is an important difference between the seasonal cycle and business cycles, however. The BOJ does not always accommodate output, price, and portfolio shocks, instead allowing the interest rate to change, and at times it even actively changes the interest rate during the business cycle ("dynamic operations"). The BOJ's policy response function therefore involves a kind of regime shift between interest smoothing and dynamic operations. My simple VAR analysis suggests, however, that the trade balance has always been the main target of monetary policy. In the 1950s and 1960s, the anti-inflation stance of the BOJ seems to have been much weaker than during the post–oil shock period.

When the BOJ changes its policy stance, moreover, it affects real output. Accordingly, I reject the real business cycle theorist's view, which holds that money shocks are always nothing but the mirror image of real shocks and that money therefore plays no role in the business cycle. The analysis in section 5.4 suggests that monetary policy has substantial impacts on real output, mainly through fixed investment and imports in Japan. One remaining task is to pin down the impact of changes in the interest rate on fixed investment. It is well known that the interest elasticity of investment is typically estimated to be small or even insignificant. One possible explanation to this puzzle is that monetary policy directly affects output through working capital, but at the same time investment varies through changes in anticipations of future sales rather than financial costs. This problem awaits further investigation.

References

Bank of Japan. 1986. *A Centennial History of the Bank of Japan.* Tokyo.
Barro, R. 1977. Unanticipated money growth and unemployment in the United States. *American Economic Review,* March.
Barsky, R., and J. Miron. 1989. The seasonal cycle and the business cycle. *Journal of Political Economy,* June.
Bernanke, B. 1986. Alternative explanations of the money-income correlation. *Journal of Monetary Economics,* supplement (Carnegie-Rochester Conference Series 25).
Bernanke, B., and A. Blinder. 1992. The federal funds rate and the channels of monetary transmission. *American Economic Review,* September.
Blanchard, O., and D. Quah. 1989. The dynamic effects of aggregate demand and supply disturbances. *American Economic Review,* September.

Christiano, L., and L. Ljungqvist. 1988. Money does Granger-cause output in the bivariate money-output relation. *Journal of Monetary Economics* 22.

Fischer, S. 1977. Long-term contracts, rational expectations, and the optimal money supply rule. *Journal of Political Economy*, February.

Friedman, B. 1990. Changing effects of monetary policy on real economic activity. NBER Working Paper No. 3278. Cambridge, Mass.: National Bureau of Economic Research, March.

Friedman, M. 1968. The role of monetary policy. *American Economic Review*, March.

Friedman, M., and A. Schwartz. 1963. Monetary and business cycles. *Review of Economics and Statistics*, February.

Granger, C. W. J. 1969. Investigating causal relations by econometric models and cross-spectral methods. *Econometrica*, July.

Kaldor, N. 1970. The new monetarism. *Lloyds Bank Review*, July.

King, R., and C. Plosser. 1984. Money, credit, and prices in a real business cycle. *American Economic Review*, June.

Lucas, R. 1972. Expectation and the neutrality of money. *Journal of Economic Theory*, April.

———. 1977. Understanding business cycles. *Journal of Monetary Economics*, Supplement.

McCallum, B. T. 1983. A reconsideration of Sim's evidence concerning monetarism. *The Economics Letters* 13:167–71.

Mehra, Y. 1978. Is money exogenous in money-demand equations? *Journal of Political Economy*, April.

Miron, J. 1986. Financial panics, the seasonality of the nominal interest rate, and the founding of the Fed. *American Economic Review*, March.

Papell, D. 1989. Monetary policy in the United States under flexible exchange rates. *American Economic Review*, December.

Plosser, C. 1990. Money and business cycles: A real business cycle interpretation. NBER Working Paper No. 3221. Cambridge, Mass.: National Bureau of Economic Review, January.

Romer, C., and D. Romer. 1989. Does monetary policy matter? A new test in the spirit of Friedman and Schwartz. In *NBER Macroeconomics Annual 1989*, ed. O. Blanchard and S. Fischer. Cambridge, Mass.: MIT Press.

Roosa, R. 1956. *Federal Reserve Operations in the Money and Government Securities Market*. Federal Reserve Bank of New York, July.

Shiller, R. 1980. Can the Fed control real interest rates? In *Rational Expectations and Economic Policy*, ed. S. Fischer. Chicago: University of Chicago Press.

Sims, C. 1972. Money, income, and causality. *American Economic Review*, September.

———. 1980. Comparison of interwar and postwar business cycles: Monetarism reconsidered. *American Economic Review*, May.

Stock, J. H., and M. W. Watson. 1989. Interpreting the evidence of money-income causality. *Journal of Econometrics* 40.

Suzuki, Y., A. Kuroda, and H. Shirakawa. 1988. Monetary control mechanism in Japan. *Bank of Japan Monetary and Economics Studies*, no. 2:43–65.

Taylor, J. B. 1979. Estimation and control of a macroeconomic model with rational expectations. *Econometrica*, September.

———. 1980. Aggregate dynamics and staggered contracts. *Journal of Political Economy*, February.

———. 1989. Differences in economic fluctuations in Japan and the United States: The role of nominal rigidities. *Journal of the Japanese and International Economies*.

Yoshikawa, H. 1989. Money supply and the real economy (in Japanese). *Keizaigaku Ronshu* 55, no. 3:31–57.

Yoshikawa, H., and F. Ohtake. 1987. Postwar business cycles in Japan: A quest for the right explanation. *Journal of the Japanese and International Economies,* December.

6 An Aggregate Demand– Aggregate Supply Analysis of Japanese Monetary Policy, 1973–1990

Kenneth D. West

This paper studies the sources of the business cycle in Japan, 1973–90, focusing on the role played by money supply shocks. A secondary aim is to get a feel for whether the effects of Japanese monetary policy are roughly similar to those that would result if the Bank of Japan were operating under a simple, stylized rule or objective function.

For my analysis, I use a simple open economy aggregate demand–aggregate supply model, estimated on monthly data, January 1973 to August 1990. The six variables in the model are output, price, money supply, oil prices, foreign (U.S.) output, and the real yen/dollar exchange rate. The reduced form of the model is an unrestricted vector autoregression, and identification of the underlying linear simultaneous equations system is achieved in part with covariance restrictions of the sort first suggested by Blanchard and Watson (1986).

The model yields a decomposition of movements in the variables in the system into five underlying shocks: demand, cost, money supply, oil, and a residual foreign shock. It is found that movements in output are mainly attributable to demand and foreign shocks, movements in foreign output and the real exchange rate to foreign shocks; movements in prices are not driven overwhelmingly by any one kind of shock. For no variable apart from growth in the money supply itself are monetary shocks a particularly important source of variability, a conclusion also reached in some studies of the U.S. economy cited below. But unlike such studies, which typically find a major role for

Kenneth D. West is professor of economics at the University of Wisconsin and a faculty research fellow of the National Bureau of Economic Research.

The author thanks Anil Kashyap, John Shea, Naoyuki Yoshino, and conference participants for helpful comments and discussions; Kunio Okina for supplying data; Dongchul Cho and Fuku Kimura for research assistance; and the Graduate School of the University of Wisconsin, the National Science Foundation, and the Sloan Foundation for financial support.

monetary policy in the recession of 1982 and perhaps elsewhere, I find that money supply shocks in Japan do not appear to play an especially prominent role in any of the cyclical turning points that have occurred in the sample.

These findings are obviously consistent with Friedman's (1985, 27) monetarist view that the Bank of Japan has aimed above all for "highly stable and highly dependable" money growth, putting relatively light weight on the state of the economy when determining monetary policy. The findings are also consistent with what I call the "textbook view" that the monetary authority should set the money supply rule by maximizing an objective function that aims at stabilizing output and prices (and, perhaps, other variables such as the exchange rate or the money supply itself as well); Bryant (1990) and, implicitly, Hamada and Hayashi (1985) attribute a sophisticated version of this view to the Bank of Japan. The bank's operating instruments (M_2, in the present paper) will then be set as a time-invariant function of all the variables that influence the path of price and output (e.g., Chow 1983, chap. 12). A relatively small overall role of monetary shocks (where shocks are surprises in monetary policy, i.e., deviations of the money supply from the level specified in the rule), with no special prominence for such shocks at cyclical turning points, seems consistent with this textbook view.

I do not attempt to distinguish beween these interpretations by formally inverting my estimated money growth rule to obtain the weights on money, output, and price stability in a policy objective function. This is mainly because some reduced-form evidence suggests that no simple story will stand very close scrutiny: both U.S. and Japanese output growth help predict money supply growth, a fact inconsistent with an extreme monetarist view that the money supply in Japan is set in total disregard to the state of the economy (not a view that Friedman or anyone else has advocated, as far as I know). On the other hand, money growth is not predicted by inflation, oil price inflation, or changes in the real exchange rate; these three variables all help predict output and inflation and thus should influence the path of the money supply as well, if indeed the textbook view is correct.

Instead, I see how well a simple monetarist view characterizes the effects (if not the intentions) of monetary policy by simulating the behavior of the economy during 1973–90, under a counterfactual policy of constant expected money growth, keeping all shocks fixed at their estimated values. To my surprise, the behavior of output growth and inflation is practically unchanged. (This is not because any and all anticipated monetary policy has vanishingly small real effects, as shown by a simulation under a policy of adjusting the money supply in response to movements in nominal GNP.) While the simulations cast no direct light on the *intentions* of the Bank of Japan's monetary policy, it does raise the possibility that the *effects* of the activist component of its policy—if any—were small. I leave open the question as to whether in fact there is a gap between intentions and effects and, if so, why.

Before turning to the analysis, several comments on the approach might be useful to prevent misinterpretation. First, I do not calculate standard errors on the variance decompositions. Related work (West 1992) suggests that these will be quite large. So it is probably not wise to put too much weight on any single point estimate.

Second, I limit myself to inferences mechanically drawn from the estimates of my model. I assume that the Bank of Japan can perfectly control the value of M_2, up to a zero mean and serially uncorrelated shock; I abstract from problems that the bank no doubt faces with data availability, uncertainty about the values of key parameters, serial correlation in shocks, and so on. I do so not because I doubt the importance of such problems in practice, but because I do not believe that my simplified approach biases my results in an obvious way. Nonetheless, in light of the papers for this volume by Okina, Ueda, and Yoshikawa, as well as Hutchison (1986), it obviously would be useful to consider extensions of the model in which the bank's operating instrument is interest rates.

Third, the model used is essentially a textbook open economy model, with unrestricted lags put on the right-hand side of all equations to capture dynamics. Many of the features of the Japanese economy that from one or another point of view might require special treatment—the system of wage payments, the high savings rates, and so forth—are, I believe, comfortably subsumed in the standard model. See Taylor (1989), for example. Other features, such as the credit and interest rate controls that apparently have been operative, especially in the early part of the sample (Fukui 1986; Ito 1989; Kosai and Ogino 1984, chap. 6), perhaps are not as easily subsumed. But the standard model still tells a "story . . . consistent with the data," to use Blanchard's (1989, 1146) conclusion for a similar model applied to U.S. data. I interpret this as suggesting that it is reasonable in a first effort such as this to abstract from such special features, while acknowledging that much might be learned by modeling such features explicitly.

Finally, as is well known, the model is not derived from optimization; in addition here, as in, for example, Blanchard (1989) but not Taylor (1989), expectations are not explicitly modeled but instead are absorbed in distributed lags on past variables. It should be noted first of all that the fact that expectations are not explicitly modeled leads to inefficient but not inconsistent estimates of parameters, impulse response functions, or variance decompositions if, as in Taylor (1989), the "true" structural model is simply a rational expectations version of the aggregate demand–aggregate supply model. The advantage of the present approach is that it does not require detailed specification of the variables being forecast. For example, in the aggregate supply curve, is it just next month's price, as in a monthly version of Lucas (1973), or a weighted sum of the next twelve months of prices, as in a monthly version of Taylor (1989)? On the other hand, the simulations under alternative money supply rules potentially fall prey to the Lucas critique. I discuss this briefly in the relevant section of the paper.

More generally, some readers will be skeptical about estimates of an aggregate demand–aggregate supply model, with or without rational expectations. I hope that such readers will still find in this paper two results that will be useful to keep in mind in future, and perhaps more highly structured, work. I state these now, since in the body of the paper I will assume the validity of the model in interpreting the empirical results.

The first result is that at conventional significance levels the broad measure of money used here (M_2) Granger causes the real variables in the model. Eichenbaum and Singleton (1986) and Christiano and Ljungqvist (1988), among others, suggest that such a finding is inconsistent with a strict real business cycle theory. A small amount of experimentation suggests that, in possible contrast to U.S. data (e.g., Eichenbaum and Singleton 1986), this finding is robust to the method used to detrend the data.[1]

Second, while the technique used to orthogonalize shocks relies on the assumed model for its validity, one can to a limited extent think of it in terms of the atheoretical approach exemplified by Sims (1980). In this context, the procedure can be interpreted as putting oil price shocks first, the residual foreign shock last, with demand, cost, and money supply shocks in between (and no simple Sims-style statement of the order of these three shocks is possible). The fact that oil price shocks nonetheless play a small role and foreign shocks a big role in output fluctuations suggests that the results for these two shocks may be robust to alternative procedures for orthogonalizing the disturbances.

Section 6.1 describes the model, section 6.2 the data, section 6.3 the estimates, section 6.4 the sensitivity of the results to minor changes in specification, and section 6.5 the behavior of the economy under hypothetical alternative money supply rules. An appendix available on request contains some additional results omitted from the body of the paper to save space.

6.1 The Model

The variables in the model, all of which are in logs, are:

y_t = output (industrial production)
p_t = price level (WPI)
m_t = money supply (M_2 + CD)
o_t = oil prices (WPI for petroleum and coal)
y_t^* = foreign output (U.S. industrial production)
a_t = real exchange rate (yen/dollar)

---

1. On the other hand, the finding is not robust to the measure of money used. High-powered money does not Granger cause any of the three sets of real variables just listed. I believe that, in contrast to the argument Eichenbaum and Singleton (1986) and Christiano and Ljungqvist (1988), the argument in Plosser (1990) would suggest that the overall pattern of Granger causality is therefore consistent with a real business cycle view.

Let $x_t \equiv (y_t, p_t, m_t, o_t, y_t^*, a_t)'$ be the (6×1) vector of endogenous variables, with $v_t \equiv (v_{yt}, v_{pt}, v_{mt}, v_{ot}, v_{y^*t}, v_{at})'$ the corresponding vector of reduced-form innovations (one-step-ahead prediction errors), $v_t = x_t - {}_{t-1}x_t$.

Six linear simultaneous equations determine the six endogenous variables in x_t. On the right-hand side of all six are n lags of each of the six endogenous variables. Together with a constant term, this set of lags is denoted by the $(6n + 1) \times 1$ vector $z_{t-1} \equiv (1, x_{t-1}', \ldots, x_{t-n}')'$. The structural equations are

(1) $\qquad y_t = \alpha_1(m_t - p_t) + \alpha_2 a_t + \alpha_3 y_t^* + \Gamma_y' z_{t-1} + u_{dt};$

(2) $\qquad p_t = \beta_1 y_t + \beta_2 o_t + \Gamma_p' z_{t-1} + u_{ct};$

(3) $\qquad m_t = \gamma_1 v_{yt} + \gamma_2 v_{pt} + \gamma_3 v_{at} + \Gamma_m' z_{t-1} + u_{mt};$

(4) $\qquad o_t = \Gamma_o' z_{t-1} + u_{ot};$

(5) $\qquad y_t^* = \delta_1 v_{yt} + \delta_2 v_{pt} + \delta_3 v_{mt} + \delta_4 v_{ot} + \Gamma_{y^*}' z_{t-1} + u_{y^*t};$

(6) $\qquad a_t = \phi_1 v_{yt} + \phi_2 v_{pt} + \phi_3 v_{mt} + \phi_4 v_{ot} + \phi_5 v_{y^*t} + \Gamma_a' z_{t-1} + u_{at}$

The u's are mutually and serially uncorrelated disturbances, the Γ's are $(6n + 1) \times 1$ vectors of parameters.

Equation (1) is an aggregate demand curve, u_{dt} a demand shock. The demand curve may be obtained by combining IS and LM curves, substituting out for the nominal interest rate. The dependence of a standard IS curve on the real rate rather than the nominal rate is implicitly allowed, since $\Gamma_y' z_{t-1}$ will absorb any term in expected inflation.

The term in real balances $(m_t - p_t)$ in (1) comes from the LM curve, and $\alpha_1 > 0$. The terms in the real exchange rate a_t and foreign output y_t^* come from the IS curve. These terms capture the effect that a_t and y_t^* have on the trade balance. If a J-curve is operative, so that depreciation (increase in a_t) has a perverse negative effect on the trade balance in the short run, $\alpha_2 < 0$, otherwise $\alpha_2 \geq 0$. In any case, $\alpha_3 > 0$, since increases in foreign output affect exports, and thus the trade balance and aggregate demand, positively.

Equation (2) is an aggregate supply curve, u_{ct} a cost (supply) shock. Both β_1 and β_2 are positive: quantity supplied depends positively on output and negatively on oil prices. Terms in expected prices or output are absorbed in $\Gamma_p' z_{t-1}$.

Equation (3) is the money supply rule. I assume that, at the beginning of month t, the monetary authority chooses an expected value for the period t money supply, ${}_{t-1}m_t$. The difference between m_t and ${}_{t-1}m_t$ (the variable v_{mt}) might or might not depend on intramonth attempts by the Bank of Japan to influence the path of nonmonetary variables. Output and price, and perhaps the real exchange rate, are present to allow for the possibility of such intramonth attempts to target these variables (Bryant 1990). A second reason that output and price are present is that the measure of money used in the empirical work is a broad one whose period t value cannot be perfectly controlled at time ($t - 1$), but instead will depend on surprises in money demand (velocity), even if the bank makes no such intramonth attempts. A second reason that the real exchange rate is present is that its value might affect intramonth decisions about whether or not to sterilize exchange rate operations, and thus affect the value of the money supply.

The monetary rule of course might also depend in part on interest rates. Equation (3) allows for this implicitly: use the LM curve to write the nominal interest rate in terms of money, output, and prices, and possibly lagged values of these and other variables, and then substitute out for the interest rate in the monetary rule.[2] The resulting disturbance will then depend in part on velocity shocks and thus be correlated with the aggregate demand shock u_{dt}. The estimation procedure described below will, however, yield a shock to the money supply that is uncorrelated with demand shocks by construction. This is interpreted as the component of money supply shocks uncorrelated with velocity shocks. Under this interpretation, the estimation procedure is attributing entirely to demand shocks a component shared by both demand and money shocks.

In related literature (Blanchard and Watson 1986), the money supply rule is written in terms of levels rather than surprises (e.g., $\gamma_1 y_t$ rather than $\gamma_1 v_{yt}$). In the present setup, the specifications are observationally equivalent: estimates of the parameters in (1)–(6), and the implied variance decompositions, impulse response functions, and so on, are the same whether levels or surprises are used. I write (3) as a function of surprises in accord with my interpretation of monetary policy as a rule for setting $_{t-1}m_t$; in simulations below on the hypothetical effects of alternative rules over the sample period, I take both the γ_i's and the v_t's as structural and invariant to the policy rule.

Equation (4) says that the period t oil price is a predetermined variable, which in the present setup means that its innovation is contemporaneously uncorrelated with the other innovations in the model. Shapiro and Watson (1988) argue that this is reasonable because movements in oil prices are dominated by a few sharp swings. Note that the oil price being predetermined is perfectly consistent with it being Granger caused by other variables.

Equations (5) and (6) are vacuous identities, simply stating that the period t surprise in each of these variables can be written as a linear combination of other surprises, plus a term orthogonal to these surprises. The idea is that foreign output, while not modeled explicitly, is determined by a set of equations similar to those determining Japanese output. Since demand, cost, money, and oil shocks plausibly are correlated across countries, the period t surprise in foreign output will be correlated with all these shocks, as well as with any shocks to the exchange rate. The estimation procedure will attribute

---

2. If the interest rate targeted by the Bank of Japan is different from that in the LM curve (e.g., call rate versus gensaki), one must also use an equation relating the two rates to eliminate interest rates from the system. The only reason I have not explicitly used interest rates is to avoid increasing the dimensionality of an already complicated system of equations.

this common element of foreign and Japanese demand shocks, for example, to u_{dt} and similarly for other shocks. The residual u_{y*t} is thus the idiosyncratic component on foreign cycles after any common components have been absorbed by u_{dt}, u_{ct}, u_{mt}, and u_{ot}.

Similarly, the exchange rate is often thought to be set by forward-looking behavior of the sort generally presumed to determine asset prices, so, like other asset prices, its surprise will depend on the surprises of all the fundamental variables in the model (e.g., Dornbusch 1976; West 1987). The residual component u_{at} may thus be interpreted as reflecting speculative forces or variations in risk premiums uncorrelated with the fundamentals variables.

Once again, an observationally equivalent model would result if the surprises in (5) and (6) were replaced by levels. The potential effects of alternative policies for setting $_{t-1}m_t$, however, will be different in the two specifications. As written above, the reduced form equations for y_t^* and a_t will not change with a change in the rule for setting $_{t-1}m_t$, while those equations would change if levels were on the right-hand side. Since tests on the reduced form suggest that these two variables are exogenous in the Granger sense from the remaining variables (see below), in practice it probably would not make much difference which specification is used; I use surprises rather than levels in accord with my a priori view that it is implausible that the sorts of changes in the rule for setting $_{t-1}m_t$ contemplated below will much affect the coefficients in the reduced-form stochastic process for foreign output and the real exchange rate.

In equations (5) and (6), putting foreign output y_t^* before the real exchange rate a_t is arbitrary; the variance decompositions reported below simply report a contribution from "foreign terms" that is the sum of contributions of u_{y*t} and u_{at}.

To solve the model, tentatively replace the surprises in (3)–(6) with levels (e.g., replace v_{yt} in [3] with y_t). Write (1)–(6) in matrix form as

$$(7) \qquad B_0 x_t = k + B_1 x_{t-1} + \ldots + B_n x_{t-n} + u_t,$$

where B_i are 6×6 matrices, k is a 6×1 vector of coefficients on constant terms, and $(u_{dt}, u_{ct}, u_{mt}, u_{ot}, u_{y*t}, u_{at})'$ is a 6×1 vector of mutually and serially uncorrelated disturbances. Premultiplying both sides of (1)–(6) by B_o^{-1} yields a vector autoregressive reduced form,

$$(8) \qquad x_t = B_0^{-1} k + B_0^{-1} B_1 x_{t-1} + \ldots + B_0^{-1} B_n x_{t-n} + B_0^{-1} u_t$$
$$\equiv c + \Pi_1 x_{t-1} + \ldots + \Pi_n x_{t-n} + v_t,$$

where $v_t \equiv (v_{yt}, v_{pt}, v_{mt}, v_{ot}, v_{y*t}, v_{at})' = B_0^{-1} u_t$ is the 6×1 vector of reduced-form innovations. Even though surprises rather than levels appear in equations (3)–(6), one can similarly deduce that the reduced form of (1)–(6) follows an n'th-order vector autoregression, with a similar mapping from reduced form to structural disturbances; I omit the algebra for simplicity.

Given B_0 and Π_i, variance decompositions and impulse response functions can be calculated in the usual way. Π_i may be obtained by OLS. B_0 may then be obtained from the variance-covariance matrix of v_t as follows. This matrix has twenty-one distinct elements. These must determine twenty-three parameters: six variances, one for each of the elements of u_t, and the seventeen coefficients on contemporaneous variables or surprises in equations (1)–(6). Without additional information, the system is not identified. Given the wealth of studies on the determinants of the Japanese trade balance, which have produced some consensus estimates of relevant elasticities, it seems likely to be uncontroversial to impose values for α_2 and α_3, the instantaneous elasticities of aggregate demand with respect to the real exchange rate and foreign output, and so I used these studies to impose such values. This leaves twenty-one parameters to be determined from the twenty-one elements of the variance-covariance matrix of v_t.

The structure of the system is such that the information in these twenty-one elements can be exploited by standard instrumental variables techniques. The residual from estimating the oil equation (4) $u_{ot} \equiv v_{ot}$ can be used to instrument the aggregate demand equation, to obtain $\hat{\alpha}_1$. The aggregate demand and oil residuals u_{dt} and u_{ot} can then be used as instruments in the price equation; u_{dt}, u_{ct}, and u_{ot} can then be used as instruments in the money supply equation; u_{dt}, u_{ct}, u_{ot}, and u_{mt} can then be used as instruments in the foreign output equation; and the entire set of structural disturbances can be used in the real exchange rate equation.

6.2 Data

The data are monthly, January 1973 to August 1990, for a total of 212 observations, with pre-1973 data used for initial lags. The ending point of the sample was determined by data availability. The starting point was determined, first, by the evident fact that the Japanese economy has behaved quite differently post-1973 than pre-1973 and, second, by the presumption that monetary policy was rather different in the era of fixed exchange rates than in the era of floating exchange rates. The exact date January 1973 was chosen in accord with Hamada and Hayashi (1985, 109), who concluded that January 1973 is the likeliest date for a one-time shift in monetary policy in the early 1970s. Results of estimates with two other subsamples, January 1976 to August 1990 and January 1973 to March 1990, are very similar, as noted below.

Data for both the United States and Japan through mid-1988 were obtained from the OECD's *Main Economic Indicators* (MEI) as supplied on PC diskettes by VAR Econometrics, and updated by published sources as indicated below. The MEI indices of Japanese industrial production, seasonally adjusted, and the WPI for mining and manufacturing, all 1980 = 100, were converted to 1985 = 100, and together with seasonally adjusted data on monthly averages of M_2 + CD were then linked with post-1988 data published in various issues of the Bank of Japan's *Economic Statistics Monthly*.

(The MEI series is labeled "M1 + Quasimoney," but comparison with the figures in *Economic Statistics Monthly* indicates that the data are for M_2 + CD. The only seasonally adjusted data for M_2 + CD in *Economic Statistics Monthly* were for growth rates rather than levels, so I constructed a post-1988 level series using as an initial condition the last available MEI figure.) The MEI series on the end-of-month yen/dollar exchange rate was updated with data kindly supplied by Kunio Okina.

These measures of price level and money stock were chosen following Bryant (1990), who suggests that the WPI is the most appropriate single monthly price index, and Ito (1989, 1990) and Suzuki (1985), who suggest that M_2 + CD is the most appropriate single measure of the money stock from the point of view of monetary targeting.

The MEI indices of U.S. industrial production, seasonally adjusted, and the WPI, both 1980 = 100, were converted to 1987 = 100 and 1982 = 100, respectively, and then linked with post-1988 data published in the *Survey of Current Business* and the Federal Reserve Bank of St. Louis's *National Economic Trends*. All data were converted to logs, with the real exchange rate defined as log(yen/dollar) + log(U.S. WPI) − log(Japanese WPI).

Figure 6.1 has plots of the growth rates (log differences) and log levels of the data, with contraction phases of the reference cycle as defined by the Economic Planning Agency noted by shaded areas. Table 6.1 has some basic statistics. The negative first autocorrelation of output growth and the somewhat choppy pattern of autocorrelations for money growth and inflation in oil prices (rows 1, 3, and 4) are unusual features of the data (at least to one used to working with U.S. data); the jerky behavior that leads to these patterns can be seen in the graphs for these variables in figure 6.1.

6.3 Empirical Estimates

6.3.1 Preliminaries

The empirical work began with tests for unit roots. Standard univariate-augmented Dickey-Fuller tests suggested that one difference sufficed to induce stationarity in each of the variables; a version of the Johansen (1988) test for cointegration, extended to include trend as well as constant terms, found, according to p-values kindly supplied by James H. Stock, no evidence of cointegration. Details on these tests are available upon request. I thus simply differenced all variables before proceeding with the empirical work. For example, y_t is the growth rate of output. I nonetheless generally refer to y_t as simply "output," except where this might cause confusion. Results from specifications estimated in levels rather than differences were quite similar, as noted below.

Using the differenced data, I estimated three different VARs, with six,

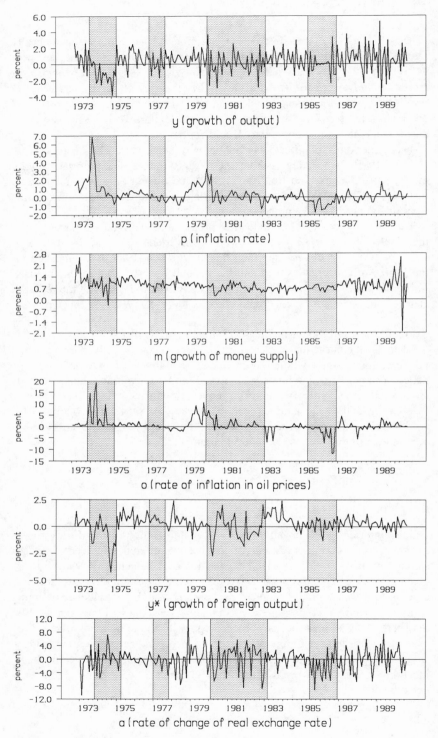

Fig. 6.1 Basic data

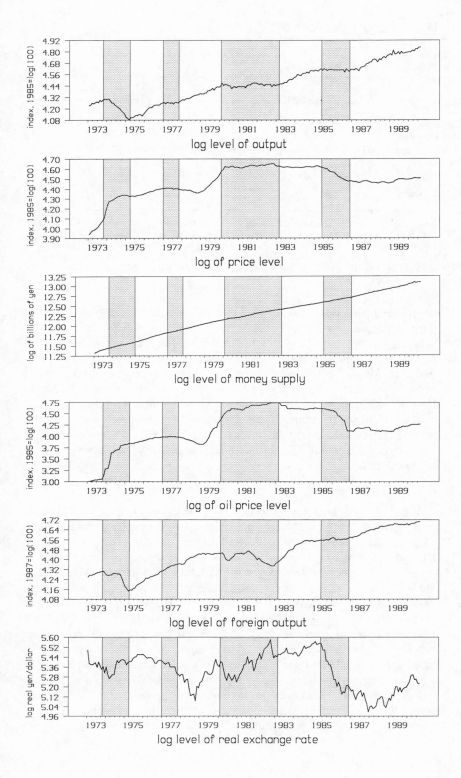

Table 6.1   **Basic Statistics**

	Mean	Standard Deviation	Autocorrelations				
			1	2	3	4	5
(1) y	0.304	1.444	−0.271	0.186	0.262	−.068	0.131
(2) p	0.274	1.000	0.780	0.596	0.491	0.458	0.423
(3) m	0.845	0.410	−0.008	0.294	0.219	0.148	0.110
(4) o	0.599	3.090	0.496	0.298	0.417	0.396	0.239
(5) y^*	0.211	0.897	0.510	0.353	0.262	0.157	0.087
(6) a	−0.130	3.367	−0.026	0.009	0.068	0.004	0.007

Note: The statistics are based on 212 monthly observations from January 1973 to August 1990. Variables: y = rate of growth of output (index of industrial production, mining, and manufacturing, seasonally adjusted, 1985 = 100); p = rate of inflation (WPI); m = growth rate of M_2 + CD, seasonally adjusted; o = rate of inflation in oil prices (WPI for petroleum and coal); y^* = rate of growth of U.S. output (index of industrial production, seasonally adjusted, 1987 = 100); a = percentage change in real exchange rate (yen/dollar).

twelve, and twenty-four lags of each right-hand-side variable, plus a constant term. All regressions began in January 1973, with the twenty-four-lag regression, for example, reaching back to January 1971 for lags to put on the right-hand side. Likelihood ratio tests using the degrees of freedom adjustment suggested by Sims (1980) rejected the null of six lags in favor of the alternative of twelve ($\chi^2(216) = 274.2$, p-value = .003), but did not reject the null of twelve lags in favor of the alternative of twenty-four ($\chi^2(432) = 311.4$, p-value = 1.00). In addition, both Q-statistics (reported below) and the individual autocorrelations of the residuals suggested that a lag length of twelve sufficed to reduce the residuals in each equation to white noise. I thus set the lag length to twelve.

6.3.2   Reduced Form

The model suggests that, except in special cases, anything that Granger causes money, oil prices, foreign output, and the real exchange rate ought to Granger cause output and prices as well (though of course there may be such Granger causality to output and prices even in the absence of Granger causality to the right-hand-side endogenous variables in equations [1] and [2]). Table 6.2, panel A, presents F-statistics suggesting that this is essentially the case: at conventional significance levels, at least one of money, oil prices, and foreign output is Granger caused by each of the six variables (rows 3–5), and, indeed, all six variables Granger cause output (row 1), and all but foreign output Granger cause prices (row 2). The standard errors for sums of distributed lags reported in table 6.2, panel B, yield compatible implications for when movements in one variable help predict movements in another.

Note that money Granger causes both output and prices (table 6.2, panel A, rows 1 and 2, column 3), suggesting the possibility that monetary policy may be used to influence the path of these two variables. If the monetary authority

Table 6.2   **Reduced Form**

A. Granger Causality Tests
From

To	(1) y	(2) p	(3) m	(4) o	(5) y*	(6) a	(7) y, p, m, o	(8) y*, a
(1) y	7.202 [0.000]	3.318 [0.000]	2.723 [0.002]	2.352 [0.009]	3.569 [0.000]	2.345 [0.009]	4.206 [0.000]	2.648 [0.000]
(2) p	1.131 [0.340]	5.280 [0.000]	1.926 [0.036]	2.027 [0.026]	0.784 [0.666]	4.019 [0.000]	9.936 [0.000]	2.172 [0.003]
(3) m	2.055 [0.024]	0.766 [0.685]	4.221 [0.000]	0.797 [0.653]	0.973 [0.477]	0.624 [0.819]	2.495 [0.000]	0.651 [0.889]
(4) o	2.022 [0.026]	5.334 [0.000]	1.792 [0.055]	3.236 [0.000]	1.558 [0.111]	1.786 [0.056]	5.856 [0.000]	1.801 [0.019]
(5) y*	0.981 [0.470]	1.704 [0.072]	0.725 [0.725]	1.530 [0.120]	2.596 [0.004]	1.844 [0.047]	1.468 [0.044]	3.049 [0.000]
(6) a	0.792 [0.658]	1.144 [0.330]	0.430 [0.949]	0.679 [0.769]	0.489 [0.918]	1.126 [0.344]	0.729 [0.896]	0.808 [0.722]

(7) H_A: m_t does not Granger cause y_t, $m_t - p_t$, $o_t - p_t$, y_t^*, $a_t \sim \chi^2(60) = 92.490$ [0.004]

(8) H_B: m_t does not Granger cause y_t, $m_t - p_t$, $o_t - p_t$, $\sim \chi^2(36) = 80.504$ [0.000]

B. Summary Statistics

Left-hand-side Variable	Right-hand-side Variables: Sums of Lag Coefficients						Summary Statistics		
	(1) y	(2) p	(3) m	(4) o	(5) y*	(6) a	(7) Standard Error	(8) $\bar{R}^2$	(9) Q (42)
(1) y	−0.695 (0.348)	−1.477 (0.433)	1.216 (0.420)	0.416 (0.154)	1.173 (0.311)	0.176 (0.104)	1.033	.49	33.98 [0.81]
(2) p	0.218 (0.183)	0.836 (0.228)	0.658 (0.221)	−0.085 (0.081)	−0.114 (0.163)	0.087 (0.055)	0.543	.71	23.66 [0.99]
(3) m	−0.297 (0.121)	−0.109 (0.150)	0.709 (0.146)	0.032 (0.054)	0.200 (0.108)	0.018 (0.036)	0.359	.23	20.08 [1.00]
(4) o	0.378 (0.660)	4.179 (0.822)	−1.369 (0.797)	−0.697 (0.293)	−0.540 (0.590)	0.589 (0.197)	1.960	.60	34.01 [0.81]
(5) y*	−0.029 (0.238)	0.240 (0.296)	−0.177 (0.288)	−0.143 (0.106)	0.437 (0.213)	0.006 (0.071)	0.707	.38	29.29 [0.93]
(6) a	0.573 (1.194)	0.946 (1.487)	−0.469 (1.442)	−0.412 (0.529)	−0.547 (1.066)	0.297 (0.357)	3.545	−.11	25.49 [0.98]

Notes: Panel A: The F-statistics in rows 1–6 test the null that the coefficients are zero for all lags of the variables in a given column, when the variable in a given row is on the left-hand side. p-values are given in brackets. The degrees of freedom for the tests in the first six columns are 12,139, in column 7 are 48,139, and in column 8 are 24,139. Panel B: In columns 1–6 asymptotic standard errors are in parentheses. Column 7 presents the standard error of the regression. In column 9 the p-value for the Q-statistic is in brackets.

is following a program of targeting or stabilizing output and/or prices, in general it should adjust the money supply in response to whatever variables influence the path of those two variables (see, e.g., Chow 1983, chapter 12). In light of the results in rows 1 and 2, this means in response to all the variables in the system. In a stationary world (one in which the objective function of the monetary authority and parameters of the model are unchanging), this would lead to money being Granger caused by all the variables in the system.

It appears, however, that money is Granger caused only by itself and output (row 3, columns 1 and 3). Tests on sums of distributed lag coefficients reported in table 6.2, panel B, find some predictive power in foreign output as well. But overall there is no reduced-form evidence that the money supply responds to prices, oil prices, or the real exchange rate.

One possible reason for the lack of Granger causality is that, while there is indeed a stable feedback rule consistent with targeting of output and prices, the sample is too small to accurately reflect this fact, a distinct possibility given that I am using a profligately parameterized model. But while it would not be wise to interpret the lack of Granger causality as sharp evidence against the simple textbook model of output and price targeting, it seems equally foolish to expect the estimates of this model to yield sharp implications about what the price and output targets of the Bank of Japan are, even if one's priors are that such targets are central to the bank's decision making (e.g., Bryant 1990).

Also, the fact that both output and foreign output help predict the money supply suggests that the bank does have its eyes on the economy when it determines the money supply. That this money growth is not exogenous has been argued by many, including in particular Hutchison (1986), who uses Granger causality tests such as those applied here. Once again, it would be foolish to expect the estimates of this model to yield a clear statement that the bank follows a money-targeting rule, even if one's priors are that this is essentially the case.

One final note on the reduced form: the evidence that money Granger causes real variables is quite strong. Consider rewriting the system so that money is the only nominal variable, with $m_t - p_t$ (real balances) and $o_t - p_t$ (real oil prices) joining y_t, y_t^*, and a_t as real variables. As reported in rows 7 and 8 of table 6.2, panel A, the null that money does not Granger cause any of these variables is strongly rejected, as is the null that money does not Granger cause the set of domestic variables y_t, $m_t - p_t$, and $o_t - p_t$.

6.3.3 Structural Equations

Table 6.3, panel A, has estimates of equations (1)–(6). The coefficients on y_t^* and a_t in the aggregate demand equation were imposed rather than estimated: Noland (1989) estimated a long-run elasticity of Japanese exports with respect to foreign output of about 1.4. Since exports are about 10 to 15% of GNP, and the short-run effect is presumably less than the long-run, this sug-

Table 6.3   **Structural Estimates**

A. Parameter Estimates[a]

(1) $y_t = 0.512\,(m_t - p_t) - 0.03a_t + .20y_t^* + \hat{\Gamma}_y'z_{t-1} + \hat{u}_{dt}$
$(.591)$

(2) $p_t = 0.255y_t + 0.094o_t + \hat{\Gamma}_p'z_{t-1} + \hat{u}_{ct}$
$(.047)\qquad(.023)$

(3) $m_t = -0.038v_{yt} - 0.057v_{pt} - 0.017v_{at} + \hat{\Gamma}_m'z_{t-1} + \hat{u}_{mt}$
$(.035)\qquad(.112)\qquad(.051)$

(4) $o_t = \hat{\Gamma}_o'z_{t-1} + \hat{u}_{ot}$

(5) $y_t^* = 0.065v_{yt} - 0.167v_{pt} - 0.096v_{mt} + 0.002v_{ot} + \hat{\Gamma}_{y^*}'z_{t-1} + \hat{u}_{y^*t}$
$(.060)\qquad(.119)\qquad(.169)\qquad(.032)$

(6) $a_t = 0.268v_{yt} + 2.412v_{pt} + 1.859v_{mt} - 0.344v_{ot} - 0.021v_{y^*t} + \hat{\Gamma}_a'z_{t-1} + \hat{u}_{at}$
$(.301)\qquad(.590)\qquad(.838)\qquad(.160)\qquad(.428)$

B. Summary Statistics

Equation	Right-hand-side variables: Sums of Lag Coefficients						Summary Statistics		
	y	p	m	o	y^*	a	Standard Error	$\bar{R}^2$	Q (42)
(1)	−0.408	−1.524	1.723	0.372	1.109	0.189	1.144	.36	27.64
	(0.491)	(0.481)	(0.729)	(0.184)	(0.391)	(0.122)			[0.96]
(2)	0.615	0.821	0.476	−0.032	−0.363	−0.013	0.531	.72	28.56
	(0.195)	(0.250)	(0.225)	(0.090)	(0.169)	(0.056)			[0.94]

Notes: Asymptotic standard errors in parentheses. The coefficients in equation (1) in panel A without standard errors were imposed rather than estimated. See notes to table 6.2 for additional description.
[a]$\hat{\sigma}_d = 1.144;\ \hat{\sigma}_c = 0.531;\ \hat{\sigma}_m = 0.372;\ \hat{\sigma}_o = 1.960;\ \hat{\sigma}_{y^*} = 0.706;\ \hat{\sigma}_a = 3.484.$

gests an upper bound of about 0.2 for the short-run elasticity of aggregate demand with respect to foreign output. Krugman and Obstfeld (1988, 454) report that Artus and Knight (1984) found that the six-month elasticity of the Japanese current account with respect to the real exchange rate was about -0.25, and Noland (1989) found a one-quarter elasticity of about -1 (the negative signs being consistent with a J-curve), again suggesting an aggregate demand elasticity about 10 to 15% of those figures: hence the -0.03. Some alternative imposed values for these short-run elasticities led to very similar results, as noted below.

The remaining parameters in table 6.3 were estimated by instrumental variables, as described above. The three freely estimated parameters in the aggregate demand and aggregate supply equations are all correctly signed. I do not know of estimates for Japanese data to which the estimates can be directly compared, but comparison with U.S. studies suggests that they are plausible.

Although the estimate of the instantaneous elasticity of aggregate demand with respect to real balances is fairly imprecise, the 0.512 value is bracketed by estimates from quarterly U.S. data. On the one hand, the 0.15 quarterly figure for the MPS model for the United States (Blanchard 1989, 1150) is somewhat lower. On the other hand, if one combines the Japanese money demand estimates in Hamada and Hayashi (1985, table 4.5; income elasticity ≈ 0.2 to 0.5, interest elasticity ≈ -0.01 to -0.02) with the range of interest elasticities of the IS curve found in U.S. studies (≈ -0.1 to -0.2; e.g., Friedman 1977), the implied value of the elasticity is about 2–5, somewhat higher than the estimated value of 0.512.

The estimated price elasticity of supply of about 4 ($4 \approx 1/0.255$) is bracketed by the quarterly U.S. estimates of 0.81 (Blanchard and Watson (1986, 132)) and 10–12 (Blanchard 1989, 1152). The 0.094 figure on oil prices is consistent with the monthly estimate in Blanchard (1987, 68) that a 1% increase in crude materials prices causes a 0.02% increase in consumer prices.

The three negative signs on the variables in the money supply equation are consistent with the possibility that the intramonth response of the Bank of Japan to shocks is one of "leaning against the wind"; on the other hand, the signs could as well simply reflect factors beyond the control of the authority, such as intramonth shocks to the money multiplier. In any case, none of the three estimates is significantly different from zero, so, in the absence of any a priori theoretical bounds on plausible values, it is probably not advisable to read much into the signs or magnitudes of the estimates.

As noted above, theory does not restrict the signs or values of the coefficients on the foreign output and real exchange rate equations.

Table 6.3, panel B, has estimates of sums of distributed lag coefficients in the aggregate demand and supply equations. (The sums for the other equations are exactly as presented in table 6.2, panel B.) Coefficients on contemporaneous right-hand-side variables (e.g., m_t in [1]) are included in these sums. By and large, the significance of the sums of these distributed lag coefficients is consistent with the Granger causality tests reported above.

The long-run response of a given left-hand-side variable to a permanent increase in a given right-hand-side variable can be inferred from the estimates in the table. The long-run elasticity of aggregate demand with respect to money is about 1.2 ($\approx 1.723/1.408$), with respect to prices about -1.1 ($\approx -1.524/1.408$), which is probably consistent with a long-run elasticity of aggregate demand with respect to real balances of about 1, a point estimate suggested by Hamada and Hayashi (1985, 101). The long-run elasticity of aggregate demand with respect to the real exchange rate is about 0.13 ($\approx 0.189/1.408$), comparable to the figures of about 0.15 and 0.05 implied by Artus and Knight (1984, cited in Krugman and Obstfeld 1988, 484) and Noland (1989, 177). The elasticity with respect to foreign output is about 0.8 ($\approx 1.109/1.408$), somewhat higher than the 0.14 figure implied by Noland (1989). (The stated figures for Artus and Knight and Noland were obtained by multiplying their reported elasticities by 0.10, approximately the share of imports or exports in Japanese GNP.)

The long-run price elasticity of supply is about 0.13 ($\approx [1 - 0.821]/[1 + 0.615 - 0.255]$).

Figure 6.2 plots impulse response functions (dynamic multipliers), that is, one-to-sixty-month response of the levels of output, prices, and money to demand, cost, money, and oil shocks. (The responses to u_{y^*t} and u_{at} are not given, since the breakdown of the residual foreign shock into these two components is arbitrary; plots of responses of oil prices, U.S. output, and the real

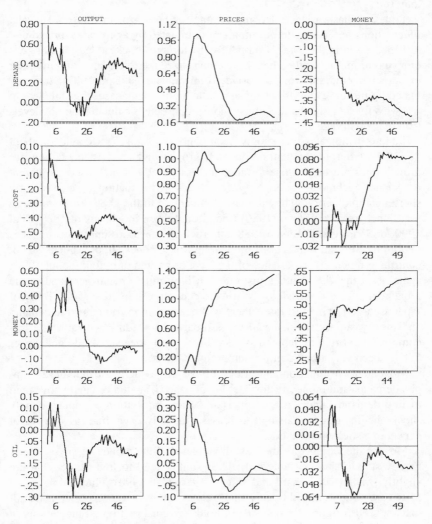

Fig. 6.2   Impulse response functions

exchange rate are omitted to save space.) While the responses are rather choppy, probably because of the negative first-order serial correlations of y_t and the choppy patterns of autocorrelations of m_t (see table 6.1), the overall patterns were as expected: demand shocks increase output and prices; cost shocks increase prices and decrease output; money shocks increase prices and output, with the long-run effect on output very close to zero. Demand shocks decrease the money supply, suggesting countercyclical stabilization; cost shocks cause fluctuations in the money stock for the first six months, but ultimately the stock increases, suggesting accommodation, at least in the long run.

Table 6.4 has variance decompositions for both growth rates and levels. Fluctuations in the growth of output are dominated by aggregate demand disturbances, and in the level of output by the foreign shock, at least at horizons of a year or more. While others have emphasized the role of the foreign sector in output fluctuations (e.g., Horiye, Naniwa, and Ishihara 1987), the estimated figure for levels strikes me as a little high. In any case, it is not clear to me why foreign shocks are much more important for fluctuations of levels than of growth rates.

Table 6.4 indicates that supply disturbances (u_c and u_o) account for about 20–25% of output fluctuations in both growth and levels. The figures for growth rates are quite close to those in West (1992), which used a different model and technique for identifying sources of fluctuations over a slightly shorter sample period. They are also comparable to the U.S. results in levels for Blanchard and Watson (1986) (though not those in Blanchard 1989, Gali 1990, or Shapiro and Watson 1988, all of which constrain supply disturbances to dominate output fluctuations in the long run). Money supply shocks do not contribute much to the variance of the level or growth of output (about 10%), again as in the U.S. studies just cited. It is useful to recall here and in the remainder of the discussion of variance decompositions that if the Bank of Japan is targeting interest rates, there will be a common component to demand and money supply shocks, and the estimation procedure will attribute this component entirely to demand shocks. Finally, oil price shocks do not appear to have been very important for output fluctuations.

Movements in inflation and prices are roughly equally attributable to supply, demand, and money factors (table 6.4); the U.S. studies cited above tend to find demand factors more important. The contribution of money supply shocks begins quite small and increases gradually over time, as one might expect in a sticky price model.

Most of the variance of the growth and level of the money supply is due to money supply shocks (table 6.4); U.S. studies tend to find figures that are slightly smaller (Blanchard and Watson 1986; Gali 1990). Fluctuations in oil prices are not dominated by any single shock, at least at long horizons (recall that the 100% figure for one month holds by construction). Fluctuations in U.S. output and the real exchange rate are dominated by foreign shocks. The

Table 6.4   **Variance Decompositions**

	Growth Rates					Log Levels				
Months	u_d	u_c	u_m	u_o	$u_{y*} + u_a$	u_d	u_c	u_m	u_o	$u_{y*} + u_a$
					Output					
1	87.2	8.1	1.6	0.6	2.4	87.2	8.1	1.6	0.6	2.4
2	74.4	15.9	1.4	2.8	5.5	80.3	6.3	3.6	1.2	8.6
3	71.3	16.5	1.7	2.8	7.7	73.5	4.4	3.1	1.8	17.2
6	64.8	15.6	3.1	6.4	10.0	54.4	2.2	6.4	0.9	36.1
12	60.9	13.4	7.2	5.9	12.6	34.5	4.3	12.3	0.6	48.4
24	57.3	11.9	11.8	7.6	11.5	15.7	15.2	12.8	2.8	53.6
60	57.8	11.3	11.9	8.0	11.0	14.6	23.2	6.4	2.0	53.8
					Prices					
1	20.6	69.4	0.4	9.0	0.6	20.6	69.4	0.4	9.0	0.6
2	27.4	54.8	0.7	9.6	7.5	27.1	59.5	0.7	10.0	2.7
3	32.4	50.4	1.1	9.2	6.9	32.2	53.8	1.0	9.8	3.1
6	33.0	43.6	2.5	10.0	10.9	40.2	44.7	2.3	6.6	6.3
12	29.3	37.6	10.0	8.9	14.2	40.2	37.6	3.2	3.3	15.6
24	27.3	31.9	17.7	8.4	14.8	27.0	33.3	19.3	1.3	19.0
60	27.6	31.0	17.5	8.3	15.6	11.6	35.2	40.6	0.5	12.1
					Money					
1	3.1	0.8	94.1	0.0	2.1	3.1	0.8	94.1	0.0	2.1
2	3.3	1.4	89.9	1.3	4.1	2.6	0.5	94.8	0.8	1.4
3	5.5	1.7	87.5	1.4	3.9	4.2	0.5	92.9	1.4	1.1
6	5.9	2.4	81.6	2.7	7.4	5.2	0.2	91.2	1.4	2.0
12	10.8	2.9	73.2	4.4	8.7	9.8	0.2	86.3	0.6	3.1
24	14.1	3.2	67.3	4.9	10.5	23.5	0.1	72.8	0.7	2.9
60	15.8	3.6	64.5	5.3	10.7	27.2	0.9	66.8	0.3	4.9
					Oil Prices					
1	0.0	0.0	0.0	100.0	0.0	0.0	0.0	0.0	100.0	0.0
2	2.4	0.3	1.8	93.8	1.6	1.1	0.2	0.9	97.1	0.8
3	10.1	4.2	2.2	79.9	3.5	7.5	2.4	2.1	85.6	2.3
6	13.7	20.5	1.9	54.3	9.6	19.2	19.7	1.8	51.6	7.7
12	14.7	17.1	6.8	43.6	17.8	28.3	23.9	2.6	20.4	24.8
24	14.0	16.0	12.6	39.9	17.4	25.2	25.1	9.2	8.3	32.2
60	14.9	15.7	12.8	38.8	17.7	14.7	27.3	24.8	4.5	28.7
					U.S. Output					
1	0.2	1.7	0.2	0.2	97.8	0.2	1.7	0.2	0.2	97.8
2	2.3	2.0	0.4	0.4	95.0	1.4	2.2	0.4	0.4	95.7
3	2.4	1.9	1.8	0.3	93.6	1.1	2.2	0.2	0.4	96.1
6	2.8	2.2	2.3	3.5	89.2	0.9	2.9	0.2	2.5	93.5
12	5.8	3.7	4.3	4.0	82.3	1.2	1.9	1.5	3.7	91.7
24	10.7	9.3	4.6	4.4	71.0	4.0	7.4	2.1	4.6	82.0
60	11.9	9.1	7.9	4.5	66.6	2.5	8.4	8.6	4.0	76.7
					Real Exchange Rate					
1	4.3	7.3	4.6	0.7	83.1	4.3	7.3	4.6	0.7	83.1
2	4.7	7.4	4.7	0.8	82.5	3.2	8.8	5.6	0.5	81.9

(continued)

Table 6.4   (continued)

	Growth Rates					Log Levels				
Months	u_d	u_c	u_m	u_o	$u_{y^*} + u_a$	u_d	u_c	u_m	u_o	$u_{y^*} + u_a$
3	4.8	7.7	5.1	0.8	81.6	3.2	7.9	7.2	0.5	81.3
6	4.8	8.9	4.7	0.9	80.7	2.5	3.9	7.7	0.7	85.2
12	5.2	10.5	7.7	1.9	74.7	2.5	5.0	7.0	2.3	83.1
24	7.3	10.7	10.5	2.1	69.5	5.3	5.3	5.1	2.8	81.6
60	9.3	10.5	10.8	2.4	67.1	6.2	4.5	4.5	3.2	81.6

Notes: Standard errors are not available. Computation is described in text.

result for output is as in West (1992), but not for the exchange rate, whose movements West found to be dominated by cost shocks.

Money supply shocks, then, do not account for a large share of the variance in any of the variables in the model, except the money supply itself. It is nonetheless possible that such shocks are important at cyclical turning points: Gali (1990, tables 4, 5), for example, finds that money supply shocks account for less than 15% of the variance of U.S. output at business cycle horizons, but attributes to such shocks the leading role in the 1981–82 recession. Table 6.5 however, suggests that this is not the case for Japan.

Table 6.5 computes causes of peak to trough changes in the (log) levels of output and prices.[3] To read the table, consider row 1. The peak (November 1973) to trough (March 1975) fall of the index of industrial was 19.32% in this contraction (column 1). The estimates of the model indicate that as of November 1973 the index was predicted to be only 11.71% lower in March 1975 (column 2), implying that the index fell 7.62% more than predicted (column 3). Of this forecast error, 45% (i.e., about -3.43 of the -7.62 that appears in column 3) is accounted for by demand shocks, 23% by cost shocks, 15% by money shocks, 5% by oil shocks, and 12% by foreign shocks. In columns 4–8, negative signs mean that the indicated shock was of the opposite sign of the forecast error in column 3.

One contraction involved such a small (in absolute value) forecast error for output (row 2, column 3) that the estimates in columns 4–8 are very sensitive to small changes in the estimate of column 3. The estimates in rows 1, 3, and 4 are not as sensitive, and the figures in column 6 in these rows indicate that money supply shocks have not played a dominant role in movements in output over any of the contractions in the sample (and, more generally, contractions

3. Since the growth rate rather than the level of output appears to be a coincident indicator in Japan, there might be a choice of subperiods that would be more revealing about the effects of monetary shocks on the level of output, but I know of no source for cyclical phases in the level of output in Japan.

Table 6.5   Percentage Changes during Contractions

	(1)	(2)	(3)	(4)	(5)	(6)	(7)	(8)
					Components of (3) (%)			
	Actual	Forecast	(1)−(2)	Demand	Cost	Money	Oil	Foreign
			Level of Output					
(1) 1973:11–1975:3	− 19.32	− 11.71	− 7.62	45	23	15	5	12
(2) 1977:1–1977:10	0.60	1.79	− 1.19	328	− 24	42	− 7	− 240
(3) 1980:2–1983:2	1.89	8.82	− 6.93	− 11	5	− 2	9	99
(4) 1985:6–1986:11	− 1.43	7.84	− 9.27	27	12	22	0	39
			Price Level					
(5) 1973:11–1975:3	24.96	24.71	0.25	− 547	1236	− 624	− 169	204
(6) 1977:1–1977:10	− 0.12	5.99	− 6.11	98	15	4	− 6	− 12
(7) 1980:2–1983:2	6.81	1.19	5.62	49	− 21	59	− 22	35
(8) 1985:6–1986:11	− 13.95	− 1.19	− 12.76	52	− 26	15	− 3	62

Notes: The dates given are the peak and trough of the four contractions in the sample. Column 1 gives the actual percentage change in the variable during that contraction. Column 2 gives the percentage change over that row's contraction as forecast at the peak using parameters estimated over the whole sample. Column 3 gives the difference between columns 1 and 2. Columns 4 to 8 decompose column 3 into the five uncorrelated shocks in the model, expressed as a percenttage of column 3; a minus sign means that the shocks had a sign opposite to the entry in column 3. The numbers in columns 4 to 8 may not add to 100, due to rounding.

are not attributable to a single type of shock).[4] Row 7 does indicate that money supply shocks had a substantial impact on the unexpected component of the change in the price level in the contraction of February 1980 to March 1982. (I ignore row 5, again because the figure in column 3 for that row is so small that small changes in it lead to large changes in the estimates in columns 4–8.)

I conclude, then, that money supply shocks have not played a dominant role in output fluctuations, either over the sample as a whole or over any of the contractions that have occurred in the sample; they have been somewhat more prominent in accounting for price and inflation fluctuations.

6.4   Sensitivity of Results

In this section, I briefly summarize the results of a set of experiments undertaken to see whether the results are sensitive to minor changes in specification. The experiments are listed in panel A of table 6.6. Specification A is the one used in previous tables and is repeated here solely to facilitate comparison. Specifications B and C impose different values for the short-run elasticities of aggregate demand with respect to foreign output and the real exchange rate (see equation [1]). Specification D imposes a random walk on the real ex-

4. The relatively small contribution of oil shocks in row 1 is puzzling.

Table 6.6　　　**Effects of Alternative Specifications**

A. Alternative Specifications[a]

	Sample Period	α_2, α_3	Levels, Trend	Other
A	1973:1–1990:8	$-.03, .20$	no, no	
B	1973:1–1990:8	$-.20, .20$	no, no	
C	1973:1–1990:8	$-.03, .05$	no, no	
D	1973:1–1990:8	$-.03, .20$	no, no	Real exchange rate is random walk
E	1976:1–1990:8	$-.03, .20$	no, no	
F	1973:1–1990:3	$-.03, .20$	no, no	
G	1973:1–1990:8	$-.03, .20$	no, no	High-powered money instead of M_2
H	1973:1–1990:8	$-.03, .20$	yes, yes	
I	1973:1–1990:8	$-.03, .20$	yes, no	

B. Granger Causality[b]

	(1) y_t	(2) p_t	(3) m_t	(4) H_A	(5) H_B
		Causality at .05 (.10) Level to		p-value for	
A–D	y, p, m, o, y^*, a	p, m, o, a	y, m	0.004	0.000
E	y, m, o, y^*	$(y), a$	$(y), m$	0.012	0.000
F	y, p, m, o, y^*, a	p, m, o, a	y, m	0.003	0.000
G	y, p, o, y^*, a	$p, (m), a$	$m, (o), y^*$	0.145	0.218
H	y, p, m, o, y^*, a	$p, (o), a$	$(y), m$	0.001	0.000
I	$y, p, (m), o, y^*, a$	$p, (m), a$	$(y), m$	0.013	0.001

C. Variance Decompositions of Levels at Twenty-Four Month Horizon[c]

	y_t			p_t			m_t		
	$u_d + u_{y^*} + u_a$	$u_c + u_o$	u_m	$u_d + u_{y^*} + u_a$	$u_c + u_o$	u_m	$u_d + u_{y^*} + u_a$	$u_c + u_o$	u_m
A	69	18	13	46	35	19	26	1	73
B	66	22	12	60	20	20	23	1	75
C	69	18	13	46	35	20	27	1	72
D	70	17	12	45	35	20	28	1	72
E	69	16	16	55	36	8	35	4	62
F	67	17	16	49	34	17	33	1	66
G	69	27	4	65	33	2	53	10	37
H	56	37	7	51	39	10	41	16	42
I	66	29	5	55	44	2	40	32	28

[a]The results for specification A, which is the one used in previous tables, are repeated for convenience of comparison. Specifications B and C impose different values of the parameters α_2 and α_3, which are defined in equation (1). Specification D sets to zero all the coefficients in the reduced-form equation for a_t. Specifications E and F try different sample periods. Specification G substitutes high-powered money for M_2. In specifications A–G all variables are in differences; in specifications H and I all variables are in levels, with a trend term in all equations in specification H.

[b]In the first three columns, each variable that Granger causes the indicated variable at the .10 but not .05 level is given in parentheses; the other listed variables Granger cause at the .05 or lower level. The last two columns report the results of the hypothesis tests and are defined in rows (7) and (8) of table 6.2.

[c]Totals may not add to 100, due to rounding.

change rate a_t, a result consistent with the reduced-form evidence presented above.[5] Specifications E and F try different sample periods. January 1976 to August 1990 was studied because Hamada and Hayashi (1985) and Suzuki (1985) suggest that the Bank of Japan changed its policy in response to the first oil shock; January 1973 to March 1990 was studied to eliminate possible effects of the huge fluctuation in money growth from April 1990 to May 1990 (see figure 6.1). Specification G substitutes high-powered money for M_2. Specification H assumes trend stationarity of all variables, and estimates with a trend term and twelve lags of the levels of all variables in all equations. Specification I assumes difference stationarity of all variables, allowing for the possibility of cointegration. In this specification, all equations had thirteen lags of all variables; the hypothesis tests were performed on the first twelve lags, so that an asymptotic normal distribution could be used in the hypothesis tests in panel B (see Sims, Stock, and Watson 1990).

Some Granger causality tests are summarized in panel B; results for specifications A–D are of course identical. With the exception of specification G, when high-powered money was used instead of M_2, money Granger causes real variables (panel B, columns 1, 4, and 5). (In contrast to U.S. data, then, this causality result holds for various techniques for inducing stationarity [Stock and Watson 1989].) The variance decompositions in panel C indicate that money supply shocks nonetheless do not seem to account for much of the movement in output, although they do account for most of the movement in the money supply.

I conclude that my basic result, that money seems to Granger cause real variables but nonetheless does not account for much of the movement in output, is unlikely to be very sensitive to minor changes in imposed parameters, sample period, or technique to induce differencing. On the other hand, the causality result is sensitive to the measure of the money stock. As noted above, however, Ito (1989, 1990) and Suzuki (1985) suggest that M_2 is a better measure of the money stock from the point of view of monetary targeting.

6.5   Effects of Alternative Money Supply Rules

A number of authors have suggested that the Bank of Japan uses its operating instruments with its eyes focused on "final" (as distinct from intermediate) targets. The targets that have been proposed, at least for the post-OPEC-I era, include "control of inflation" above all, along with "avoidance of pronounced cyclical swings in output and aggregate demand" and targeting of the real exchange rate and balance of payments (Bryant 1990, 32); "price stability and

---

5. The model was estimated by the instrumental variables technique described above; since a_t is not exactly orthogonal to past data in the sample, slightly different estimates would be obtained if I had used a different method of extracting parameter estimates from the variance-covariance matrix of the reduced-form residuals.

the maintenance of an adequate level of demand" (Hamada and Hayashi 1985, 83); "price stability" and "a high and stable exchange rate" (Fukui 1986, 110).

Bryant (1990, 33–34), Hamada and Hayashi (1985, 116), and Ito (1989) seem to doubt that the bank places much weight on deviations of any given monetary aggregate from its targeted value. On the other hand, Fukui (1986, 110–11) and Suzuki (1985, 9) seem to view the money supply as an intermediate target that gets considerable weight. And Friedman (1985, 27) lauds the bank for a "fairly consistent" policy of keeping money growth "relatively steady" (i.e., relative to the United States and Great Britain).

What does the money supply rule estimated above reveal about such descriptions? The reduced-form and structural evidence presented so far is strongly suggestive of neither a simple story of money supply targeting nor the simple textbook one of straightforward targeting of output and prices (perhaps with secondary weight placed on the money supply). I therefore doubt the wisdom of attempting to invert the estimated rule, to deduce an underlying objective function that maps one-to-one into the seventy-three parameters of the rule. Instead, to maintain a focus on simple and easy-to-understand objective functions, I simulate the behavior of the economy over the sample period under the apparently counterfactual assumption of a simple objective function.

This objective function is consistent with constant expected money growth. I assume that the monetary authority can perfectly control $_{t-1}m_t$ but not m_t. For simplicity, I abstract from the Lucas critique. I take as given the set of shocks and assume that the estimates of the parameters of equations (1)–(6) are invariant to such a change in regime. (In footnote 7, I briefly speculate on the possible biases from this simplification.) The coefficients in the reduced-form equations for y_t, p_t, and, of course, m_t will change; those for o_t, y^*_t, and a_t will not. The simulated time series process for all six variables of course is different from the actual.

The objective function corresponding to constant expected money growth aims to minimize the variance of money growth, since under this set of assumptions it is easy to see that minimizing the variance of m_t means setting $_{t-1}m_t$ to a constant. This constant was set to the estimated sample mean of money growth.

Table 6.7 has the sample means and standard deviations for the growth of nominal output and for each of the six endogenous variables from the actual (columns 1 and 4) and simulated (columns 2 and 5) data, as well as correlations between the actual and simulated data (column 7); columns 3, 6, and 8 will be described in a moment. As may be seen in columns 1 and 2, the simulated and actual data have nearly identical means. Perhaps surprisingly, they also have very similar standard deviations (columns 4 and 5)[6] and, with the

---

6. The standard deviation of the money supply (.291) differs from the value of $\hat{\sigma}_m$ given in table 6.3 (0.372) only because the latter was calculated using a degrees of freedom adjustment.

Table 6.7   **Effects of Alternative Money Supply Rules**

	Means			Standard Deviations			Correlation with Actual	
	(1) Rule a	(2) Rule b	(3) Rule c	(4) Rule a	(5) Rule b	(6) Rule c	(7) Rule b	(8) Rule c
(1) y	0.304	0.305	0.298	1.444	1.372	1.558	0.964	0.776
(2) p	0.274	0.279	0.273	1.000	0.962	1.105	0.919	0.713
(3) m	0.845	0.845	0.842	0.410	0.291	0.569	0.710	0.197
(4) o	0.599	0.596	0.594	3.090	3.108	3.590	0.940	0.764
(5) y^*	0.211	0.210	0.211	0.897	0.939	1.038	0.969	0.841
(6) a	-0.130	-0.136	-0.132	3.367	3.461	3.822	0.979	0.877
(7) $y + p$	0.578	0.584	0.571	1.787	1.716	1.922	0.957	0.774

Notes: Money supply rule a is the one actually estimated. Rule b sets expected money growth to a constant. Rule c sets expected money growth according to $_{t-1}m_t = \mu_1 + \lambda(_{t-1}y_t + {}_{t-1}p_t - \mu_2)$, where $\mu_1 = 0.845$, $\mu_2 = 0.578$, and $\lambda = -0.25$. The figures in columns 1 and 4 are simply the sample moments from the data. The figures reported in the remaining columns are computed from a simulation under the indicated rule.

predictable exception of the money supply, are very highly correlated (column 7). Moreover, the actual and simulated data are so close that it is difficult to tell one from the other when they are plotted. See figure 6.3, in which the actual data are represented by the solid line, the simulated by a dashed line; when the software that generated the graph decided that the simulated and actual were too close to be distinguished by eye (as happens especially for output growth), it plotted only a dashed line.

According to the estimated model, then, whether or not the Bank of Japan was concerned above all else with stability of money growth, its policies had effects on the economy quite similar to those that would have occurred had the bank followed a rule of constant expected money growth. To interpret this tentative conclusion, let us begin by considering the possibility that the effects of anticipated monetary policy are so small that a wide range of money supply rules will lead to qualitatively similar behavior of output and prices.

Consider, then, performing the same counterfactual simulation with a different alternative policy, similar in spirit though very different in detail to one proposed by McCallum (1988) for U.S. monetary policy. Let expected money growth be determined by

$$_{t-1}m_t = \mu_1 + \lambda(y_t + p_t - \mu_2),$$

where μ_1 and μ_2 are constants, μ_2 is a target rate for the growth of nominal output, and λ is a negative parameter. I set μ_1 to the sample mean of money growth, μ_2 to the sample mean of nominal output growth, and $\lambda = -0.25$ (a value that McCallum [1988] found worked well for the United States in his more sophisticated feedback rule).

Columns 3, 6, and 8 have the resulting sample means, standard deviations,

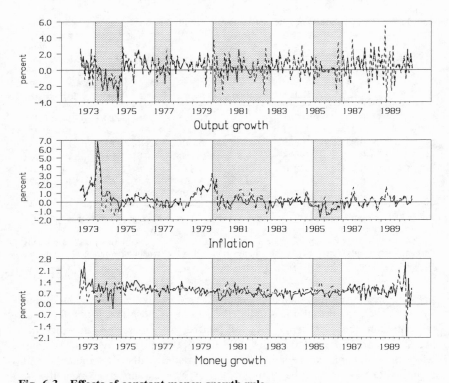

Fig. 6.3   Effects of constant money growth rule

Note: The actual data are represented by a solid line; the simulated data are represented by a dashed line. When the actual and simulated data are too close to distinguish (as happens especially for output growth), a dashed line represents both.

and correlations with the actual data. As may be seen, the means are, once again, largely unchanged, but now the standard deviations are slightly and the correlations greatly different, not only for money growth but for output, inflation, and nominal output growth as well. Anticipated monetary policy, then, does have effects sufficiently large that the estimates suggest that at least one alternative policy would have led to very different behavior.[7]

7. Even if rational expectations had been modeled explicitly, as in, for example, Taylor (1989), my aggregate demand–aggregate supply model might well still suggest that a hypothetical switch to a constant money growth rule would little change output and price behavior. The expectations that are relevant are of future prices and output. That the path of these variables is essentially unchanged under the new rule, when expectational effects are ignored, indicates that rational forecasts of these variables are similarly unchanged—that is, if we were to write the forecasts as distributed lags on the variables in the model, the coefficients in these distributed lags would not change much. This suggests (to me, at least) that a rational expectations version of the model may also have an equilibrium in which the distributed lag coefficients are not much different. This means that the coefficients on lagged variables in equations (1)–(6) will change little, which is exactly the assumption required to validate the exercise above.

Such an argument does not apply to the second money supply rule, which for well-known

Now, nothing in table 6.7 calls for the conclusion that the Bank of Japan must have been concentrating solely on stable money growth. Indeed, a simple continuity argument indicates that similar results would obtain if the hypothetical objective function were one of stable money growth together with, say, stable prices and output, provided the weight on money growth was sufficiently large. And it is possible in principle that an objective function that places little or no weight on stability of money growth but measures output and inflation stability in a complicated and sophisticated fashion would lead to a monetary rule whose simulated effects are as similar to those of the actual rule as are those of the constant expected money growth rule.

I thus do not interpret the results in table 6.7 and the previous section as arguing strongly for Friedman's (1985) view that, even if the Bank of Japan has not followed monetarist doctrine to the letter, it has followed the doctrine in spirit. I interpret these results as raising the intriguing possibility that, insofar as the bank was pursuing activist stabilization policy, such policy had little overall effect on the economy. An interesting question for future research is why this seems to be the case.

References

Artus, J. R., and M. D. Knight. 1984. Issues in the assessment of the exchange rates of industrial countries. Occasional Paper No. 29. Washington, DC: International Monetary Fund.

Blanchard, O. J. 1987. Aggregate and individual price adjustment. *Brookings Papers on Economic Activity* 1:57–109.

———. 1989. A traditional interpretation of macroeconomic fluctuations. *American Economic Review* 80:1146–64.

Blanchard, O. J., and M. W. Watson. 1986. Are business cycles all alike? In *The American Business Cycle: Continuity and Change,* ed. R. J. Gordon, 123–56. Chicago: University of Chicago Press.

Bryant, R. C. 1990. Model representations of Japanese monetary policy. Brookings Institution, Washington, DC. Manuscript.

Chow, G. C. 1983. *Econometrics.* New York: McGraw-Hill.

Christiano, L. J., and L. Ljungqvist. 1988. Money does Granger-cause output in the bivariate money-output relation. *Journal of Monetary Economics* 22:217–35.

Dornbusch, R., 1976. Expectations and exchange rate dynamics. *Journal of Political Economy* 84:1161–76.

Eichenbaum, M., and K. J. Singleton. 1986. Do equilibrium real business cycles explain postwar U.S. business cycles? In *NBER Macroeconomics Annual,* ed. S. Fischer, 91–135. Cambridge: MIT Press.

Friedman, B. 1977. The inefficiency of short-run monetary targets for monetary policy. *Brookings Papers on Economic Activity* 1:293–335.

---

reasons might, in a rational expectations environment, lead to dramatic additional changes in the reduced form beyond those allowed in the simulation.

Friedman, M. 1985. Monetarism in rhetoric and practice. In *Monetary Policy in Our Times,* ed. A. Ando, H. Eguchi, R. Farmer, and Y. Suzuki, 15–28. Cambridge: MIT Press.

Fukui, T. 1986. The recent development of the short-term money market in Japan and changes in the techniques and procedures of monetary control used by the Bank of Japan. In *Changes in Money Market Instruments and Procedures: Objectives and Implications,* 94–126. Basel, Switzerland: Bank for International Settlements.

Gali, J. 1990. How well does the IS-LM model fit postwar U.S. data? Columbia University, New York. Manuscript.

Hamada, K., and F. Hayashi. 1985. Monetary policy in postwar Japan. In *Monetary Policy in Our Times,* ed. A. Ando, H. Eguchi, R. Farmer, and Y. Suzuki, 83–121. Cambridge, MA: MIT Press.

Horiye, Y., S. Naniwa, and S. Ishihara. 1987. The charges of Japanese business cycles. *Bank of Japan Monetary and Economic Studies* 5:49–100.

Hutchison, M. M. 1986. Japan's "money focused" monetary policy. *Federal Reserve Bank of San Francisco Economic Review,* no. 3, 33–46.

Ito, T. 1989. Is the Bank of Japan a closet monetarist? Monetary targeting in Japan, 1978–1988. University of Minnesota, Minneapolis. Manuscript.

———. 1990. Chapter VI: Financial markets and monetary policy. University of Minnesota, Minneapolis. Manuscript.

Johansen, S. 1988. Statistical analysis of cointegration vectors. *Journal of Economic Dynamics and Control* 12:231–54.

Kosai, Y., and Y. Ogino. 1984. *The Contemporary Japanese Economy.* New York: M. E. Sharpe.

Krugman, P. R., and M. Obstfeld. 1988. *International Economics.* Glenview, IL: Scott, Foresman and Company.

Lucas, R. E., Jr. 1973. Some international evidence on output-inflation tradeoffs. *American Economic Review* 73:326–34.

McCallum, B. T. 1988. Robustness properties of a rule for monetary policy. *Carnegie-Rochester Conference Series* 29:173–203.

Noland, M. A. 1989. Japanese trade elasticities and the J-curve. *Review of Economics and Statistics* 71:175–78.

Plosser, C. I. 1990. Money and business cycles: A real business cycle interpretation. NBER Working Paper No. 3221. Cambridge, MA: National Bureau of Economic Research, January.

Shapiro, M. D., and M. W. Watson. 1988. Sources of business cycle fluctuations. In *NBER Macroeconomics Annual,* ed. O. Blanchard and S. Fischer, 111–48. Cambridge, MA: MIT Press.

Sims, C. A. 1980. Macroeconomics and reality. *Econometrica* 48:1–49.

Sims, C. A., J. H. Stock, and M. Watson. 1990. Inference in linear time series models with some unit roots. *Econometrica* 58:113–44.

Stock, J. H., and M. W. Watson. 1989. Interpreting the evidence on money-income causality. *Journal of Econometrics* 40:161–82.

Suzuki, Y. 1985. Japan's monetary policy over the past ten years. *Bank of Japan Monetary and Economic Studies* 3:1–9.

Taylor, J. B. 1989. Monetary policy and the stability of macroeconomic relationships. Stanford University, Stanford, CA. Manuscript.

West, K. D. 1987. A standard monetary model and the variability of the deutsche-mark-dollar exchange rate. *Journal of International Economics* 23:56–76.

———. 1992. Sources of cycles in Japan, 1975–1987. *Journal of the Japanese and International Economies* 6:71–98.

Contributors

John Y. Campbell
Woodrow Wilson School
Robertson Hall
Princeton University
Princeton, NJ 08544

Yasushi Hamao
Graduate School of Business
Columbia University
409 Uris Hall
New York, NY 10027

Takeo Hoshi
Graduate School of International
  Relations and Pacific Studies
University of California, San Diego
La Jolla, CA 92093

Kunio Okina
Research and Statistics Department
Bank of Japan
C.P.O. Box 203
Tokyo 100-91 Japan

David Scharfstein
Sloan School of Management
Massachusetts Institute of Technology
Room E52-433
Cambridge, MA 02139

Kenneth J. Singleton
Graduate School of Business
Stanford University
Stanford, CA 94305

Kazuo Ueda
Department of Economics
University of Tokyo
7-3-1 Hongo, Bunkyo-ku
Tokyo 113 Japan

Kenneth D. West
Department of Economics
7458 Social Science Building
University of Wisconsin
1180 Observatory Drive
Madison, WI 53706

Hiroshi Yoshikawa
Department of Economics
University of Tokyo
7-3-1 Hongo, Bunkyo-ku
Tokyo 113 Japan

Author Index

Subject Index

Aggregate demand–aggregate supply model: description of, 164–68; estimates from, 169–81; sensitivity of estimates, 181–83

Akaike's information criterion, 106n11, 107

Anchor rate, 50–52, 60

Arbitrage: between Japanese open and interbank markets, 20, 21f; in Japanese reserve maintenance system, 50

Bank loans: control through window guidance, 8–9, 21; in Japanese transmission mechanism, 23, 28. *See also* Discount window lending; Keiretsu firms; Nonkeiretsu firms

Bank reserves: in Japan, 1, 7–8, 11–12, 27; in United States, 7–8

Bond market, Japan: development and function of, 97–100; term structure of interest rates in, 111–13. *See also* Interest rates, long-term

Bond repurchase (gensaki). *See* Gensaki rates; Money markets

Borrower and lender of last resort, 50, 54

Budget constraint, 37–38

Business cycle, 134. *See also* Reference cycle

Call market: Bank of Japan role in, 18–27; borrowing in Japanese, 18–19; definition of Japanese, 64n3; in short-term money market, 33

Call rate: central bank smoothing of, 122; change in interbank, 64; determination of equilibrium, 12; direct pegging and clearing of, 18; factors controlling, 23;

as indicator of monetary policy, 21–24, 134–51, 154; raising Japan's, 17; as short-term interest rate, 96; stability of interbank, 13–14; target level of, 16–20. *See also* Gensaki rates; Interbank rates

Certificates of deposit (CDs): proposed repurchase of, 54; in short-term money market, 33

Commercial paper (CP): market in Japan, 1, 67; operations in, 16; in short-term money market, 33; U.S. market in, 67

Consumption: coincidence of cash seasonal high with, 131; seasonal rate of change in, 127–28

Data sources: for aggregate demand–aggregate supply model, 168–69; in investment analysis, 92

Discount rate: as BOJ policy instrument, 75–76; relation to call rate, 12. *See also* Discount window lending; Window guidance

Discount window lending: by Bank of Japan, 12, 16; as daily instrument in Japan, 8; in Federal Reserve System, 10–11; as instrument of monetary policy, 2, 3; in Japan, 12

Expectations theory of term structure, 4, 103–19. *See also* Forecasting; Interest rates, long-term; Interest rates, short-term

Expenditures, seasonal, 126, 128

193